# Cypress Hill

## Tres Equis

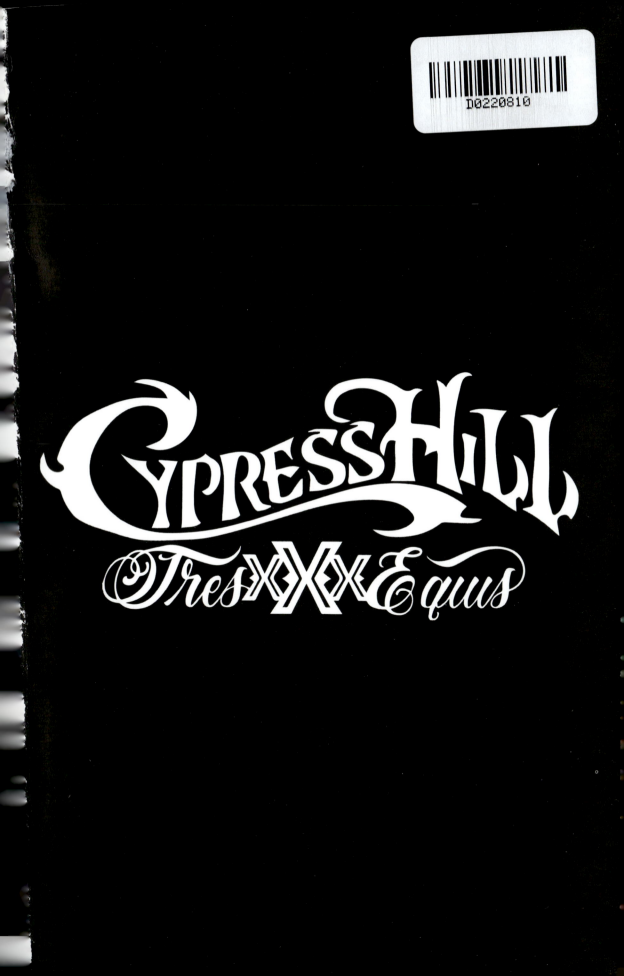

| | |
|---|---|
| **PUBLISHERS** | Joshua Frankel & Sridhar Reddy |
| **CFO & GENERAL COUNSEL** | Kevin Meek |
| **SENIOR V.P.** | Josh Bernstein |
| **V.P., RETAIL SALES & MARKETING** | Jeremy Atkins |
| **V.P., DIGITAL** | Anthony Lauletta |
| **V.P., OPERATIONS** | Dominique Rosés |
| **V.P., MARKETING** | Rebecca Cicione |
| **PRODUCTION DIRECTOR** | Courtney Menard |
| **DESIGN DIRECTOR** | Tyler Boss |
| **RETAIL SALES DIRECTOR** | Devin Funches |
| **PROJECT COORDINATOR** | Penelope Vargas |

Based on the funky true story
of Cypress Hill.


Sort of.


It's hard to say.


We were stoned.


Anyhow...it's a tribe thing.

written by.........................

chapter 1 art.....................................

chapter 2 art.....................................

chapter 3 art.....................................

chapter 4 art.....................................

chapter 5 art.....................................

chapter 6 art.....................................

color art.........................

lettering.........................

cover.........................

editorial assistant...........................

editor.........................

...............................Noah Callahan-Bever
& Gabriel Alvarez

....................Felix Ruiz

...................Jefte Palo

...................Damion Scott

...................Paris Alleyne

...Juan Gedeon & Alejandro
Enrique Santana
.......Miguel Angel Hernandez

...........................................Karla Aguilar

...........................................AndWorld Design

...........................................Ramon Villalobos

...........................................Michael Polson

...........................................Chris Robinson

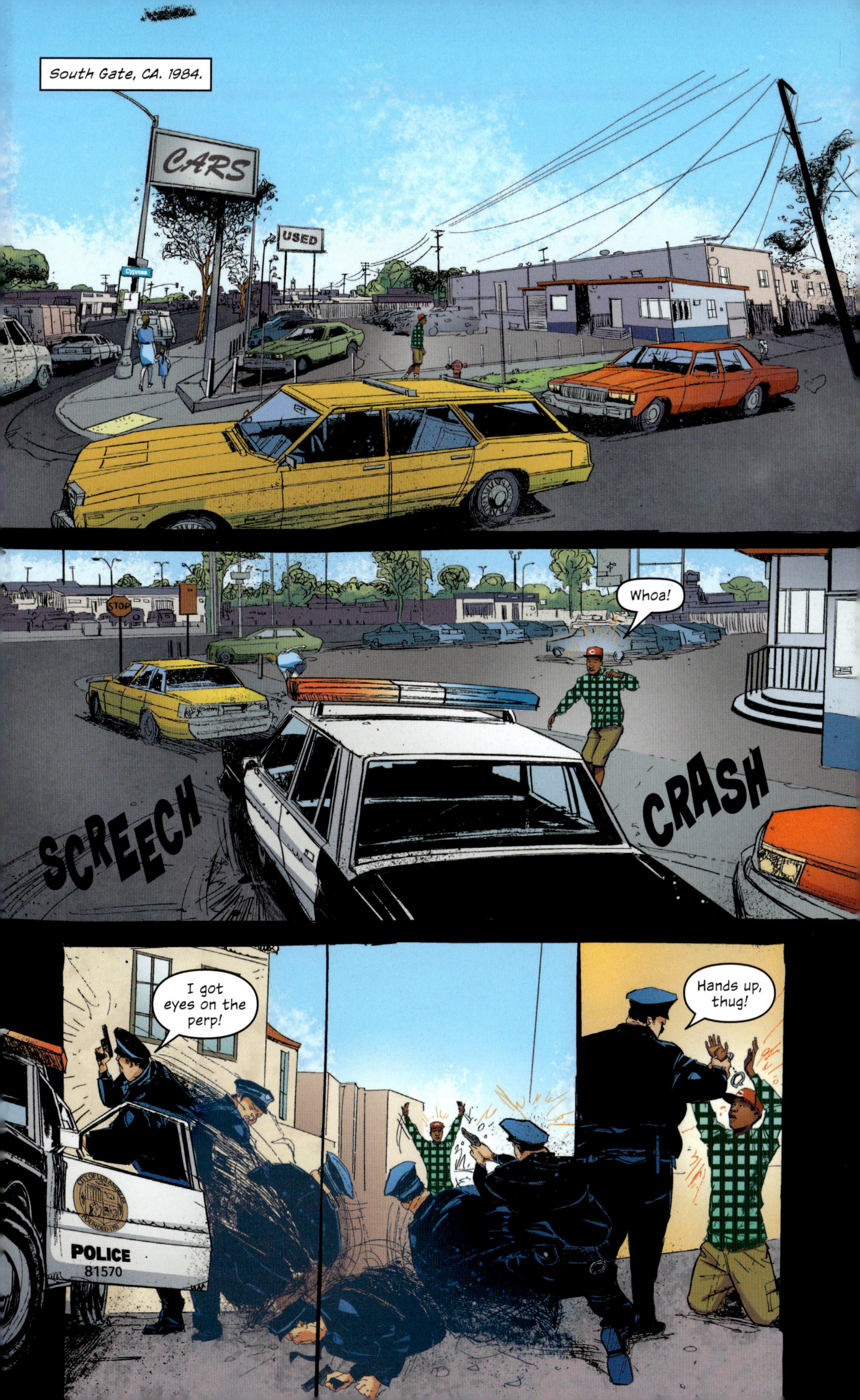
South Gate, CA. 1984.
CARS
Cypress
USED
STOP
Whoa!
SCREECH
CRASH
I got eyes on the perp!
Hands up, thug!
POLICE
81570

# Chapter One: Pigs

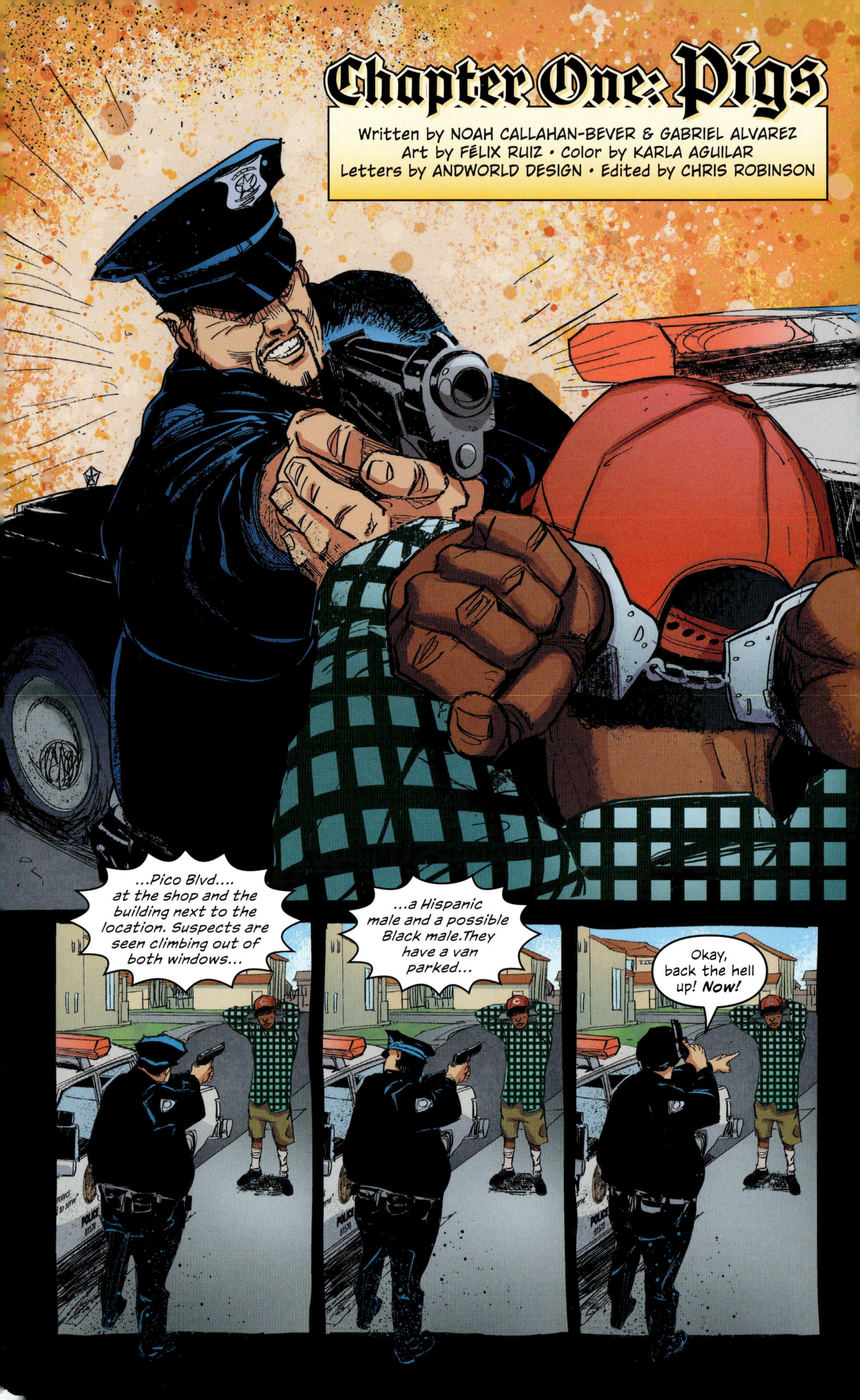

Written by NOAH CALLAHAN-BEVER & GABRIEL ALVAREZ
Art by FÉLIX RUIZ • Color by KARLA AGUILAR
Letters by ANDWORLD DESIGN • Edited by CHRIS ROBINSON
...Pico Blvd.... at the shop and the building next to the location. Suspects are seen climbing out of both windows...
...a Hispanic male and a possible Black male.They have a van parked...
Okay, back the hell up! **Now!**

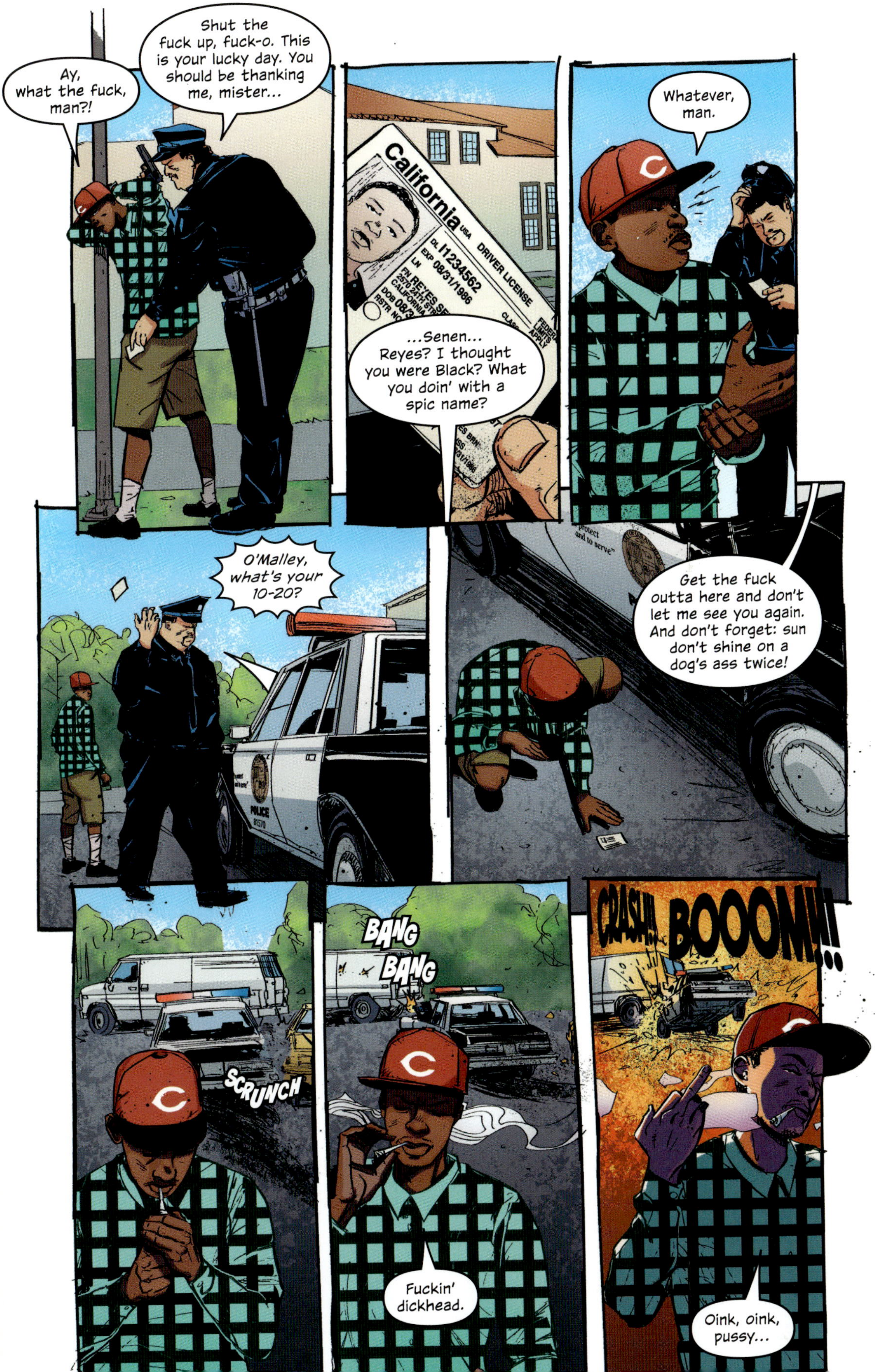

Ay, what the fuck, man?!
Shut the fuck up, fuck-o. This is your lucky day. You should be thanking me, mister...
California USA
DRIVER LICENSE
DL I1234562
EXP 08/31/1986
...Senen... Reyes? I thought you were Black? What you doin' with a spic name?
Whatever, man.
O'Malley, what's your 10-20?
Get the fuck outta here and don't let me see you again. And don't forget: sun don't shine on a dog's ass twice!
SCRUNCH
BANG
BANG
Fuckin' dickhead.
CRASH!!
BOOOM!!!
Oink, oink, pussy...

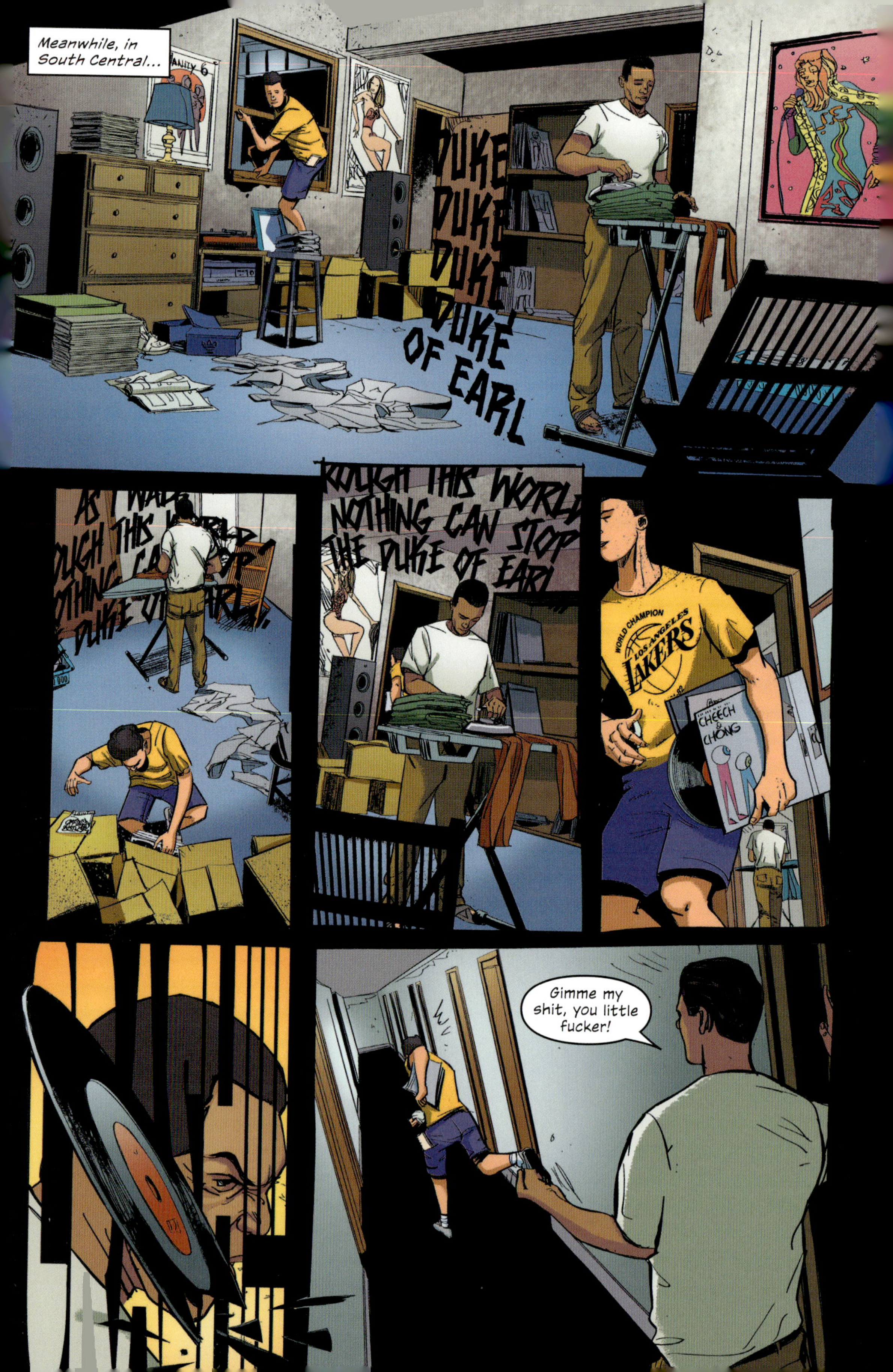

Meanwhile, in South Central...
DUKE DUKE DUKE DUKE OF EARL
ROUGH THIS WORLD NOTHING CAN STOP THE DUKE OF EARL
WORLD CHAMPION LOS ANGELES LAKERS
CHEECH & CHONG
Gimme my shit, you little fucker!

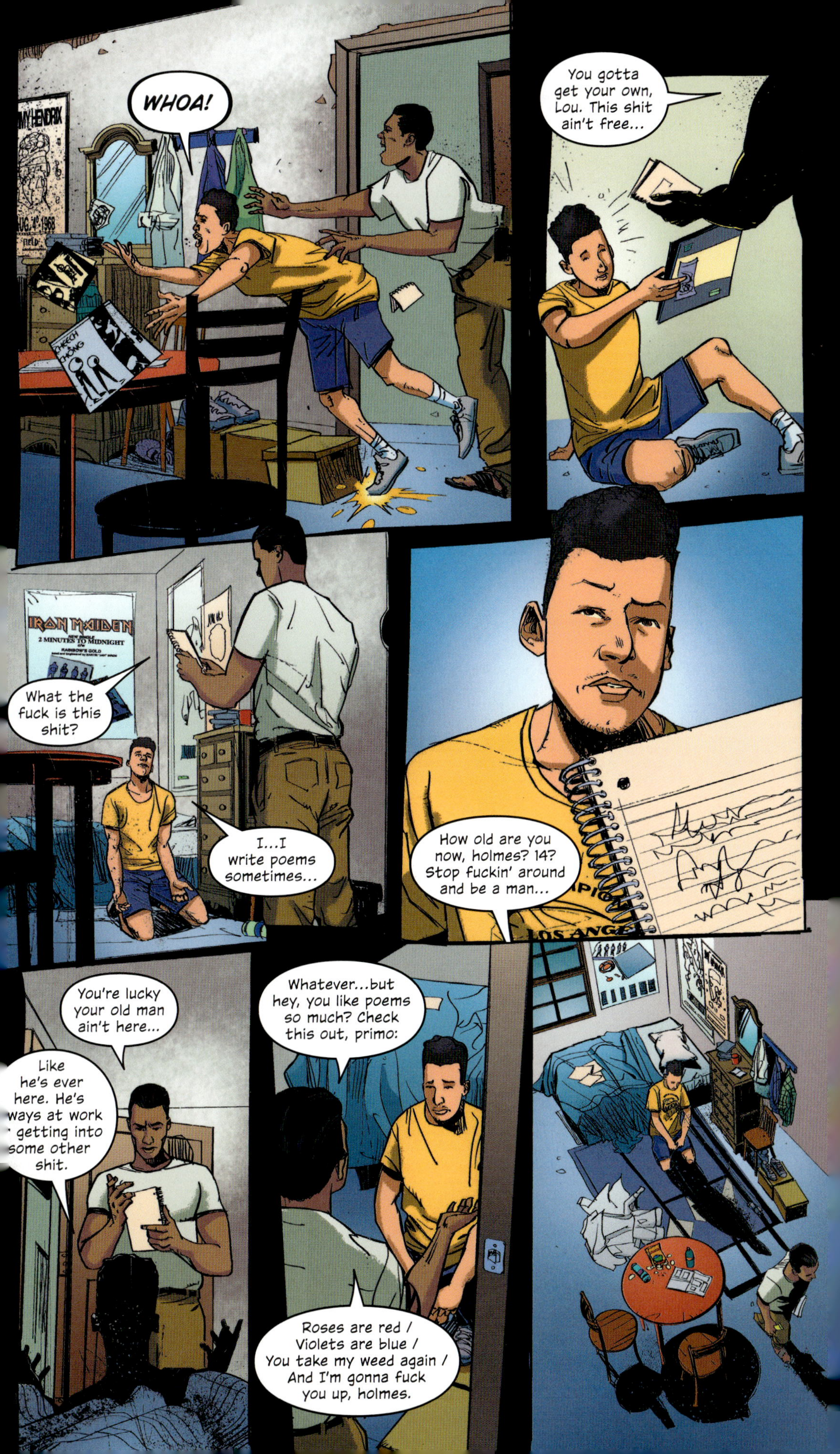
WHOA!
You gotta get your own, Lou. This shit ain't free...
What the fuck is this shit?
I...I write poems sometimes...
How old are you now, holmes? 14? Stop fuckin' around and be a man...
You're lucky your old man ain't here...
Like he's ever here. He's ways at work getting into some other shit.
Whatever...but hey, you like poems so much? Check this out, primo:
Roses are red / Violets are blue / You take my weed again / And I'm gonna fuck you up, holmes.

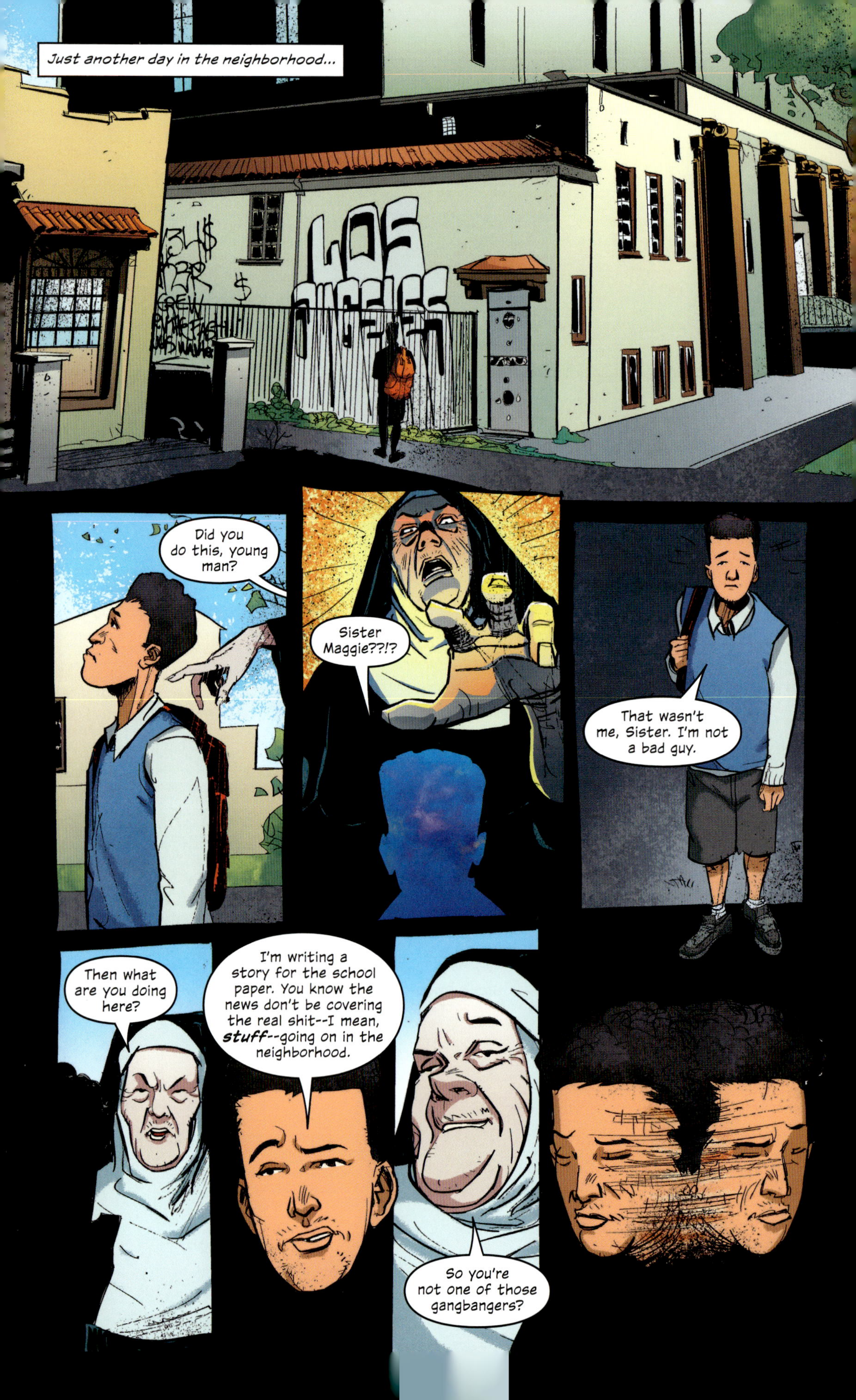
Just another day in the neighborhood...
LOS
Did you do this, young man?
Sister Maggie??!?
That wasn't me, Sister. I'm not a bad guy.
Then what are you doing here?
I'm writing a story for the school paper. You know the news don't be covering the real shit--I mean, *stuff*--going on in the neighborhood.
So you're not one of those gangbangers?

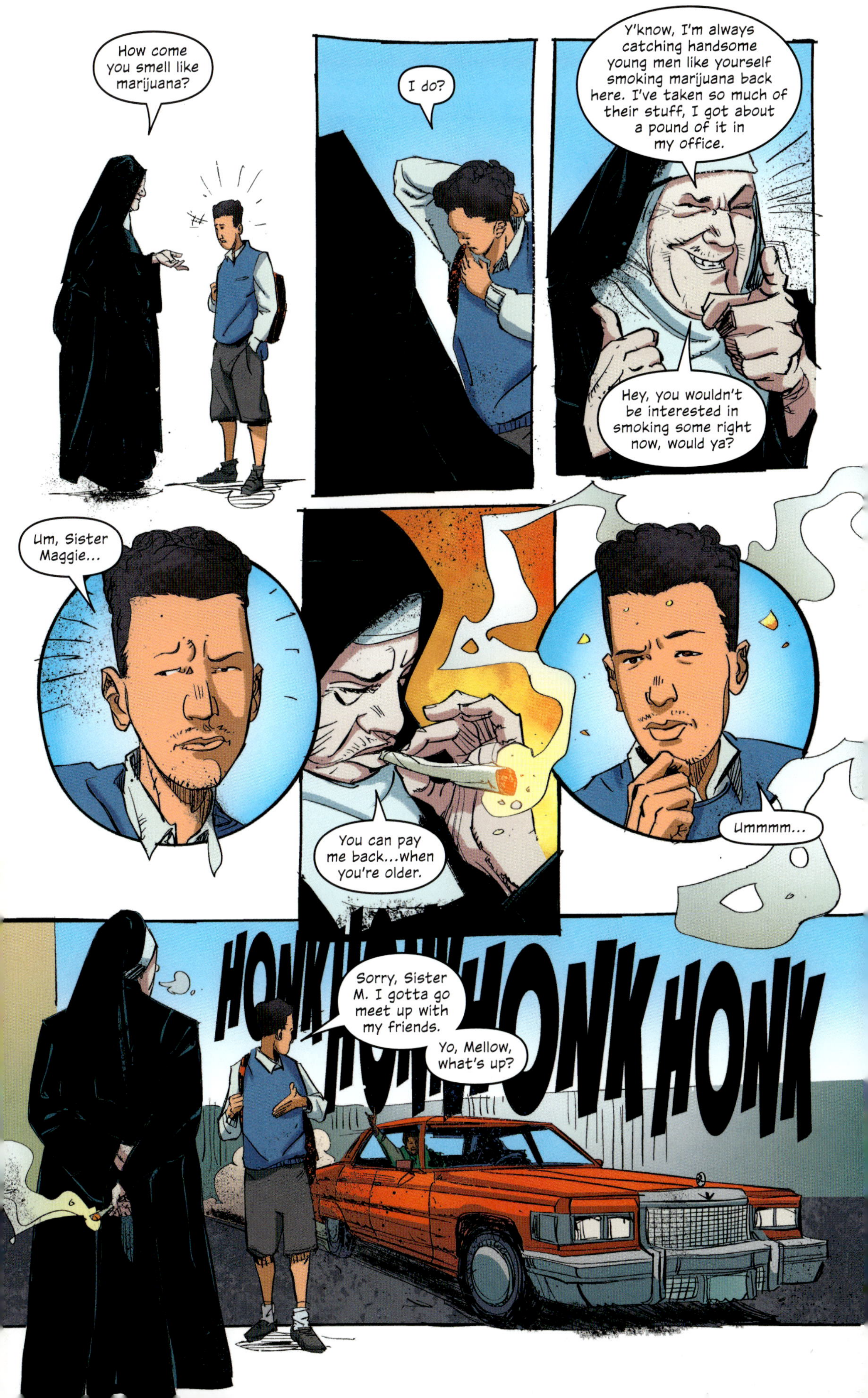
How come you smell like marijuana?
I do?
Y'know, I'm always catching handsome young men like yourself smoking marijuana back here. I've taken so much of their stuff, I got about a pound of it in my office.
Hey, you wouldn't be interested in smoking some right now, would ya?
Um, Sister Maggie...
You can pay me back...when you're older.
Ummmm...
HONK HONK HONK HONK
Sorry, Sister M. I gotta go meet up with my friends.
Yo, Mellow, what's up?

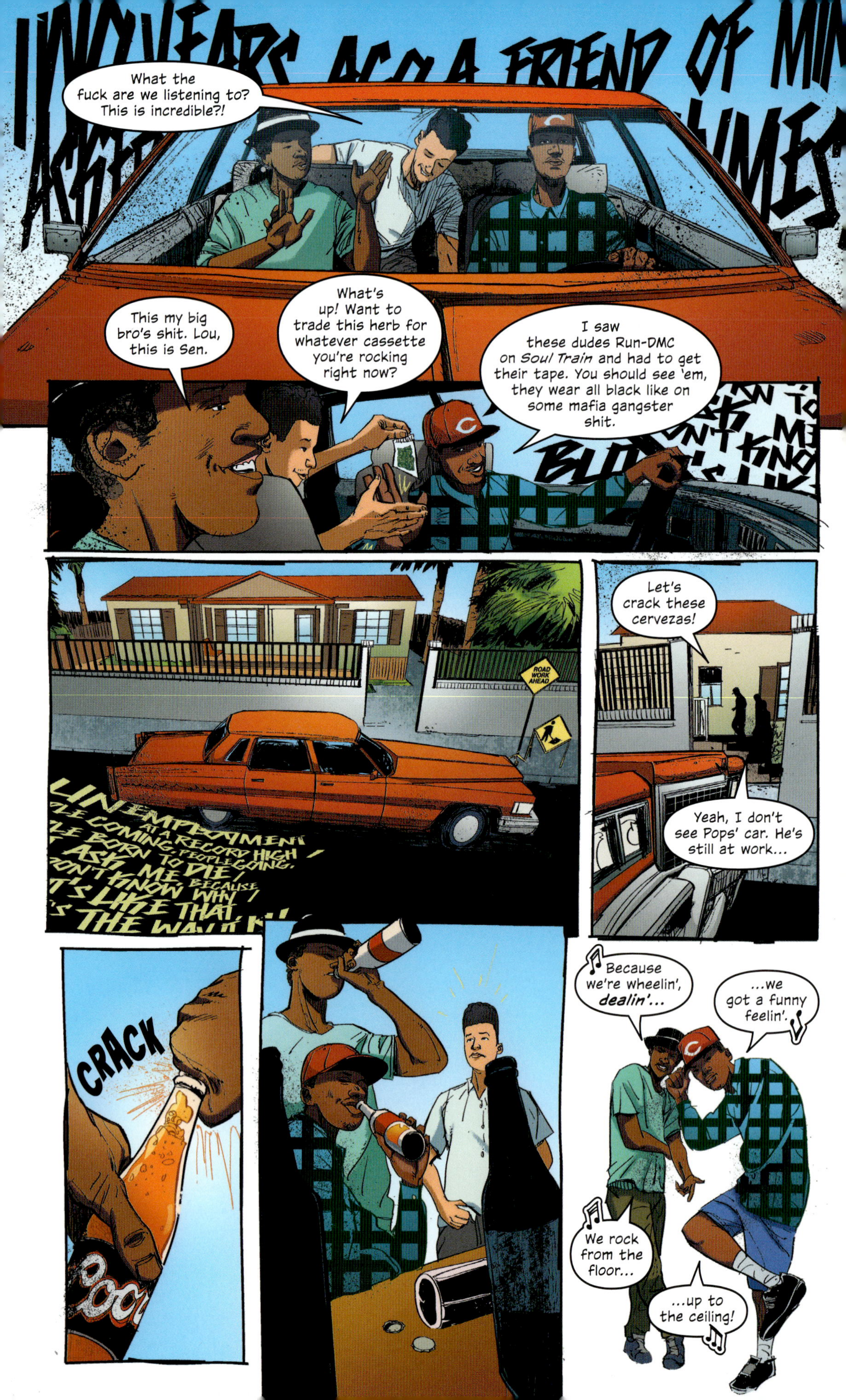
What the fuck are we listening to? This is incredible?!
This my big bro's shit. Lou, this is Sen.
What's up! Want to trade this herb for whatever cassette you're rocking right now?
I saw these dudes Run-DMC on *Soul Train* and had to get their tape. You should see 'em, they wear all black like on some mafia gangster shit.
ROAD WORK AHEAD
Let's crack these cervezas!
Yeah, I don't see Pops' car. He's still at work...
CRACK
Because we're wheelin', ***dealin'***...
...we got a funny feelin'.
We rock from the floor...
...up to the ceiling!

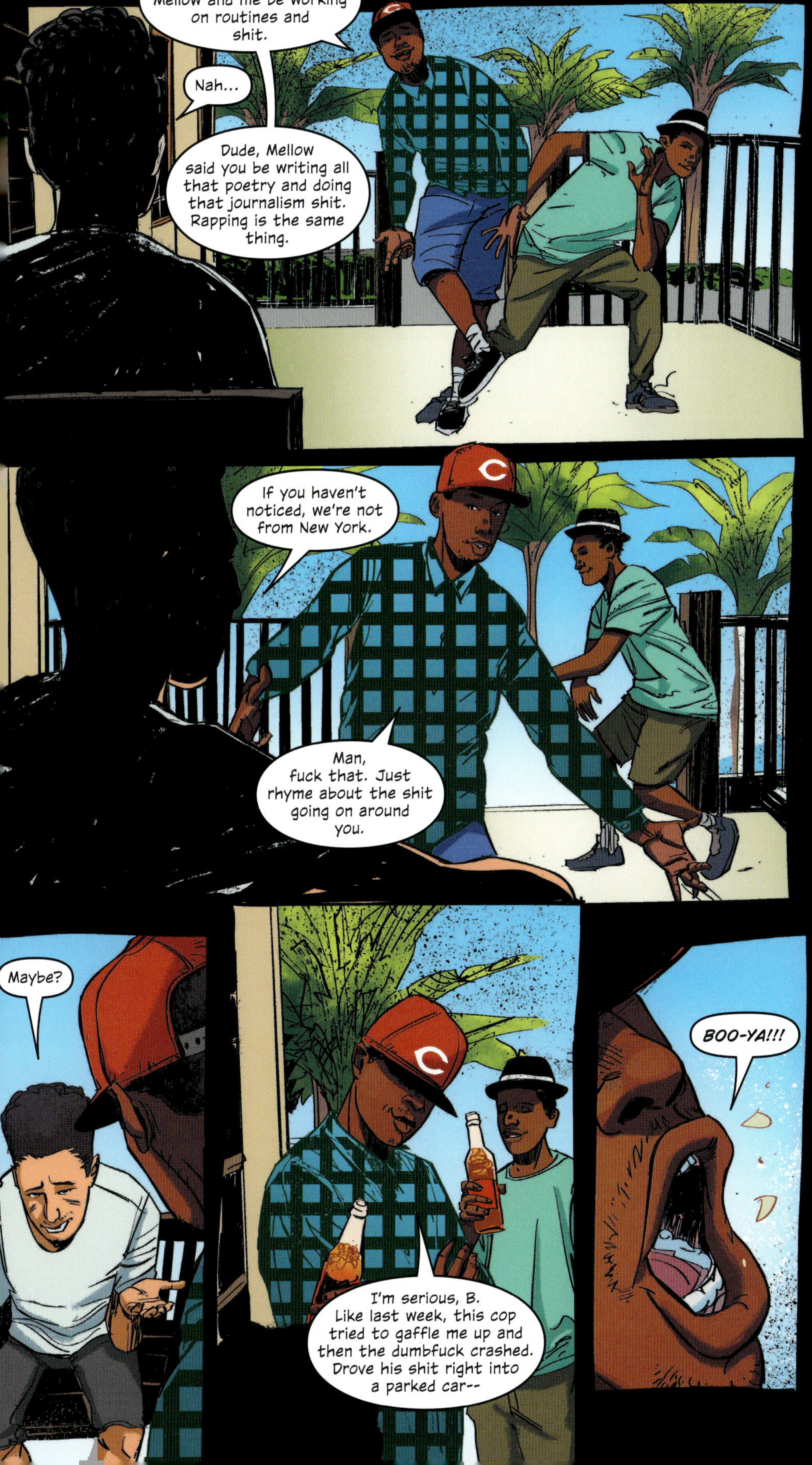
You ever think about writing raps? Mellow and me be working on routines and shit.
Nah...
Dude, Mellow said you be writing all that poetry and doing that journalism shit. Rapping is the same thing.
If you haven't noticed, we're not from New York.
Man, fuck that. Just rhyme about the shit going on around you.
Maybe?
I'm serious, B. Like last week, this cop tried to gaffle me up and then the dumbfuck crashed. Drove his shit right into a parked car--
BOO-YA!!!

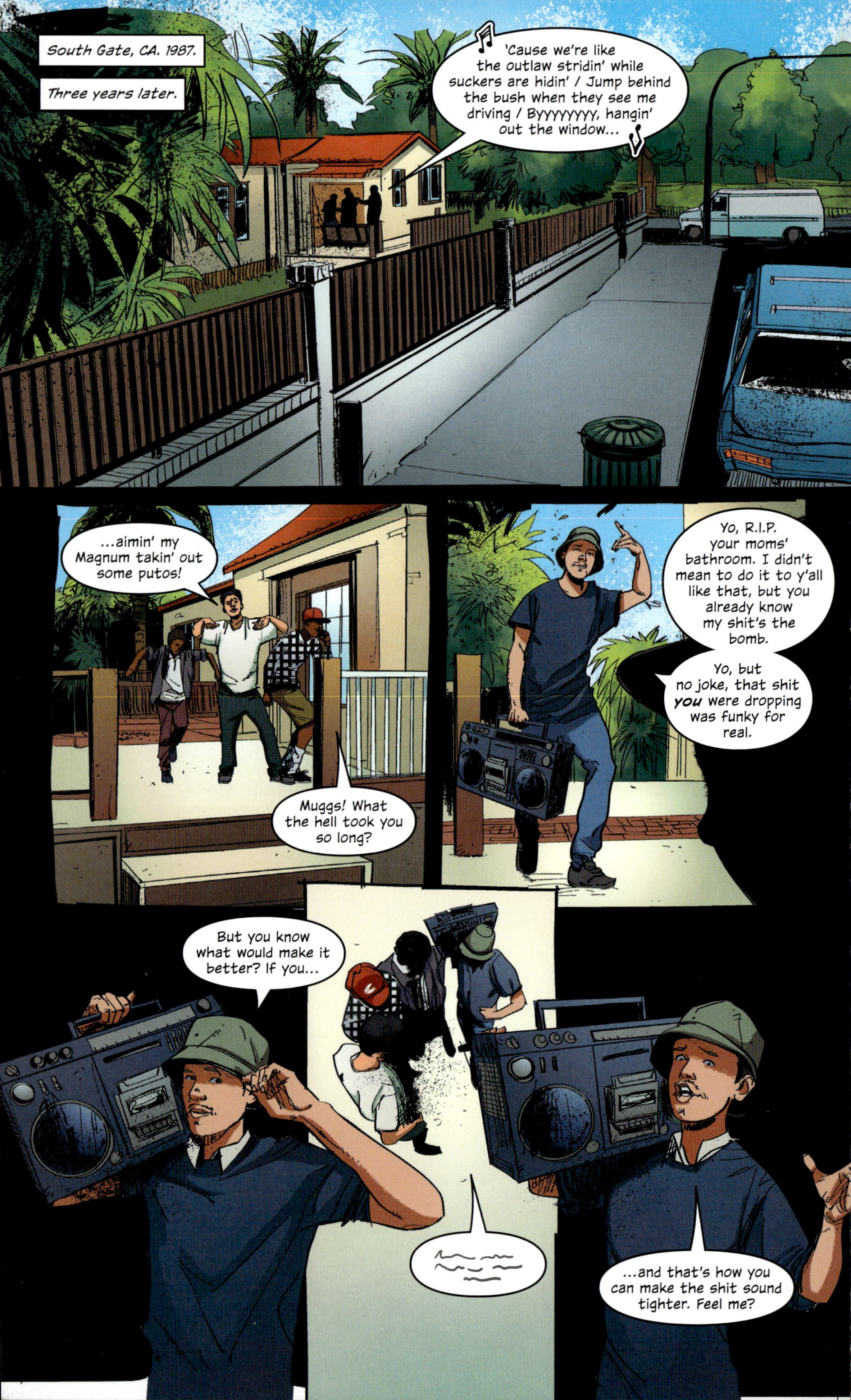
South Gate, CA. 1987.
Three years later.
'Cause we're like the outlaw stridin' while suckers are hidin' / Jump behind the bush when they see me driving / Byyyyyyyy, hangin' out the window...
...aimin' my Magnum takin' out some putos!
Muggs! What the hell took you so long?
Yo, R.I.P. your moms' bathroom. I didn't mean to do it to y'all like that, but you already know my shit's the bomb.
Yo, but no joke, that shit *you* were dropping was funky for real.
But you know what would make it better? If you...
...and that's how you can make the shit sound tighter. Feel me?

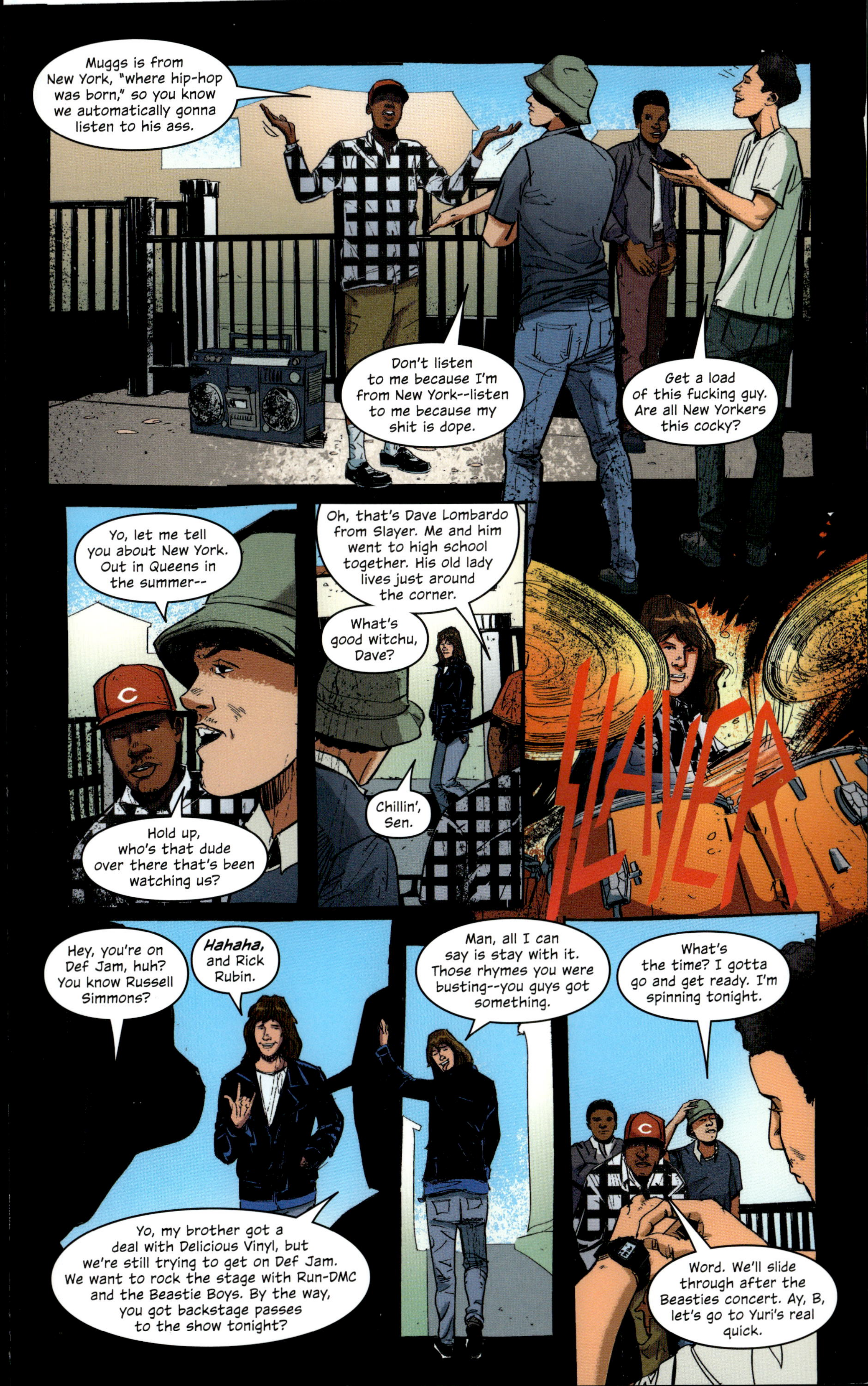

Muggs is from New York, "where hip-hop was born," so you know we automatically gonna listen to his ass.
Don't listen to me because I'm from New York--listen to me because my shit is dope.
Get a load of this fucking guy. Are all New Yorkers this cocky?
Yo, let me tell you about New York. Out in Queens in the summer--
Hold up, who's that dude over there that's been watching us?
Oh, that's Dave Lombardo from Slayer. Me and him went to high school together. His old lady lives just around the corner.
What's good witchu, Dave?
Chillin', Sen.
SLAYER
Hey, you're on Def Jam, huh? You know Russell Simmons?
*Hahaha,* and Rick Rubin.
Yo, my brother got a deal with Delicious Vinyl, but we're still trying to get on Def Jam. We want to rock the stage with Run-DMC and the Beastie Boys. By the way, you got backstage passes to the show tonight?
Man, all I can say is stay with it. Those rhymes you were busting--you guys got something.
What's the time? I gotta go and get ready. I'm spinning tonight.
Word. We'll slide through after the Beasties concert. Ay, B, let's go to Yuri's real quick.

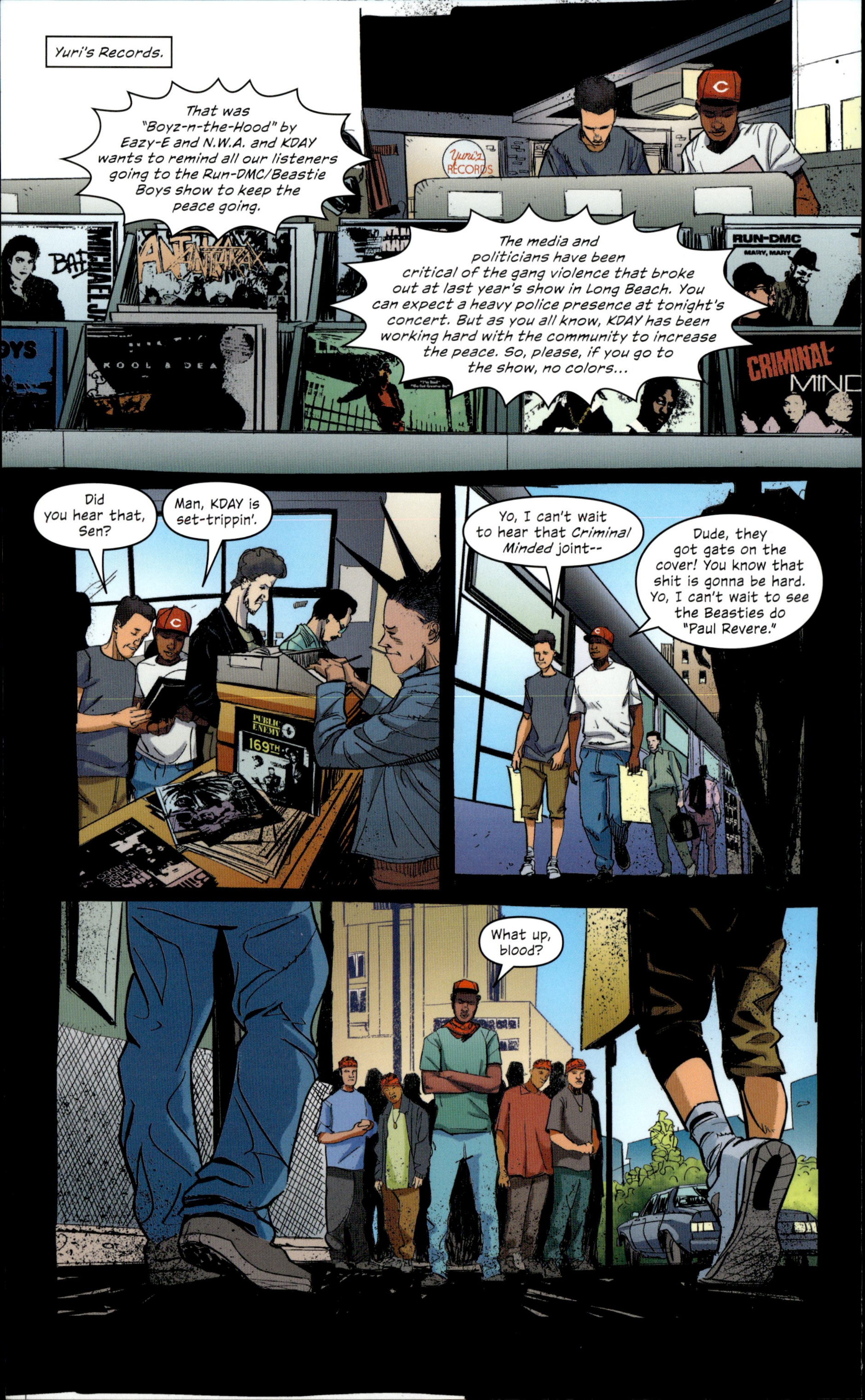
Yuri's Records.
That was "Boyz-n-the-Hood" by Eazy-E and N.W.A. and KDAY wants to remind all our listeners going to the Run-DMC/Beastie Boys show to keep the peace going.
The media and politicians have been critical of the gang violence that broke out at last year's show in Long Beach. You can expect a heavy police presence at tonight's concert. But as you all know, KDAY has been working hard with the community to increase the peace. So, please, if you go to the show, no colors...
Did you hear that, Sen?
Man, KDAY is set-trippin'.
Yo, I can't wait to hear that *Criminal Minded* joint--
Dude, they got gats on the cover! You know that shit is gonna be hard. Yo, I can't wait to see the Beasties do "Paul Revere."
What up, blood?

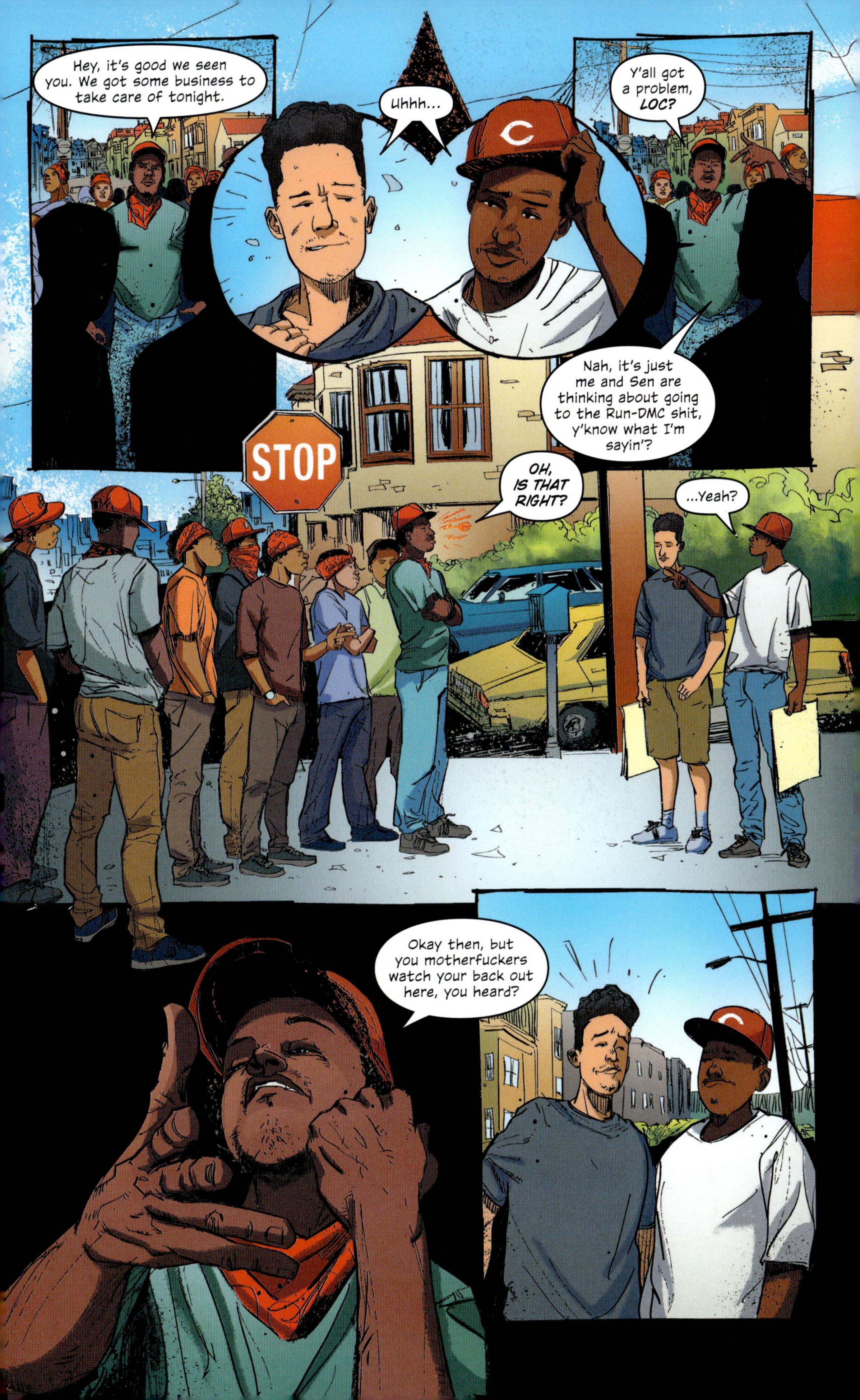
Hey, it's good we seen you. We got some business to take care of tonight.
Uhhh...
Y'all got a problem, LOC?
Nah, it's just me and Sen are thinking about going to the Run-DMC shit, y'know what I'm sayin'?
OH, IS THAT RIGHT?
...Yeah?
STOP
Okay then, but you motherfuckers watch your back out here, you heard?

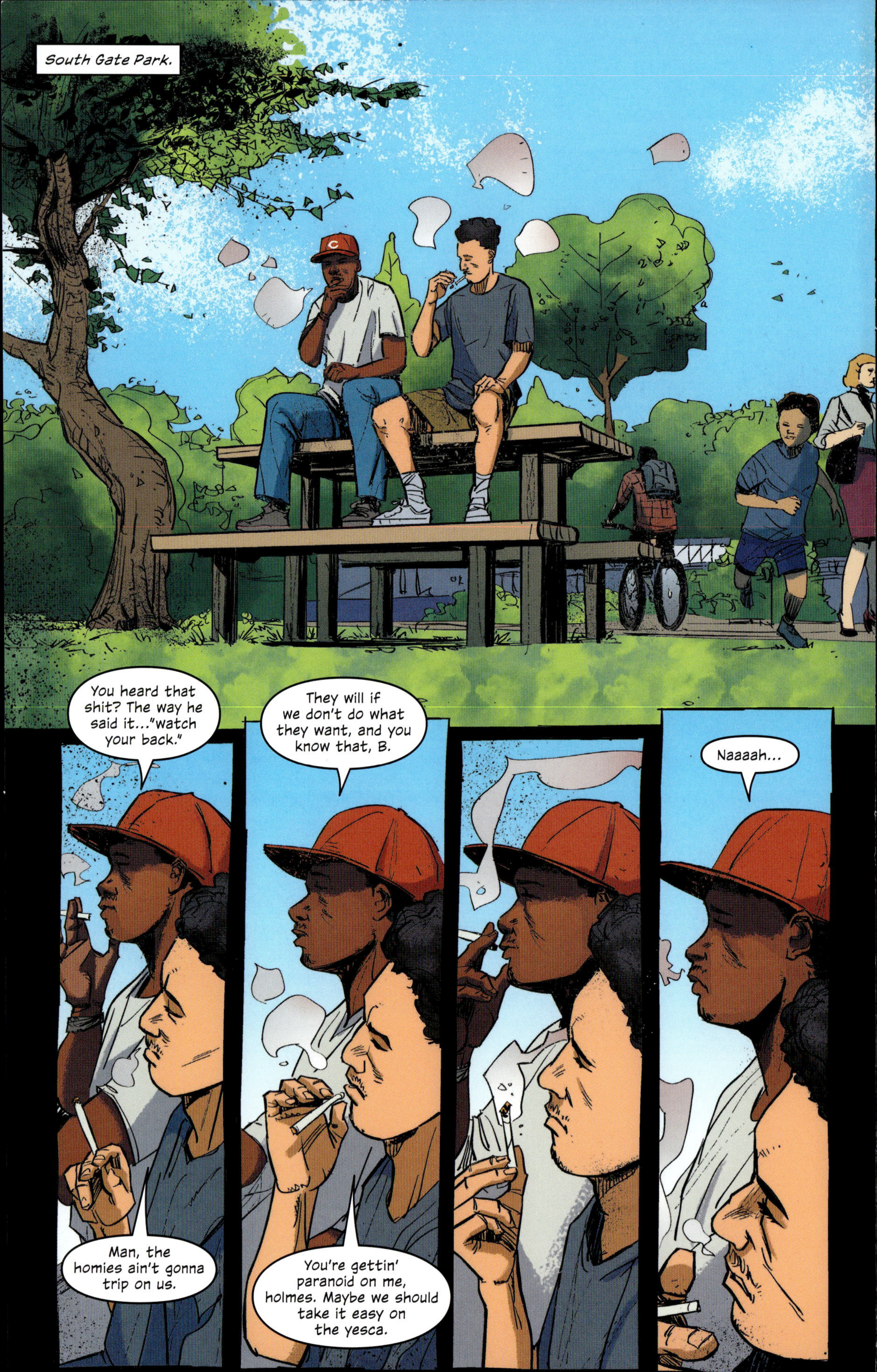
South Gate Park.
You heard that shit? The way he said it..."watch your back."
Man, the homies ain't gonna trip on us.
They will if we don't do what they want, and you know that, B.
You're gettin' paranoid on me, holmes. Maybe we should take it easy on the yesca.
Naaaah...

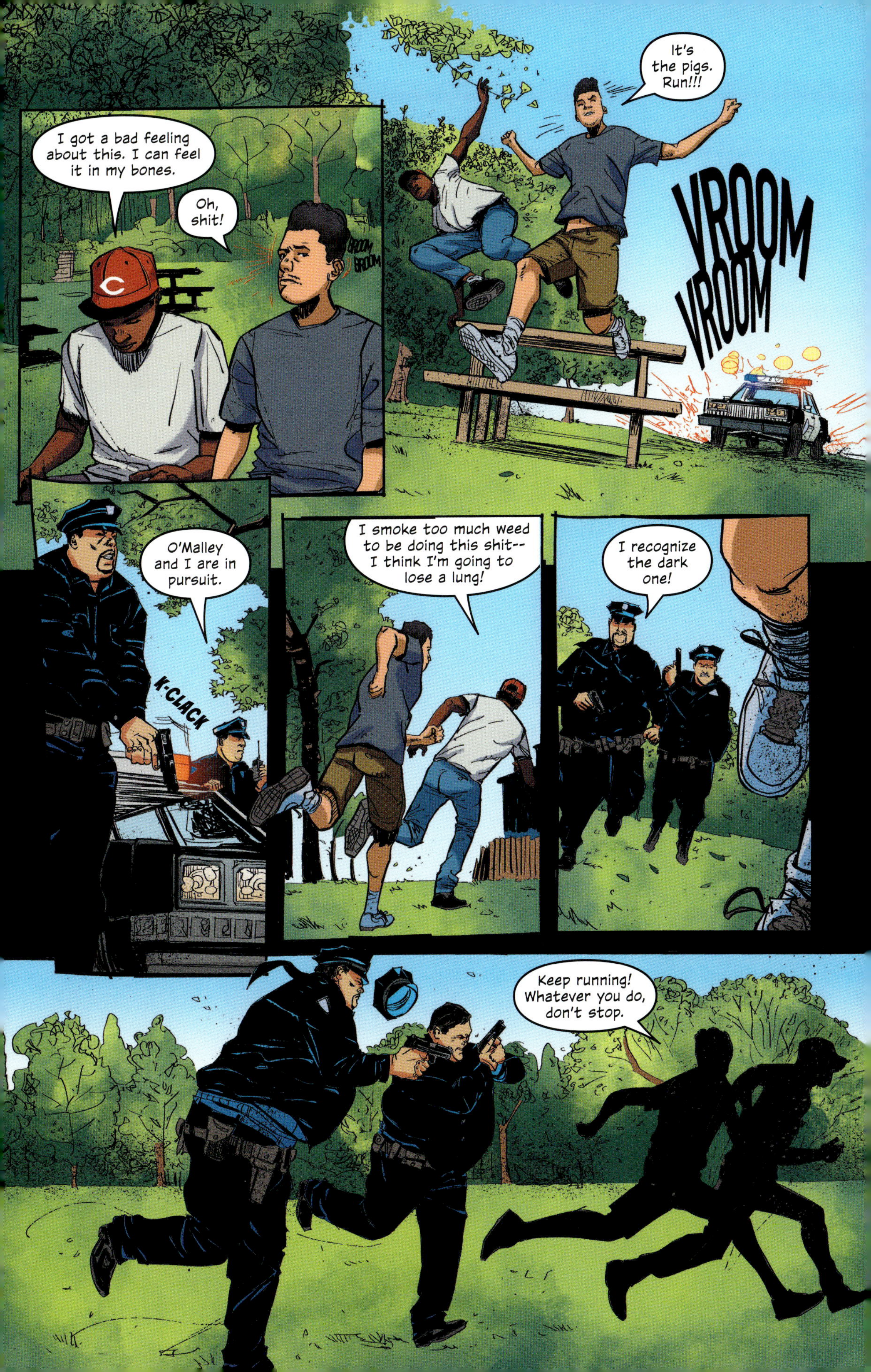
I got a bad feeling about this. I can feel it in my bones.
Oh, shit!
BROOM
BROOM
It's the pigs. Run!!!
VROOM
VROOM
O'Malley and I are in pursuit.
K-CLACK
I smoke too much weed to be doing this shit-- I think I'm going to lose a lung!
I recognize the dark one!
Keep running! Whatever you do, don't stop.

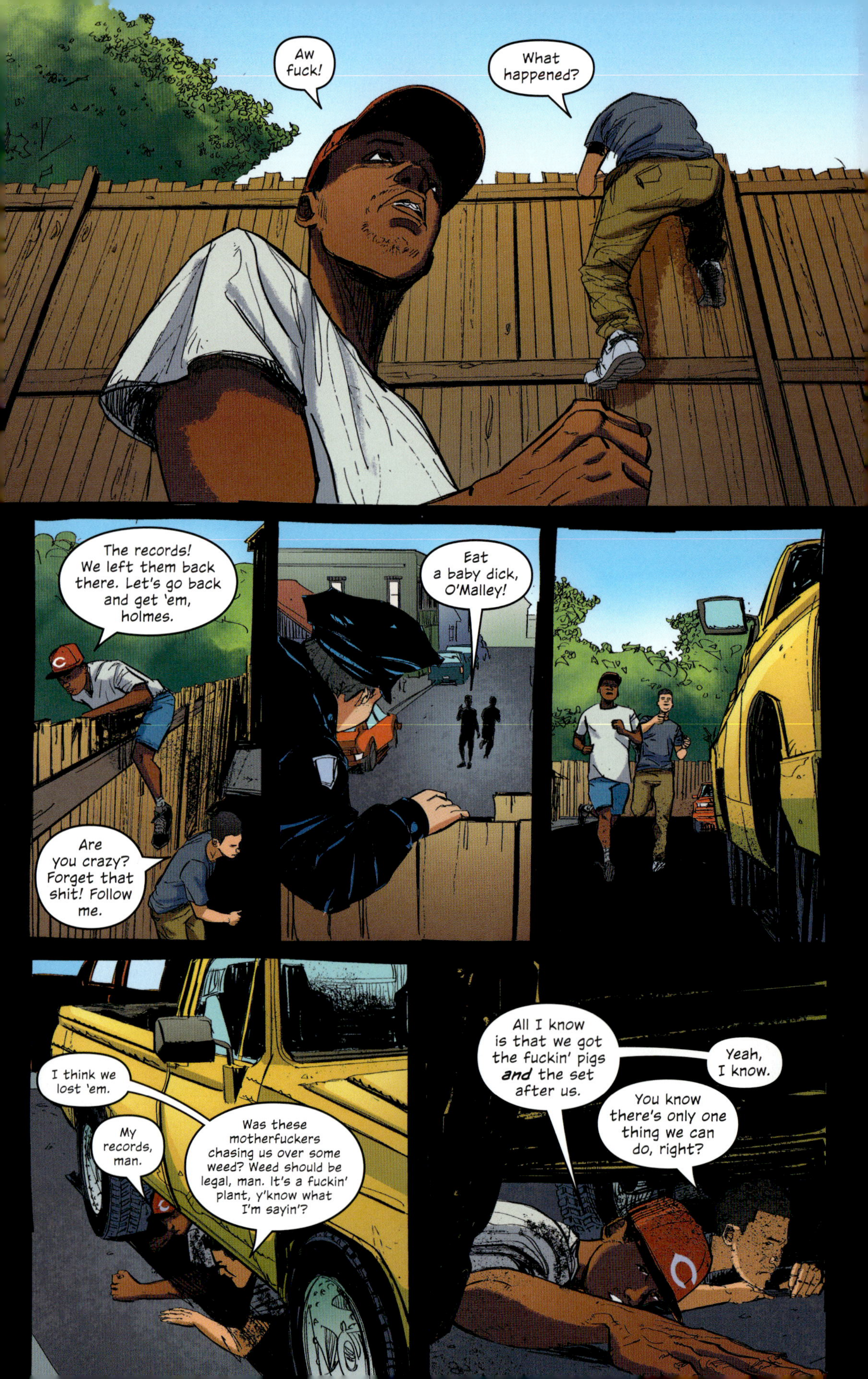
Aw fuck!
What happened?
The records! We left them back there. Let's go back and get 'em, holmes.
Are you crazy? Forget that shit! Follow me.
Eat a baby dick, O'Malley!
I think we lost 'em.
My records, man.
Was these motherfuckers chasing us over some weed? Weed should be legal, man. It's a fuckin' plant, y'know what I'm sayin'?
All I know is that we got the fuckin' pigs *and* the set after us.
Yeah, I know.
You know there's only one thing we can do, right?

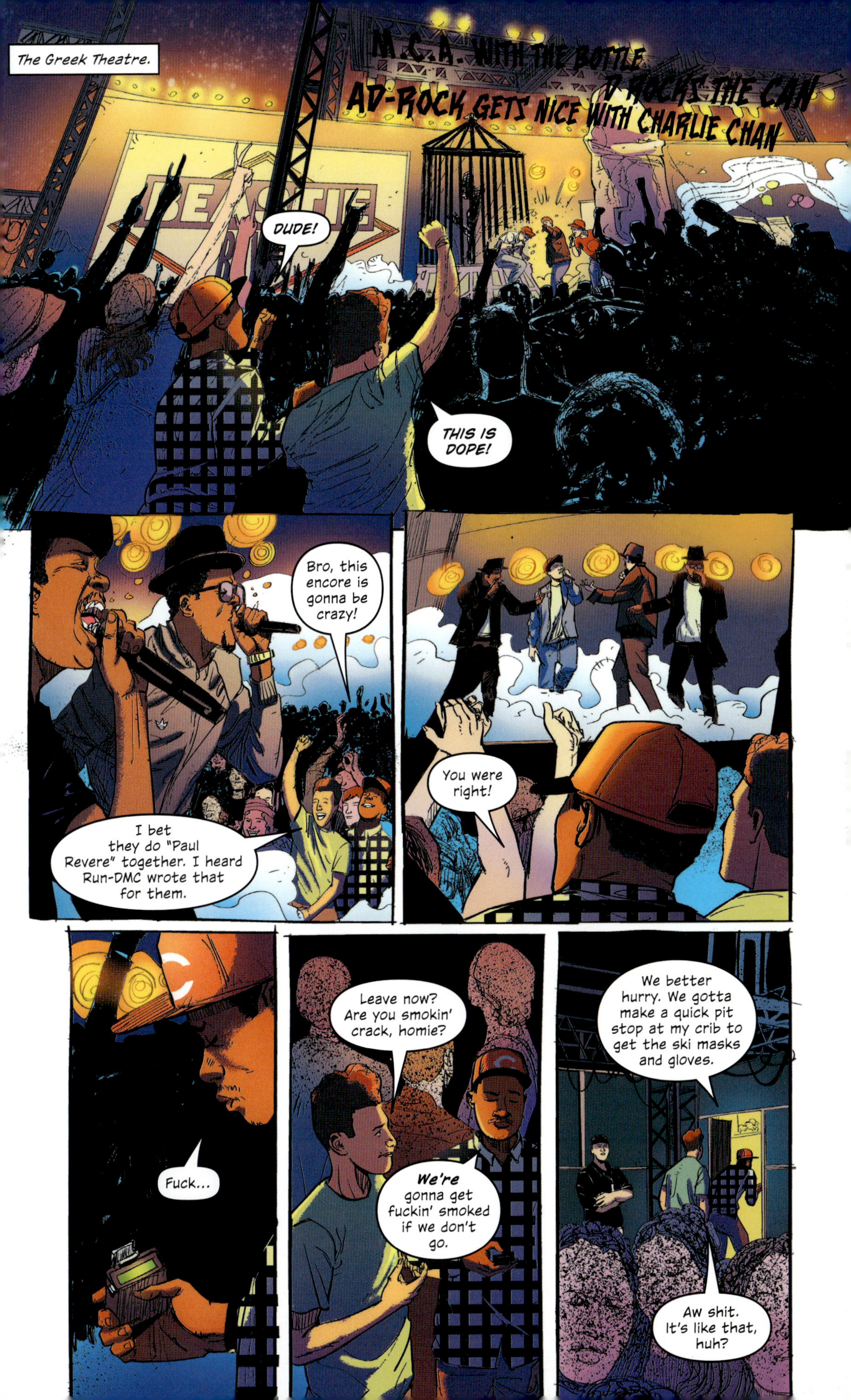
The Greek Theatre.
M.C.A. WITH THE BOTTLE
D ROCKS THE CAN
AD-ROCK GETS NICE WITH CHARLIE CHAN
DUDE!
THIS IS DOPE!
Bro, this encore is gonna be crazy!
I bet they do "Paul Revere" together. I heard Run-DMC wrote that for them.
You were right!
Fuck...
Leave now? Are you smokin' crack, homie?
*We're* gonna get fuckin' smoked if we don't go.
We better hurry. We gotta make a quick pit stop at my crib to get the ski masks and gloves.
Aw shit. It's like that, huh?

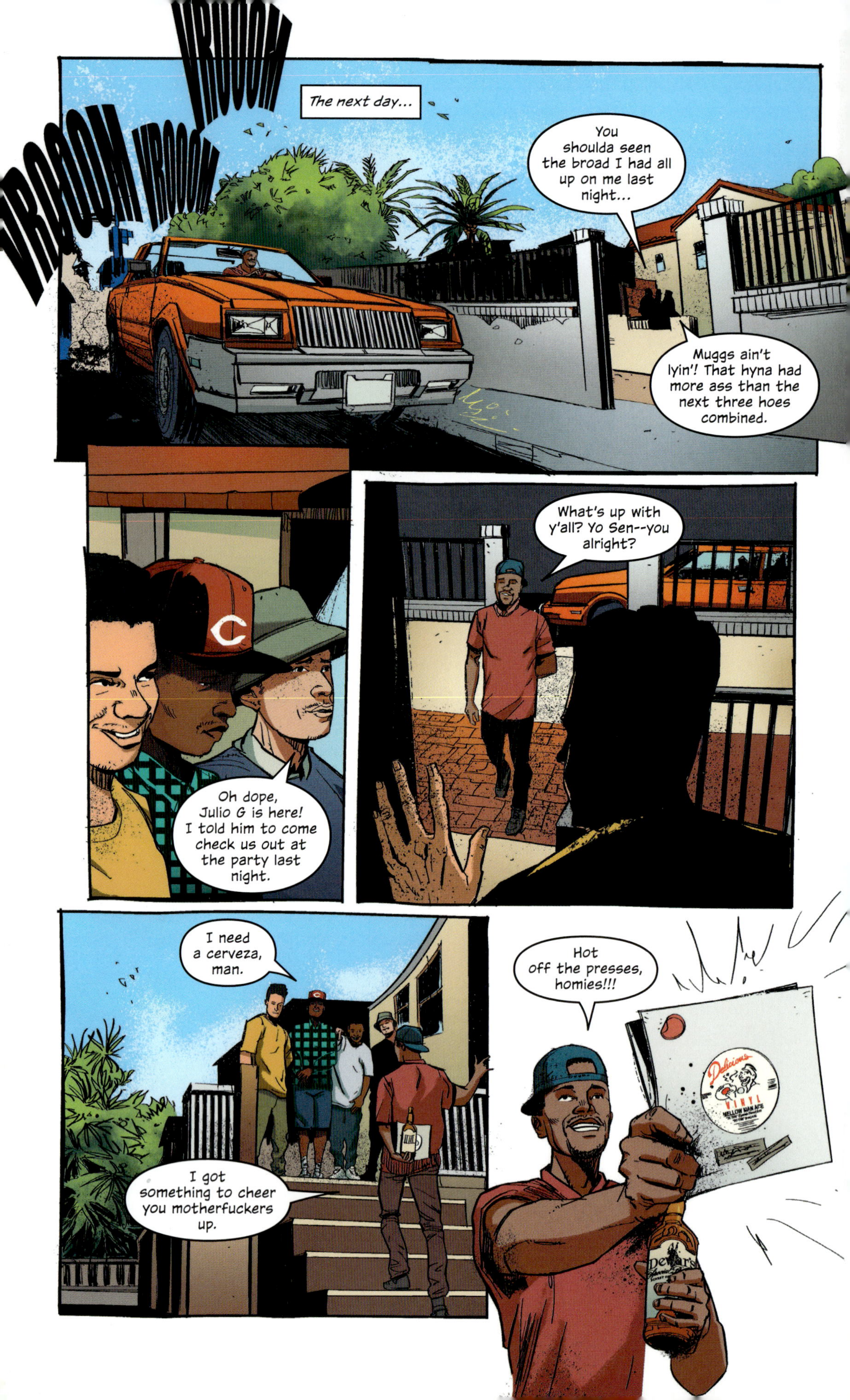
VROOOM VROOOM VROOOM
The next day...
You shoulda seen the broad I had all up on me last night...
Muggs ain't lyin'! That hyna had more ass than the next three hoes combined.
Oh dope, Julio G is here! I told him to come check us out at the party last night.
What's up with y'all? Yo Sen--you alright?
I need a cerveza, man.
I got something to cheer you motherfuckers up.
Hot off the presses, homies!!!
Delicious VINYL
MELLOW MAN ACE

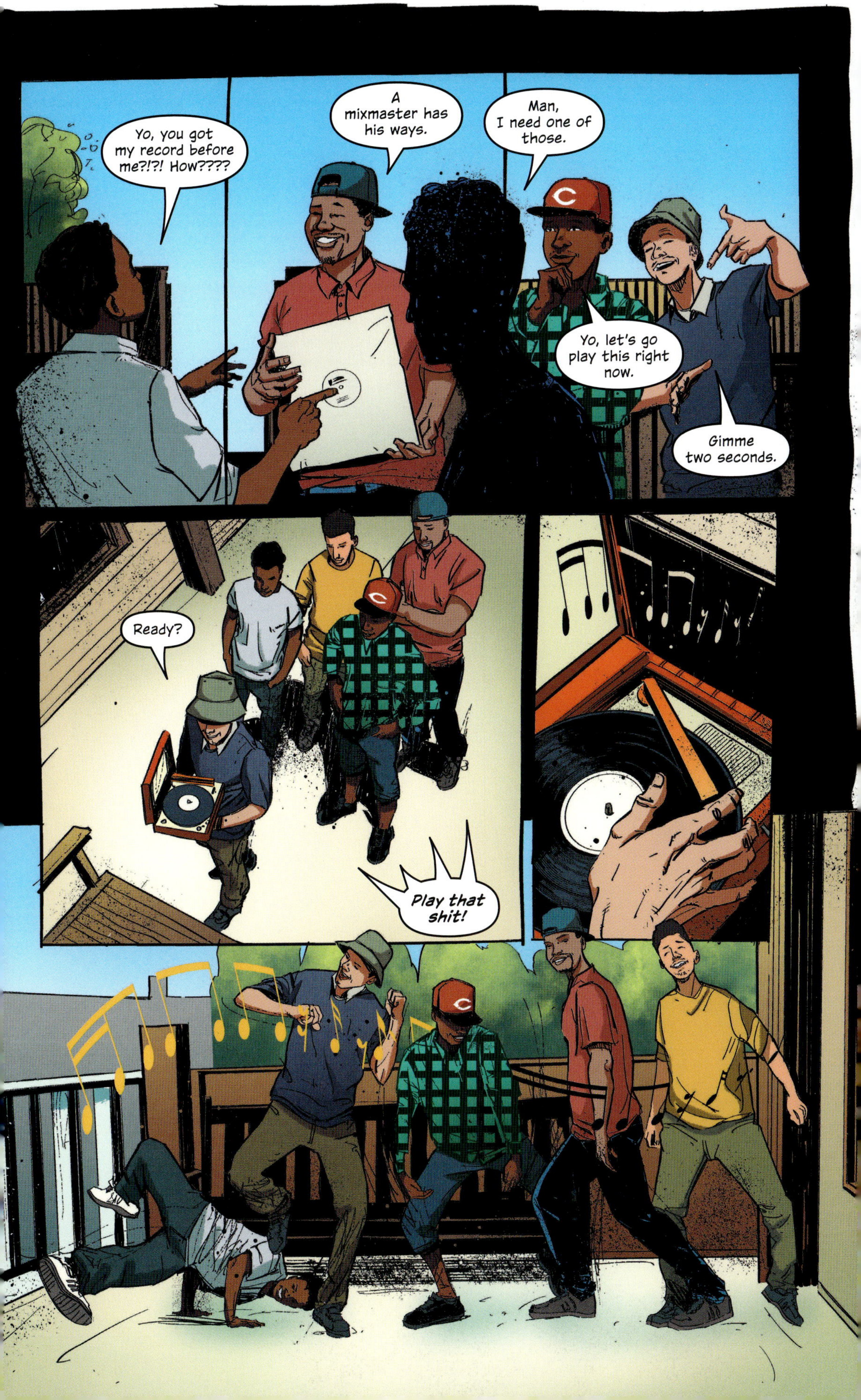
Yo, you got my record before me?!?! How????
A mixmaster has his ways.
Man, I need one of those.
Yo, let's go play this right now.
Gimme two seconds.
Ready?
Play that shit!

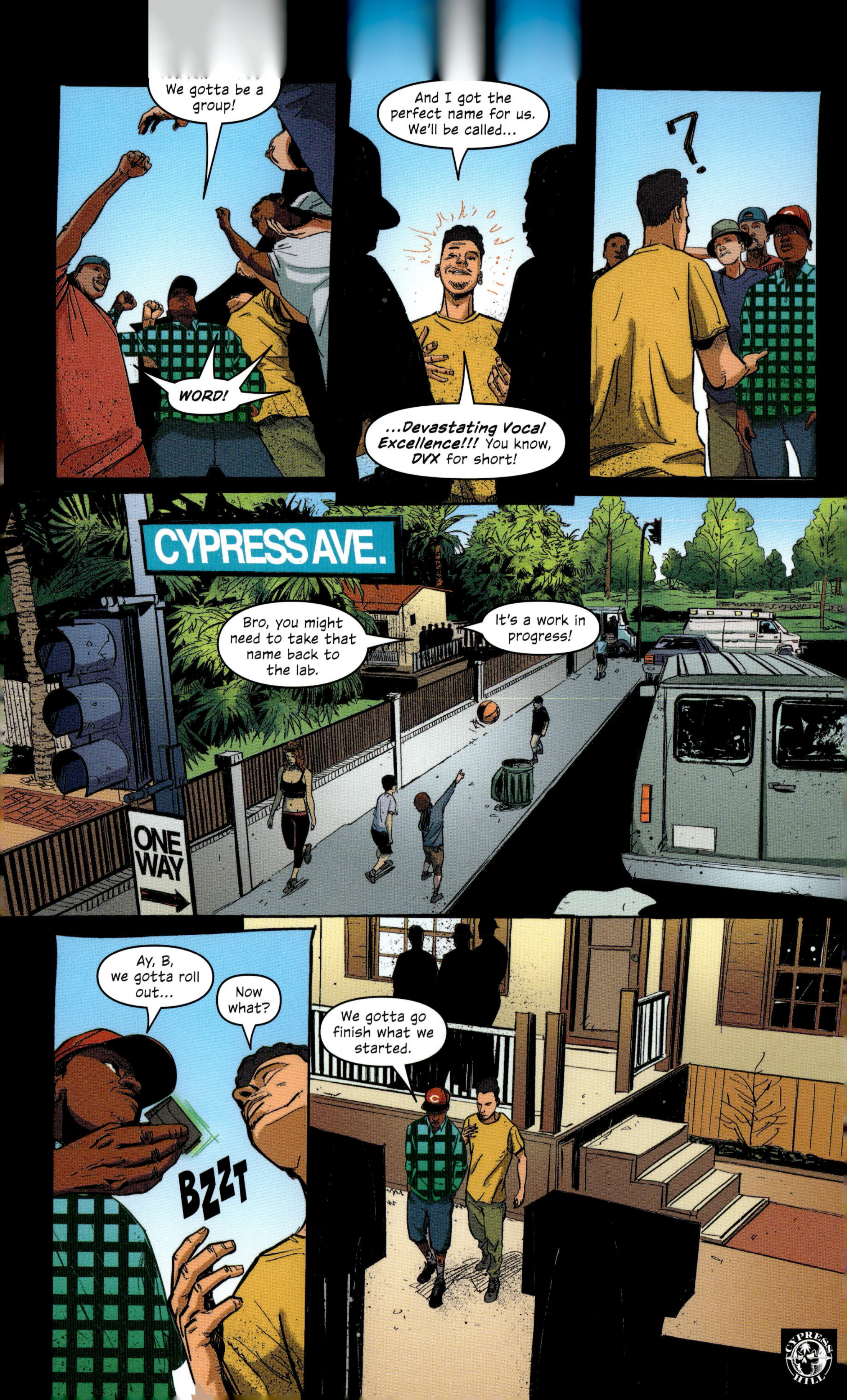
We gotta be a group!
WORD!
And I got the perfect name for us. We'll be called...
...Devastating Vocal Excellence!!! You know, DVX for short!
?
CYPRESS AVE.
Bro, you might need to take that name back to the lab.
It's a work in progress!
ONE WAY
Ay, B, we gotta roll out...
Now what?
BZZT
We gotta go finish what we started.

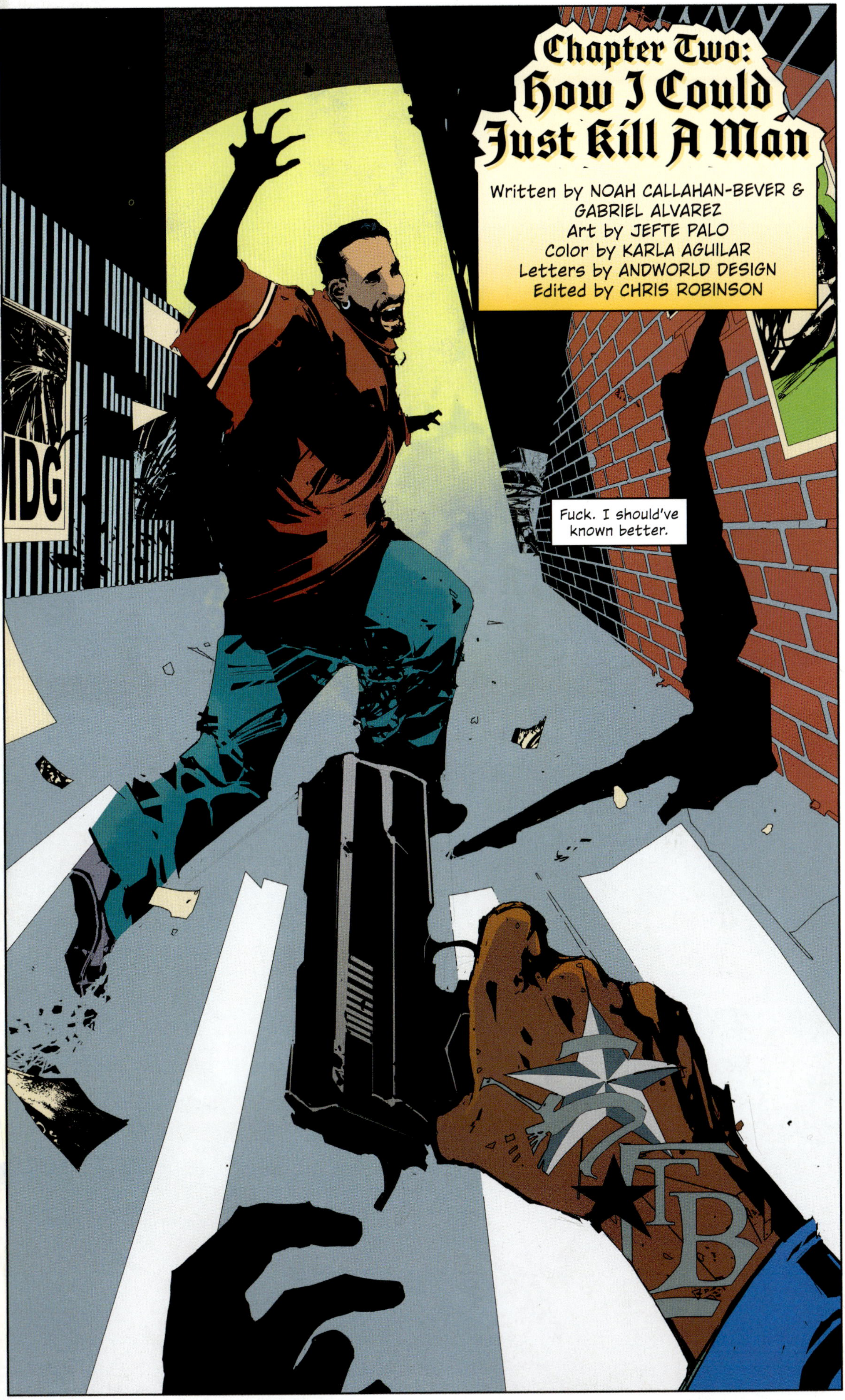
Chapter Two:
How I Could Just Kill A Man
Written by NOAH CALLAHAN-BEVER & GABRIEL ALVAREZ
Art by JEFTE PALO
Color by KARLA AGUILAR
Letters by ANDWORLD DESIGN
Edited by CHRIS ROBINSON
MDG
Fuck. I should've known better.
TB

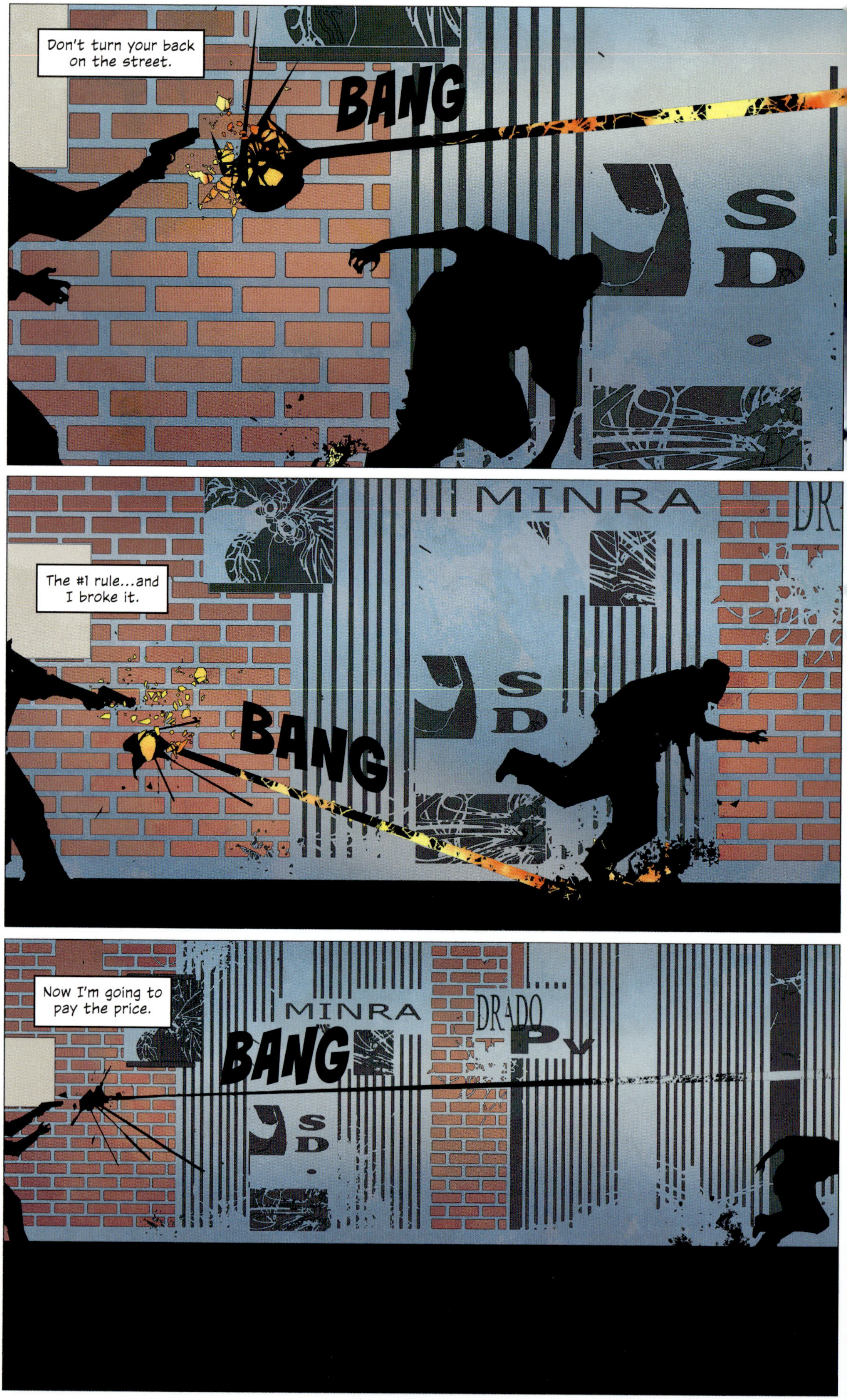
Don't turn your back on the street.
BANG
SD.
The #1 rule...and I broke it.
MINRA
DR
BANG
SD
Now I'm going to pay the price.
MINRA
DRADO
Pv
BANG
SD.

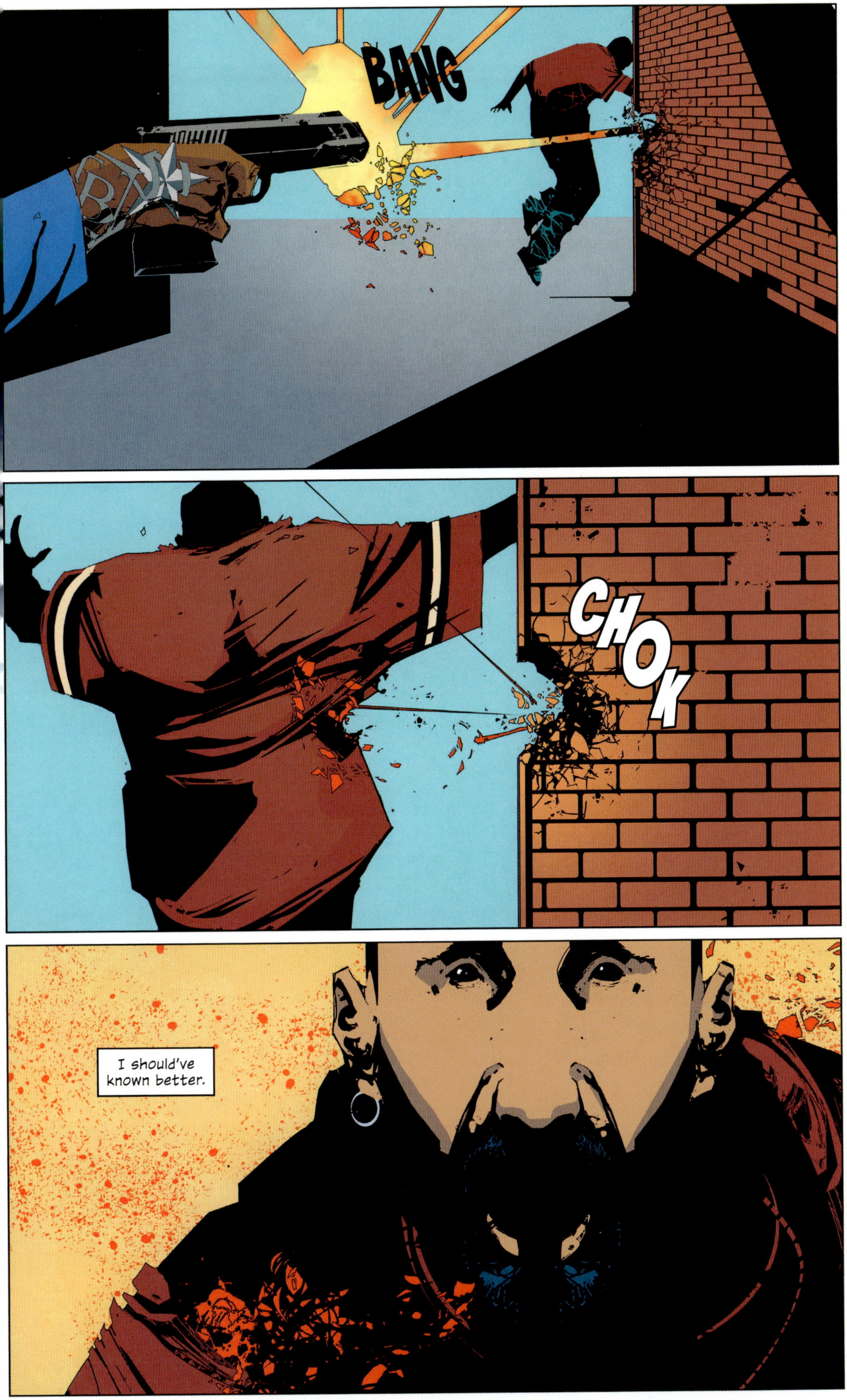
BANG
CHOK
I should've known better.

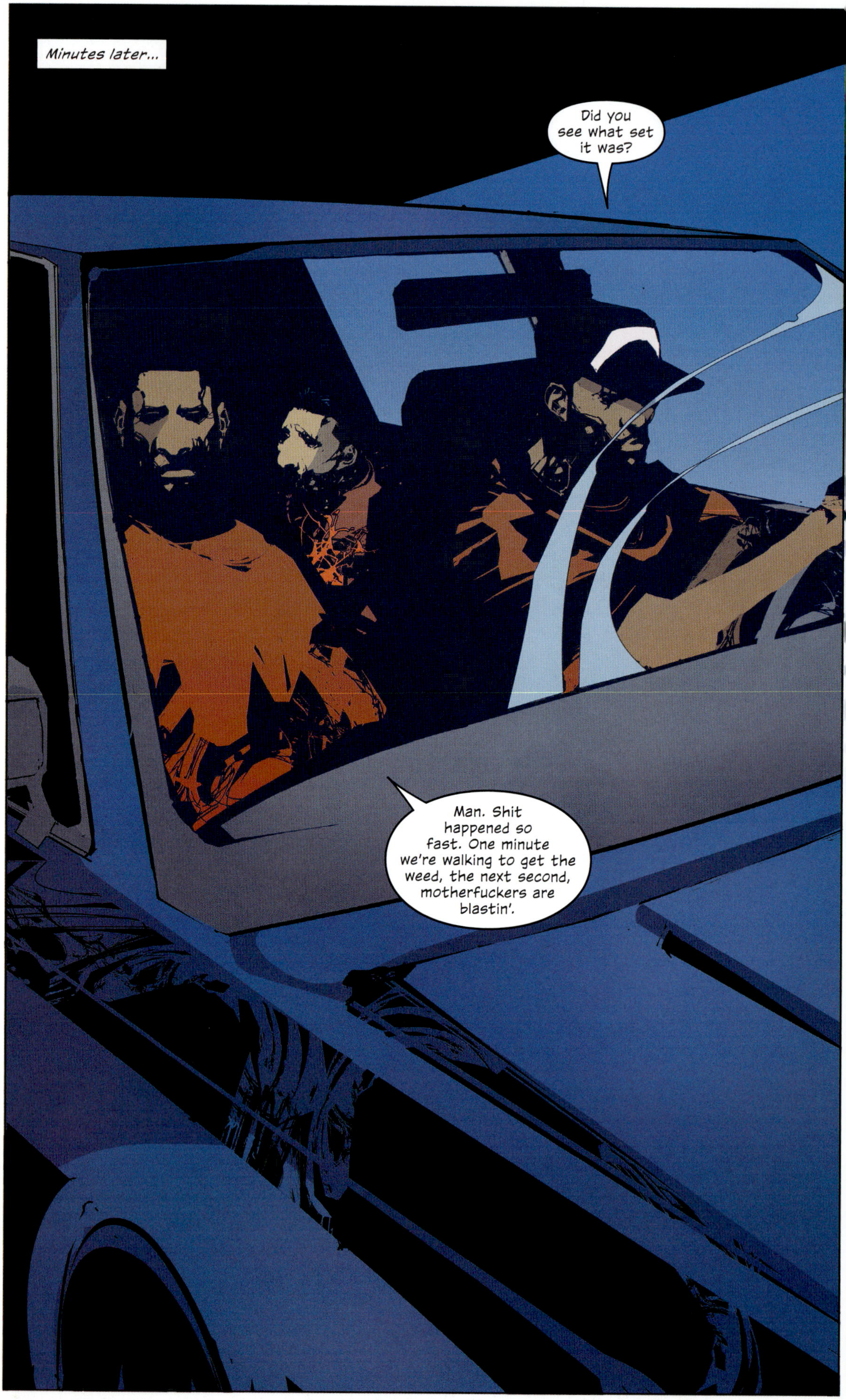
Minutes later...
Did you see what set it was?
Man. Shit happened so fast. One minute we're walking to get the weed, the next second, motherfuckers are blastin'.

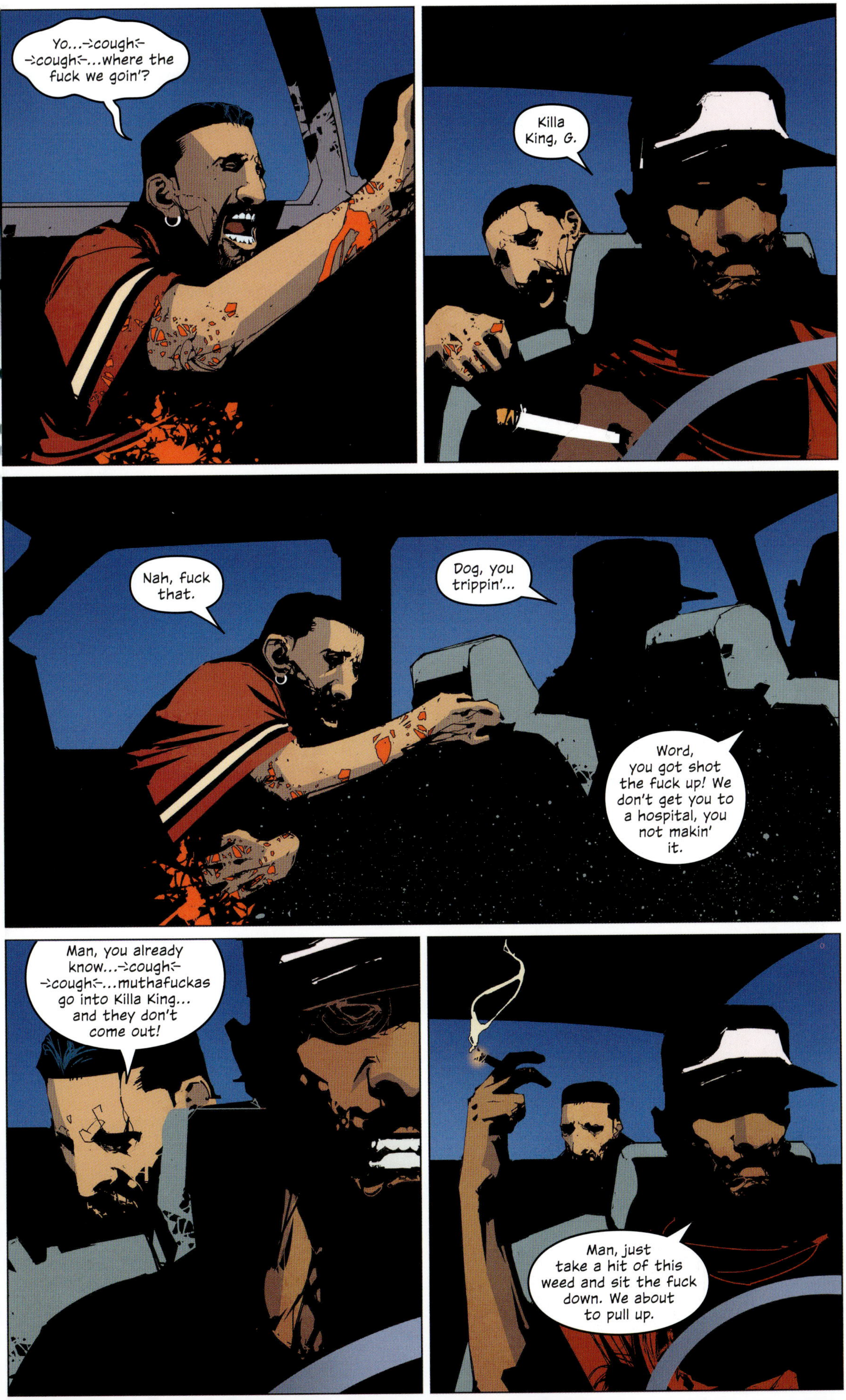
Yo...–cough–
–cough–...where the fuck we goin'?
Killa King, G.
Nah, fuck that.
Dog, you trippin'...
Word, you got shot the fuck up! We don't get you to a hospital, you not makin' it.
Man, you already know...–cough–
–cough–...muthafuckas go into Killa King... and they don't come out!
Man, just take a hit of this weed and sit the fuck down. We about to pull up.

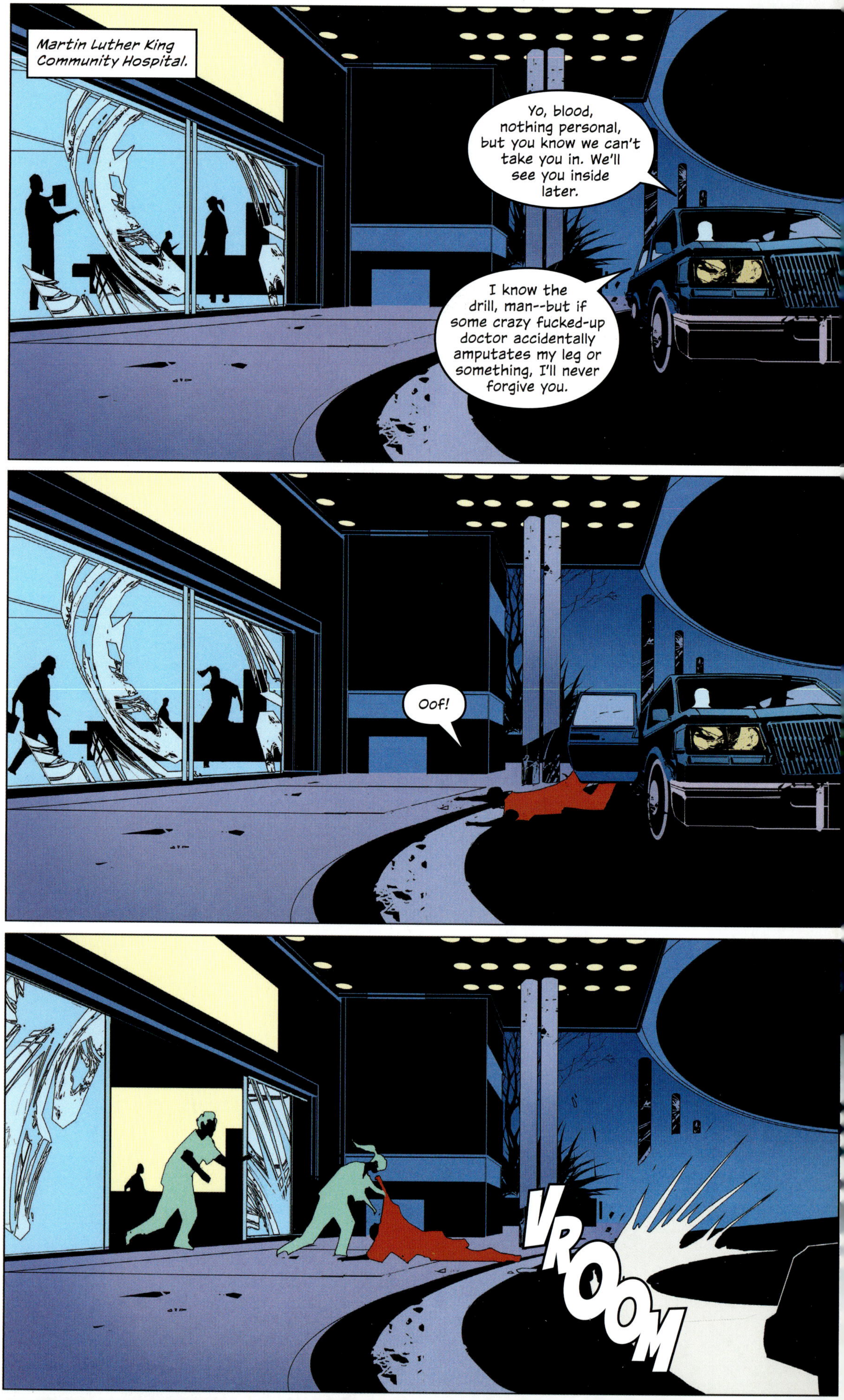
Martin Luther King Community Hospital.
Yo, blood, nothing personal, but you know we can't take you in. We'll see you inside later.
I know the drill, man--but if some crazy fucked-up doctor accidentally amputates my leg or something, I'll never forgive you.
Oof!
VROOOM

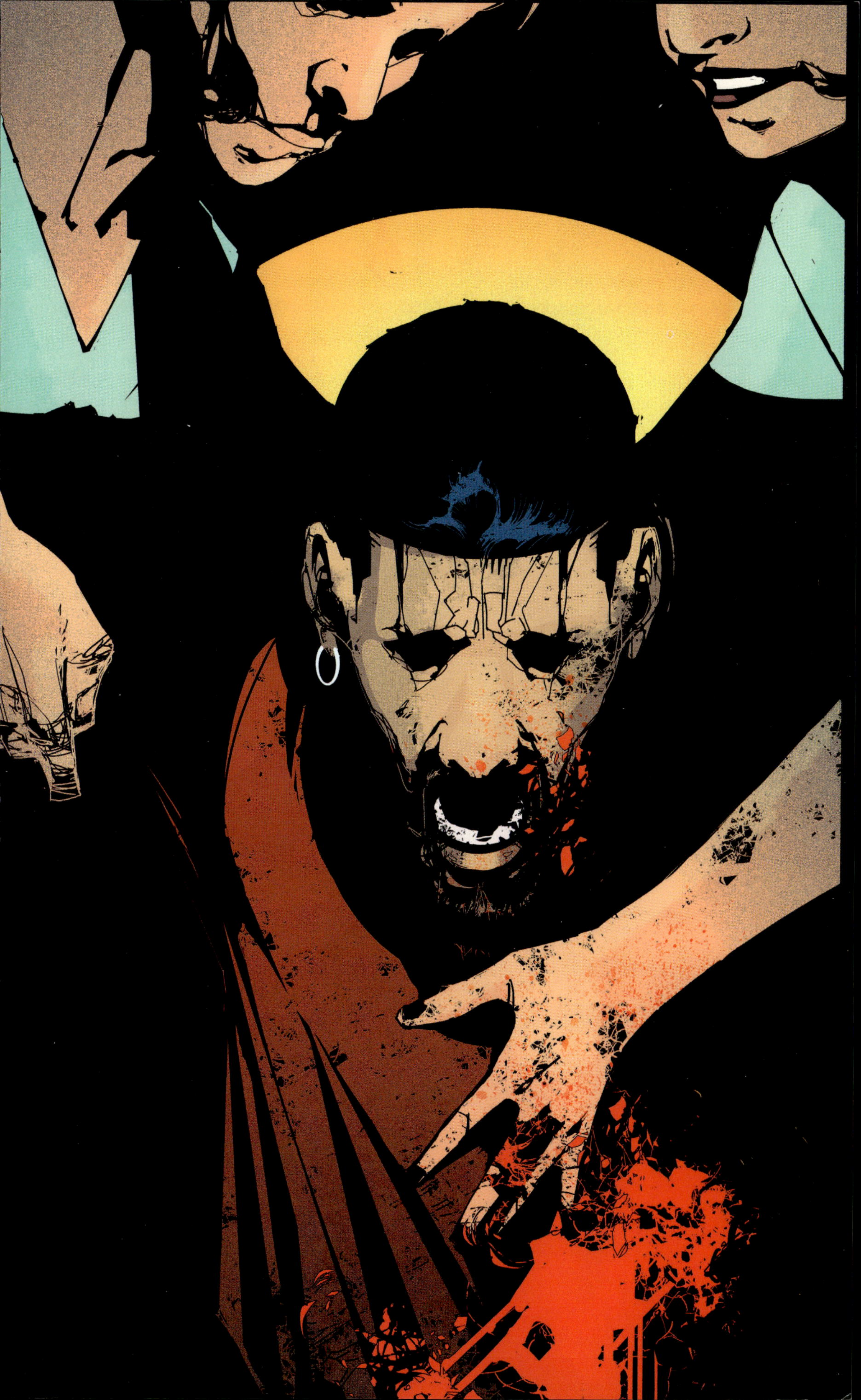

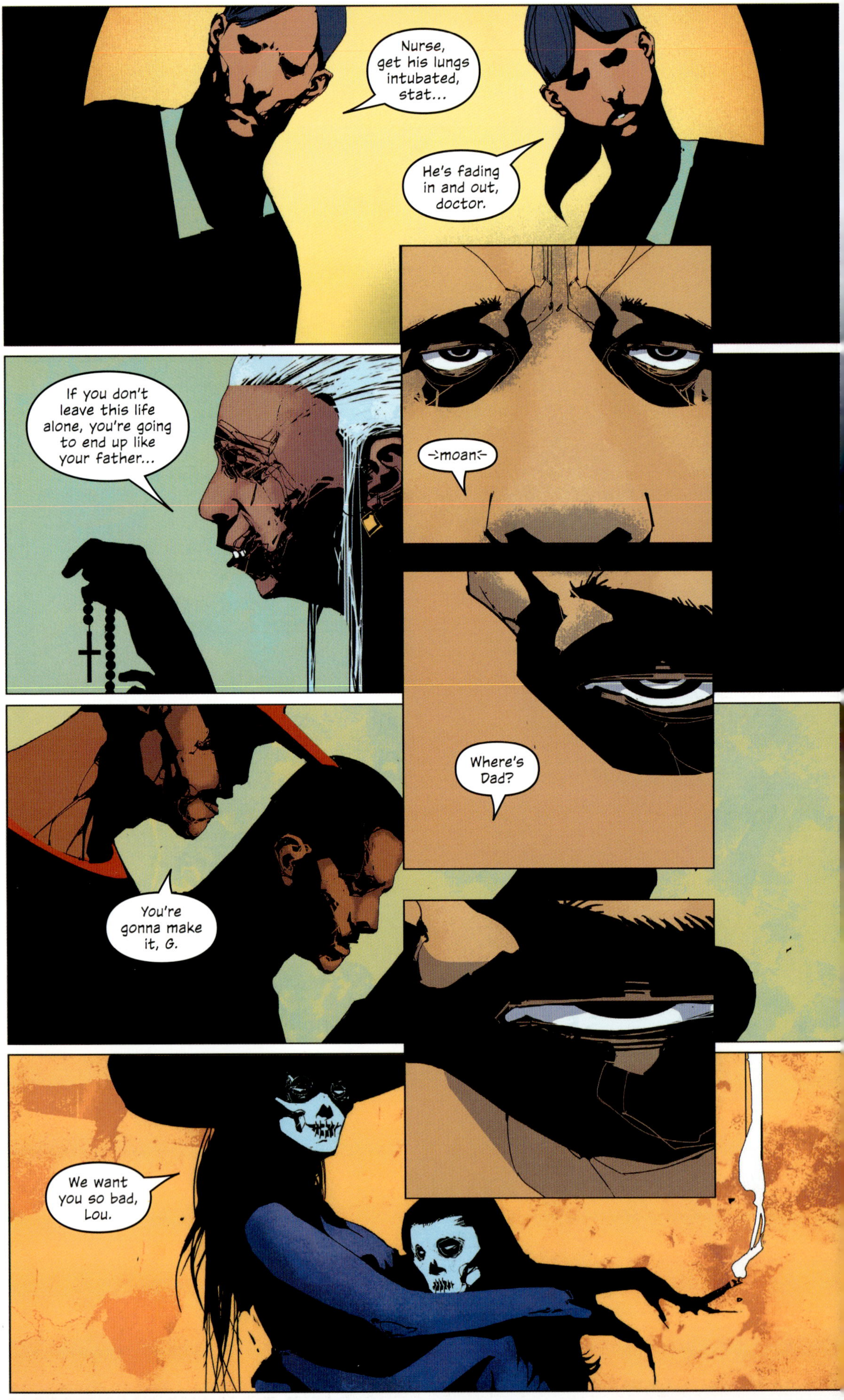
Nurse, get his lungs intubated, stat...
He's fading in and out, doctor.
If you don't leave this life alone, you're going to end up like your father...
-moan-
Where's Dad?
You're gonna make it, G.
We want you so bad, Lou.

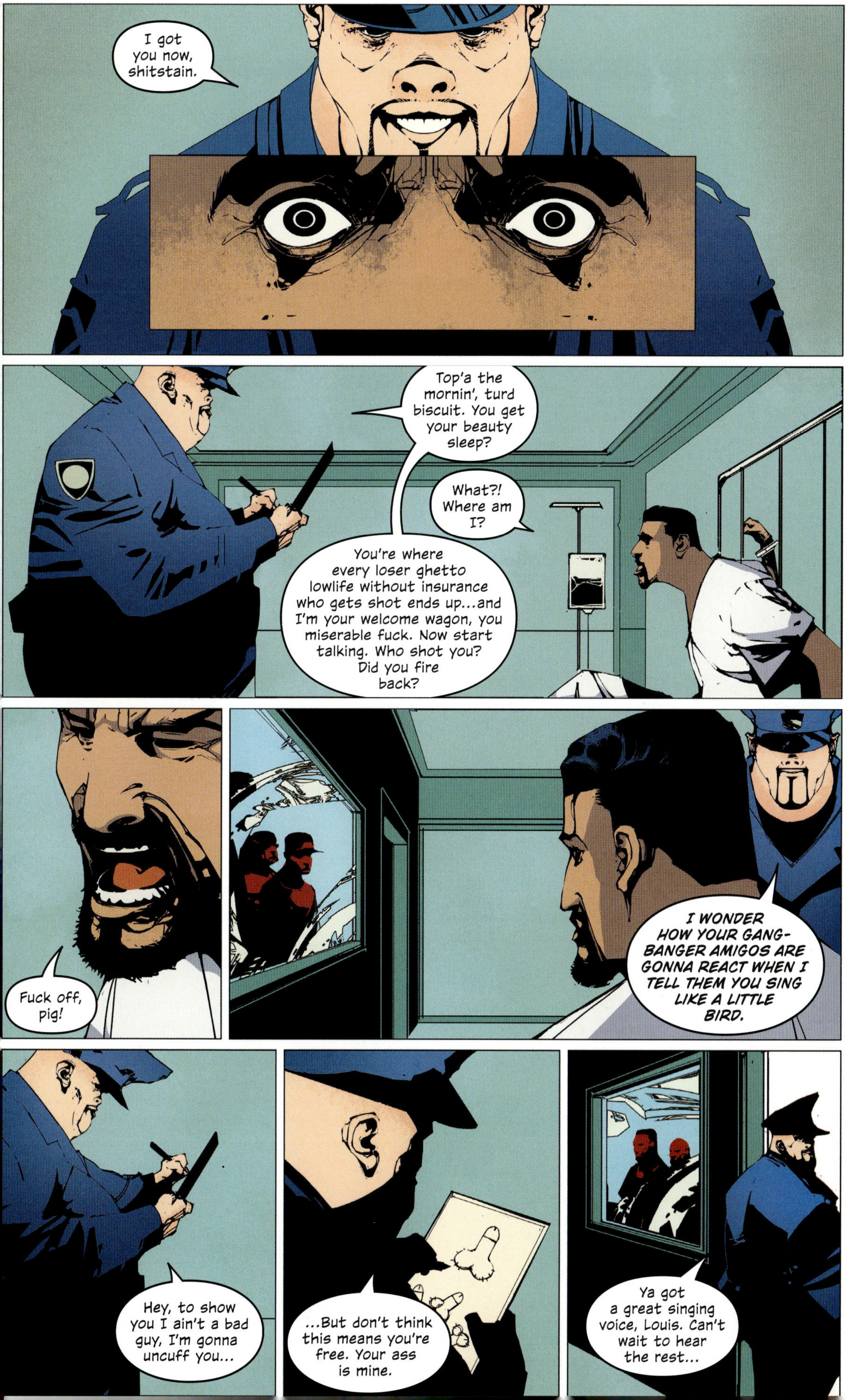
I got you now, shitstain.
Top'a the mornin', turd biscuit. You get your beauty sleep?
What?! Where am I?
You're where every loser ghetto lowlife without insurance who gets shot ends up...and I'm your welcome wagon, you miserable fuck. Now start talking. Who shot you? Did you fire back?
Fuck off, pig!
I WONDER HOW YOUR GANG-BANGER AMIGOS ARE GONNA REACT WHEN I TELL THEM YOU SING LIKE A LITTLE BIRD.
Hey, to show you I ain't a bad guy, I'm gonna uncuff you...
...But don't think this means you're free. Your ass is mine.
Ya got a great singing voice, Louis. Can't wait to hear the rest...

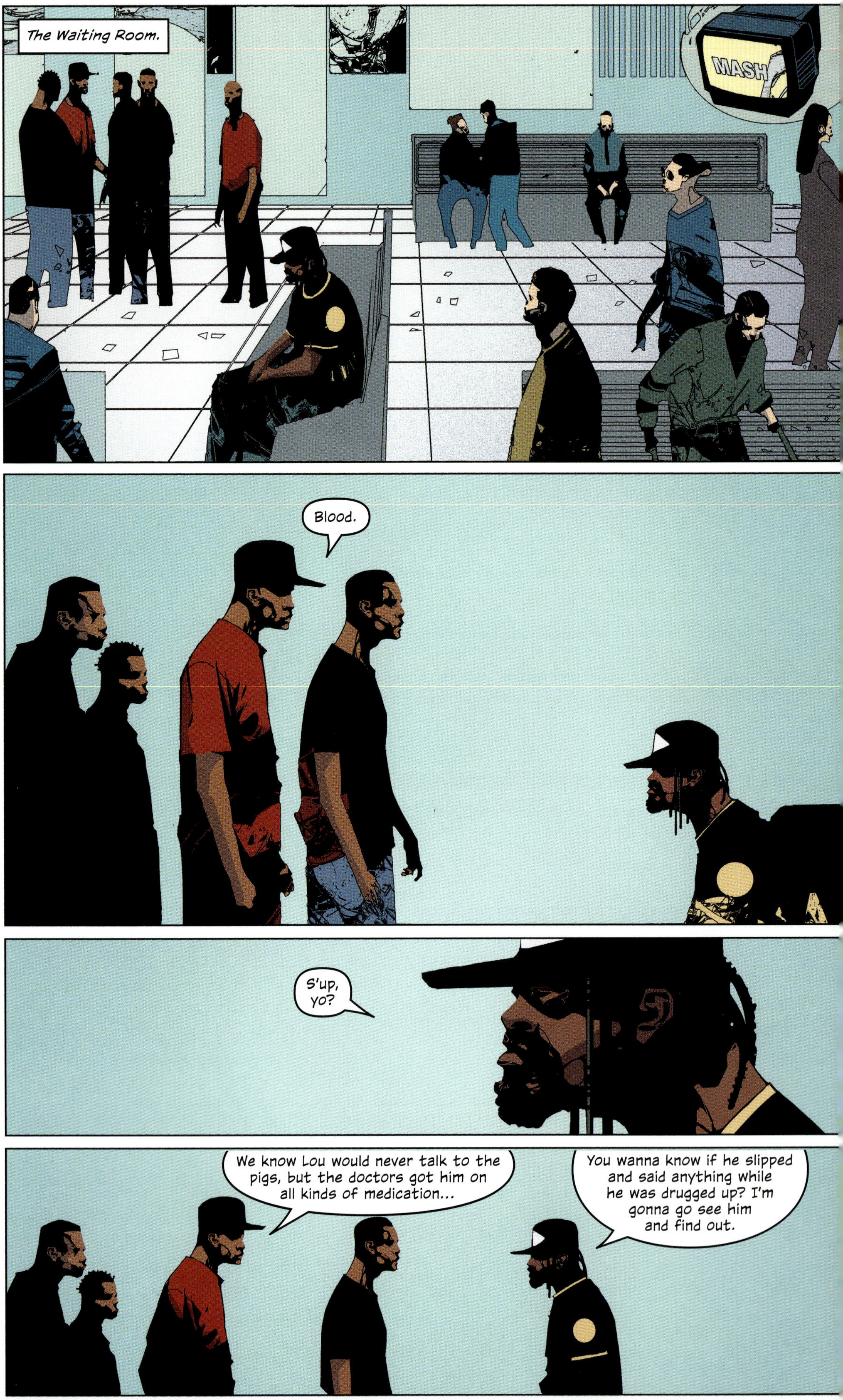
The Waiting Room.
MASH
Blood.
S'up, yo?
We know Lou would never talk to the pigs, but the doctors got him on all kinds of medication...
You wanna know if he slipped and said anything while he was drugged up? I'm gonna go see him and find out.

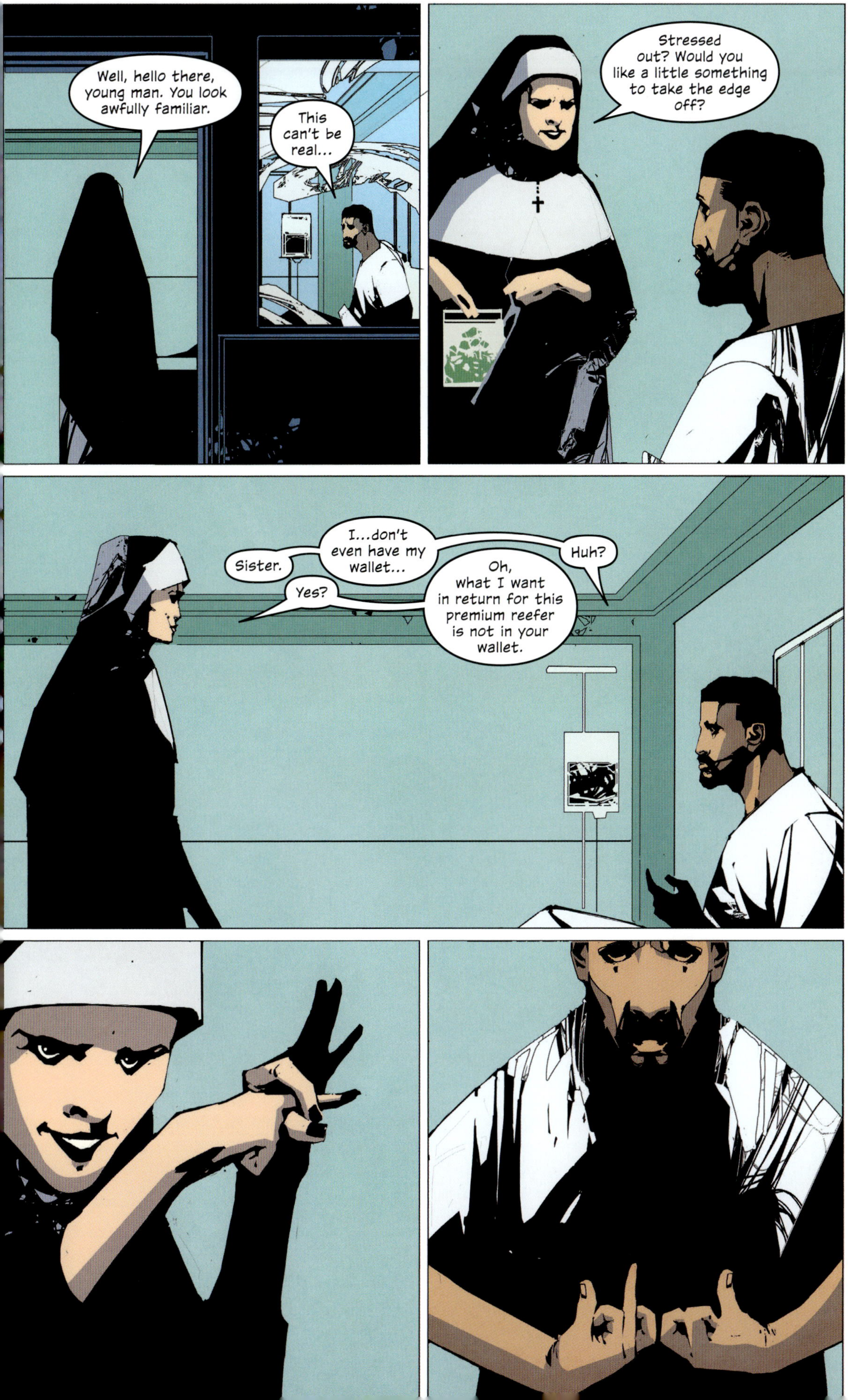
Well, hello there, young man. You look awfully familiar.
This can't be real...
Stressed out? Would you like a little something to take the edge off?
Sister.
I...don't even have my wallet...
Huh?
Yes?
Oh, what I want in return for this premium reefer is not in your wallet.

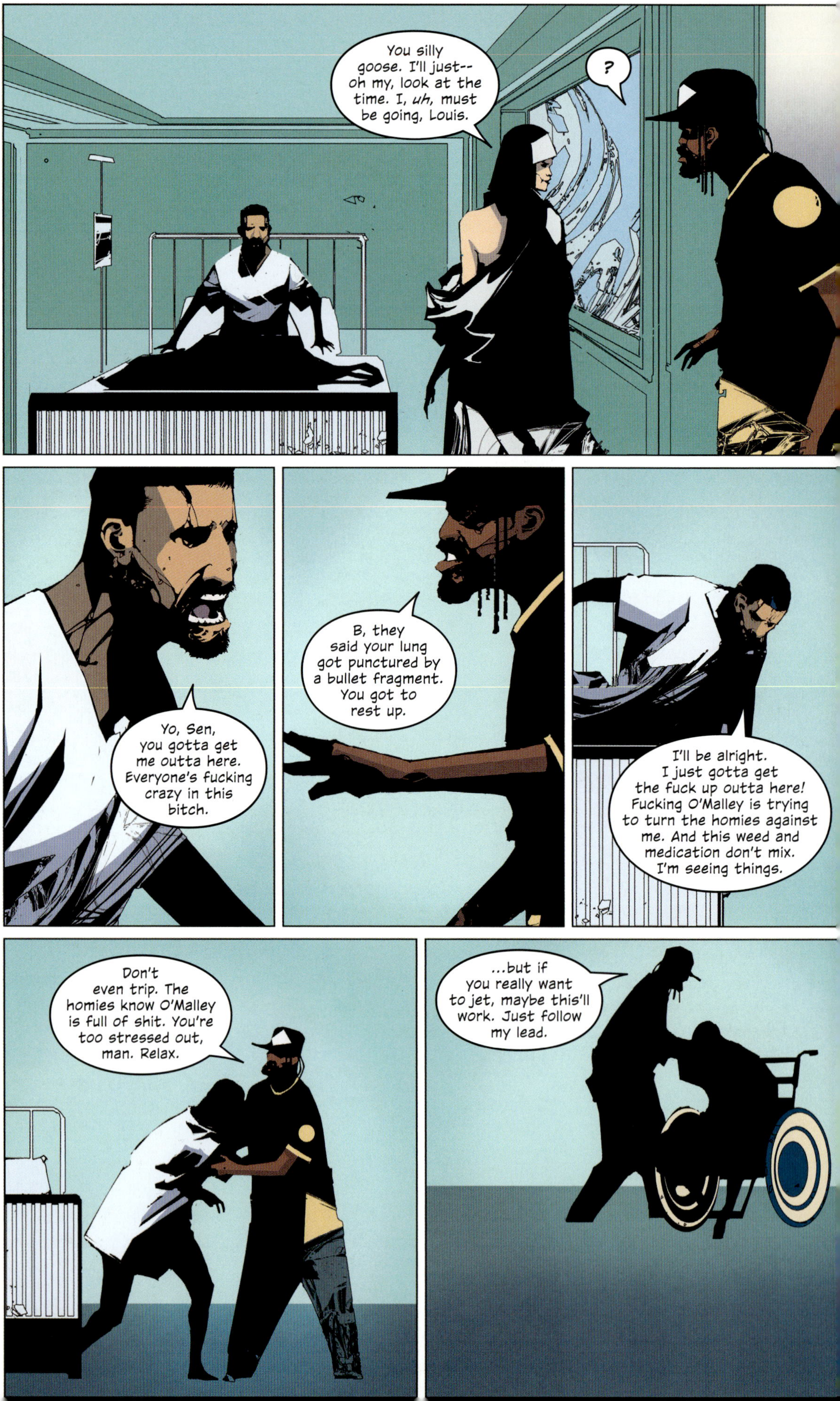
You silly goose. I'll just-- oh my, look at the time. I, *uh*, must be going, Louis.
?
Yo, Sen, you gotta get me outta here. Everyone's fucking crazy in this bitch.
B, they said your lung got punctured by a bullet fragment. You got to rest up.
I'll be alright. I just gotta get the fuck up outta here! Fucking O'Malley is trying to turn the homies against me. And this weed and medication don't mix. I'm seeing things.
Don't even trip. The homies know O'Malley is full of shit. You're too stressed out, man. Relax.
...but if you really want to jet, maybe this'll work. Just follow my lead.

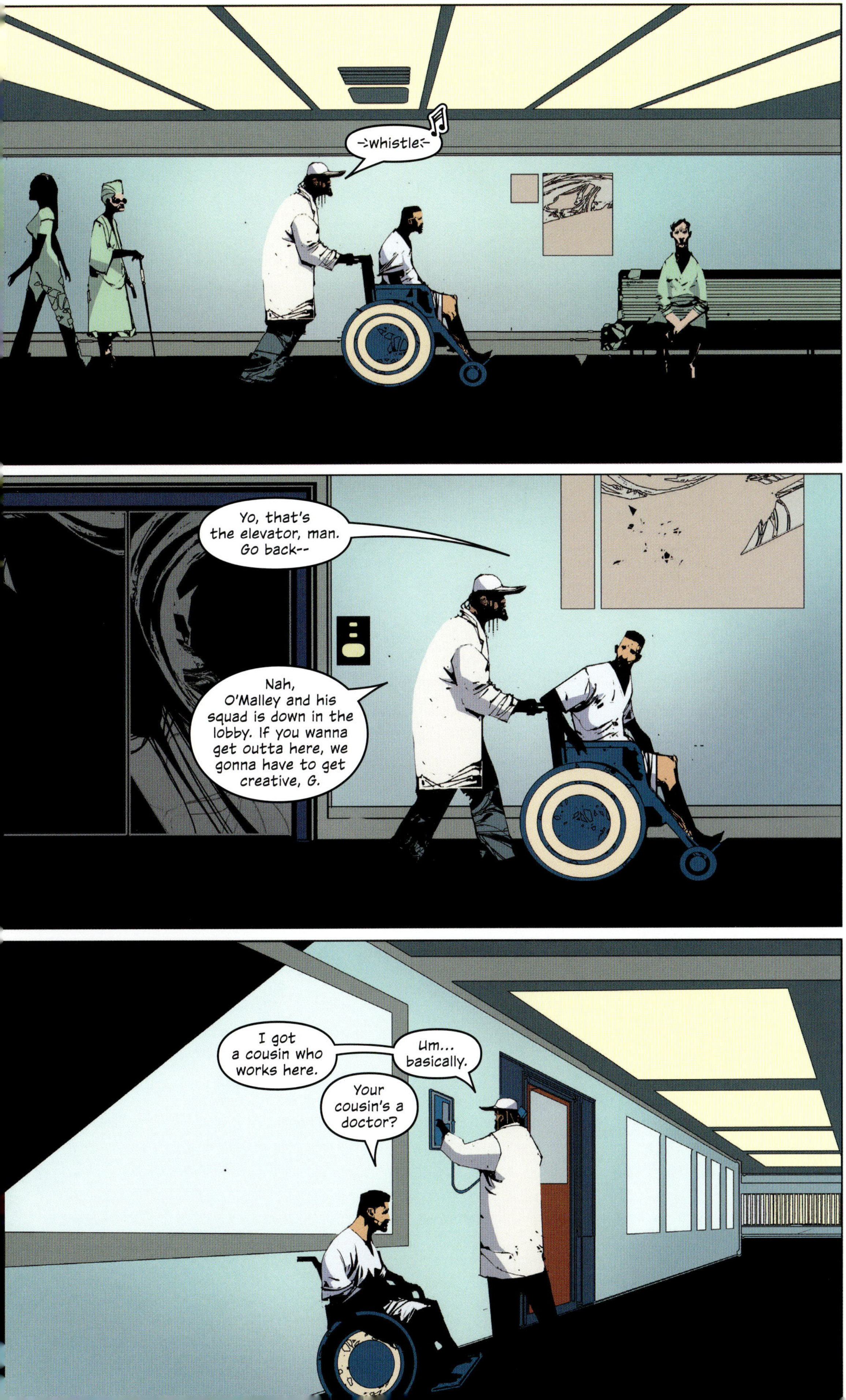
-whistle-
Yo, that's the elevator, man. Go back--
Nah, O'Malley and his squad is down in the lobby. If you wanna get outta here, we gonna have to get creative, G.
I got a cousin who works here.
Your cousin's a doctor?
Um... basically.

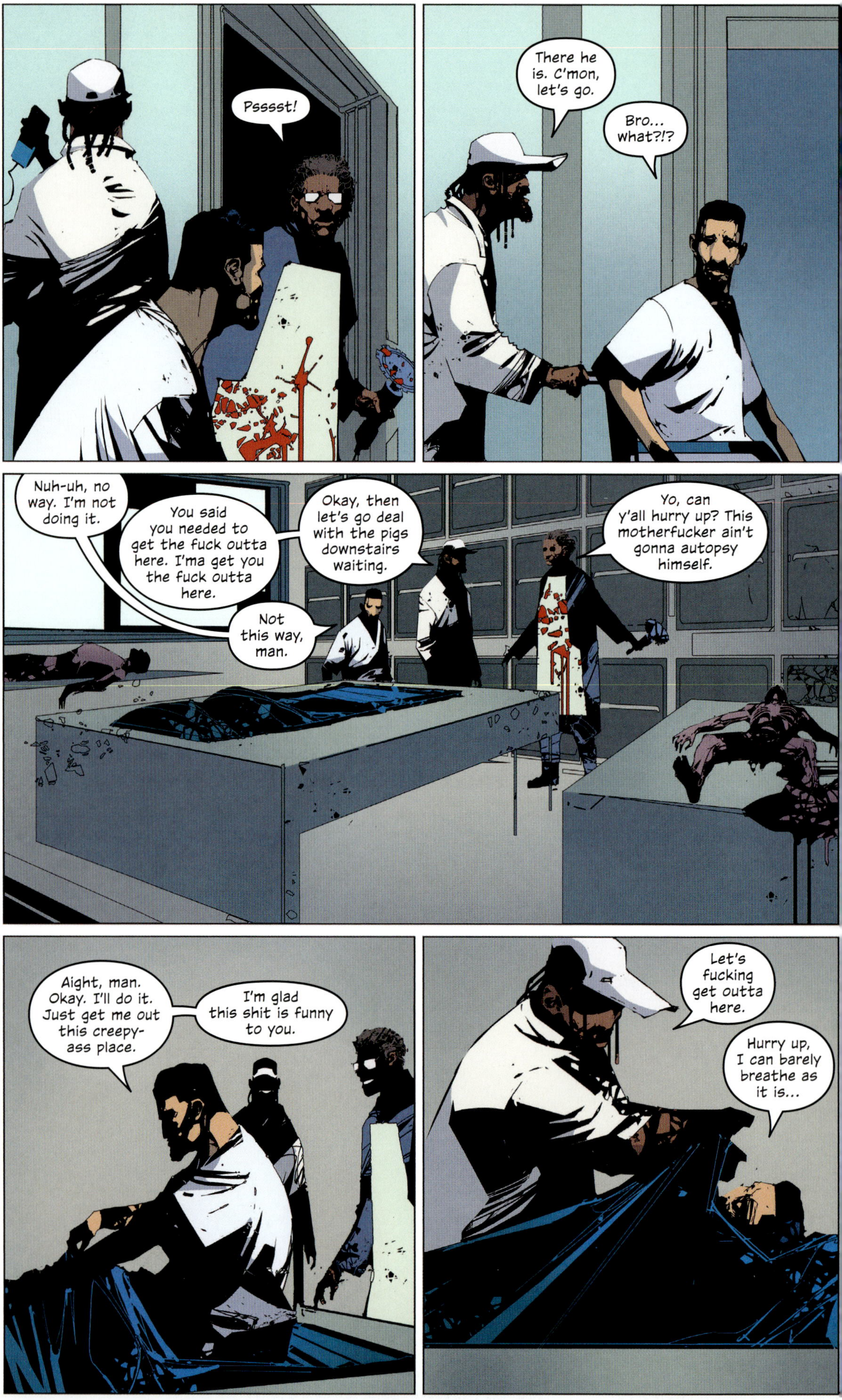
Psssst!
There he is. C'mon, let's go.
Bro... what?!?
Nuh-uh, no way. I'm not doing it.
You said you needed to get the fuck outta here. I'ma get you the fuck outta here.
Not this way, man.
Okay, then let's go deal with the pigs downstairs waiting.
Yo, can y'all hurry up? This motherfucker ain't gonna autopsy himself.
Aight, man. Okay. I'll do it. Just get me out this creepy-ass place.
I'm glad this shit is funny to you.
Let's fucking get outta here.
Hurry up, I can barely breathe as it is...

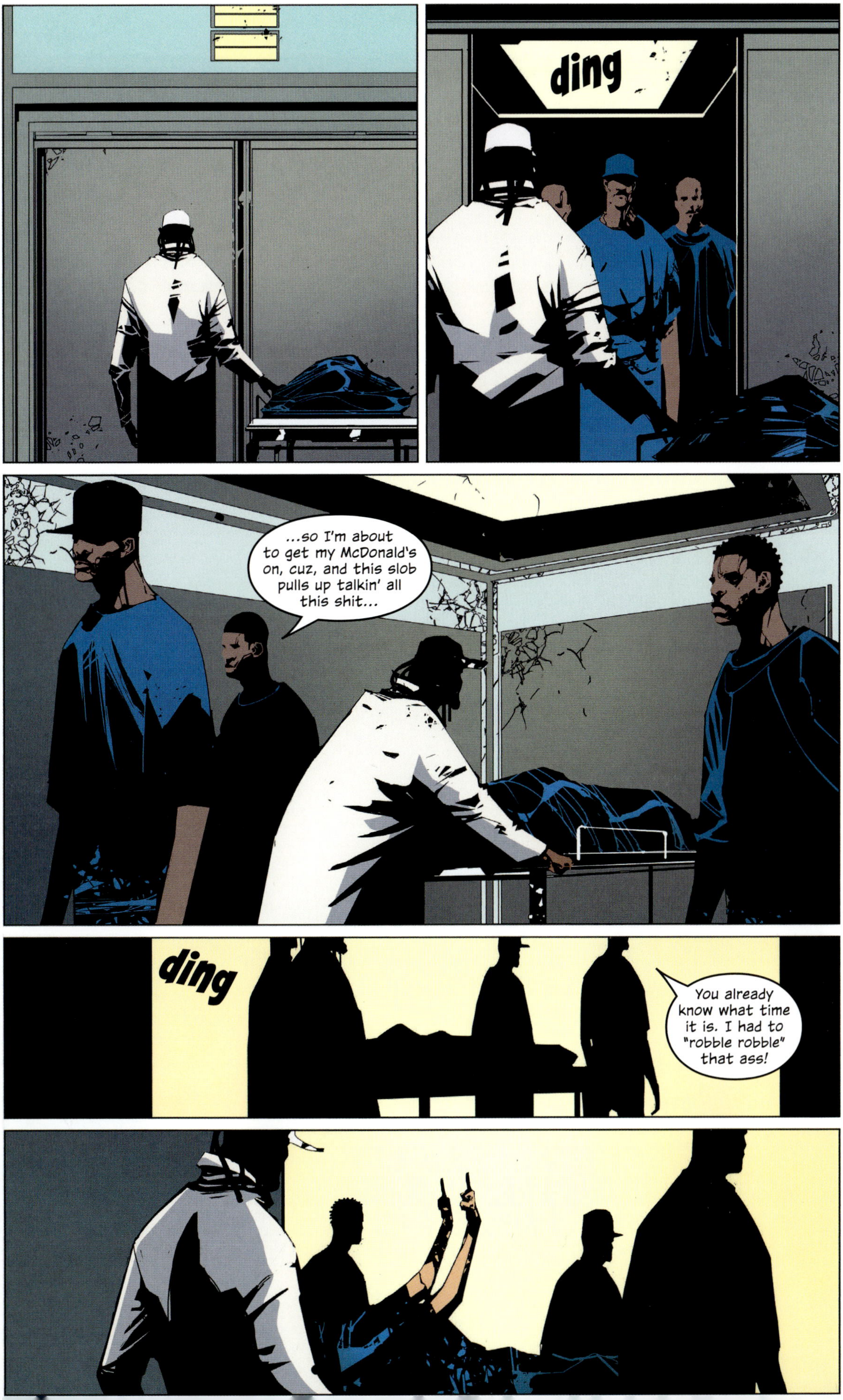
ding
...so I'm about to get my McDonald's on, cuz, and this slob pulls up talkin' all this shit...
ding
You already know what time it is. I had to "robble robble" that ass!

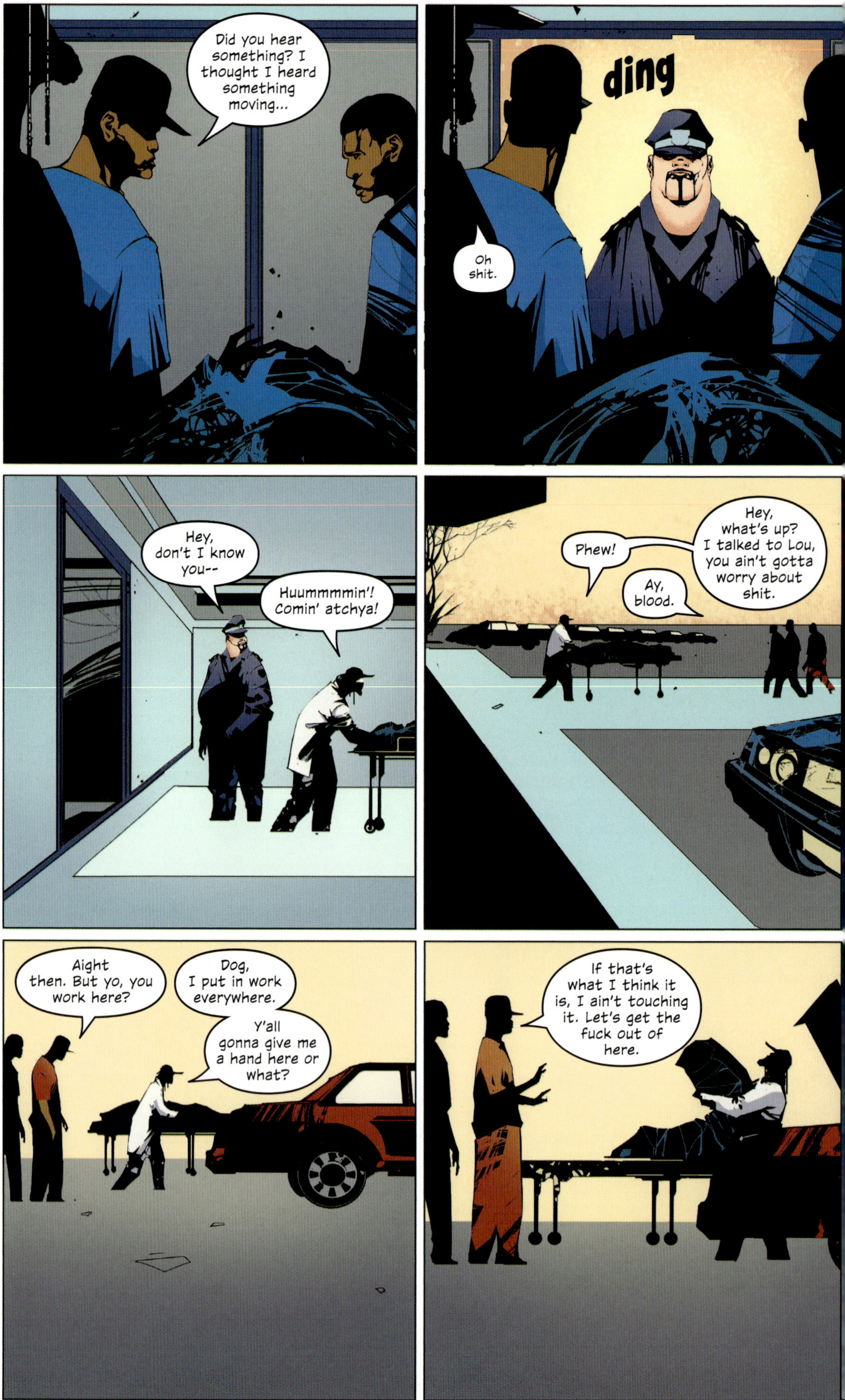
Did you hear something? I thought I heard something moving...
ding
Oh shit.
Hey, don't I know you--
Huummmmin'! Comin' atchya!
Phew!
Hey, what's up? I talked to Lou, you ain't gotta worry about shit.
Ay, blood.
Aight then. But yo, you work here?
Dog, I put in work everywhere.
Y'all gonna give me a hand here or what?
If that's what I think it is, I ain't touching it. Let's get the fuck out of here.

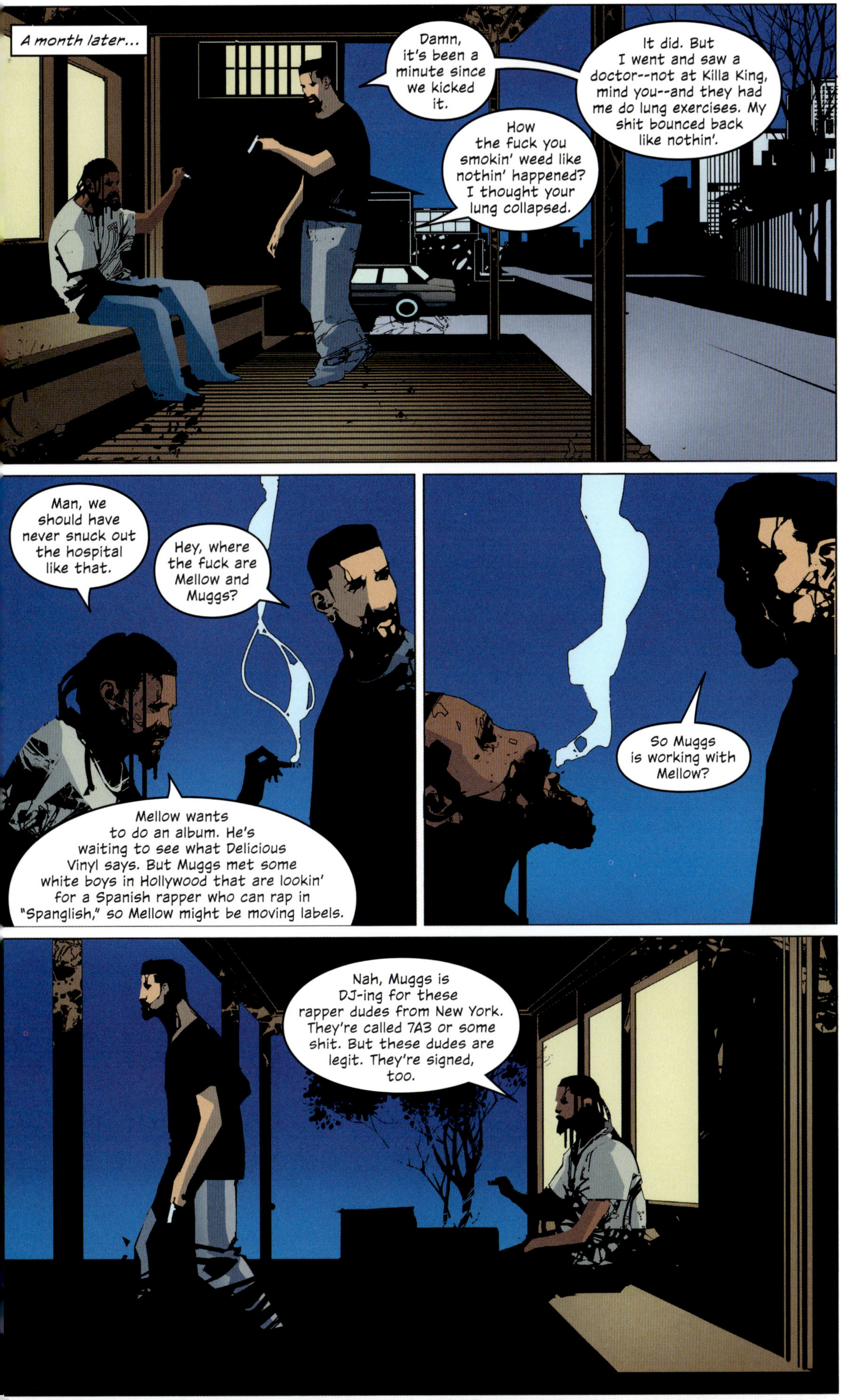
A month later...
Damn, it's been a minute since we kicked it.
How the fuck you smokin' weed like nothin' happened? I thought your lung collapsed.
It did. But I went and saw a doctor--not at Killa King, mind you--and they had me do lung exercises. My shit bounced back like nothin'.
Man, we should have never snuck out the hospital like that.
Hey, where the fuck are Mellow and Muggs?
Mellow wants to do an album. He's waiting to see what Delicious Vinyl says. But Muggs met some white boys in Hollywood that are lookin' for a Spanish rapper who can rap in "Spanglish," so Mellow might be moving labels.
So Muggs is working with Mellow?
Nah, Muggs is DJ-ing for these rapper dudes from New York. They're called 7A3 or some shit. But these dudes are legit. They're signed, too.

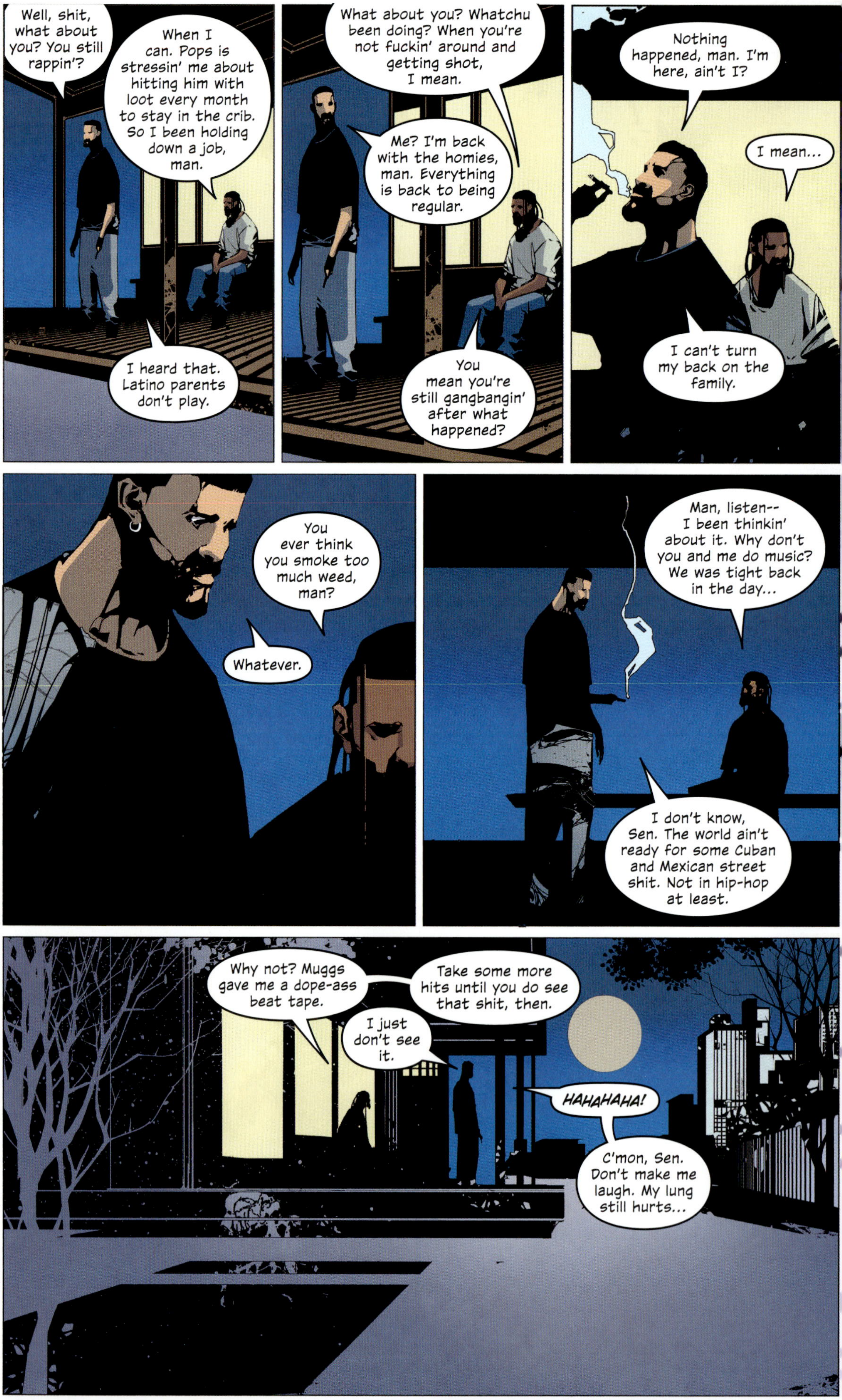
Well, shit, what about you? You still rappin'?
When I can. Pops is stressin' me about hitting him with loot every month to stay in the crib. So I been holding down a job, man.
I heard that. Latino parents don't play.
What about you? Whatchu been doing? When you're not fuckin' around and getting shot, I mean.
Me? I'm back with the homies, man. Everything is back to being regular.
You mean you're still gangbangin' after what happened?
Nothing happened, man. I'm here, ain't I?
I mean...
I can't turn my back on the family.
You ever think you smoke too much weed, man?
Whatever.
Man, listen-- I been thinkin' about it. Why don't you and me do music? We was tight back in the day...
I don't know, Sen. The world ain't ready for some Cuban and Mexican street shit. Not in hip-hop at least.
Why not? Muggs gave me a dope-ass beat tape.
I just don't see it.
Take some more hits until you do see that shit, then.
HAHAHAHA!
C'mon, Sen. Don't make me laugh. My lung still hurts...

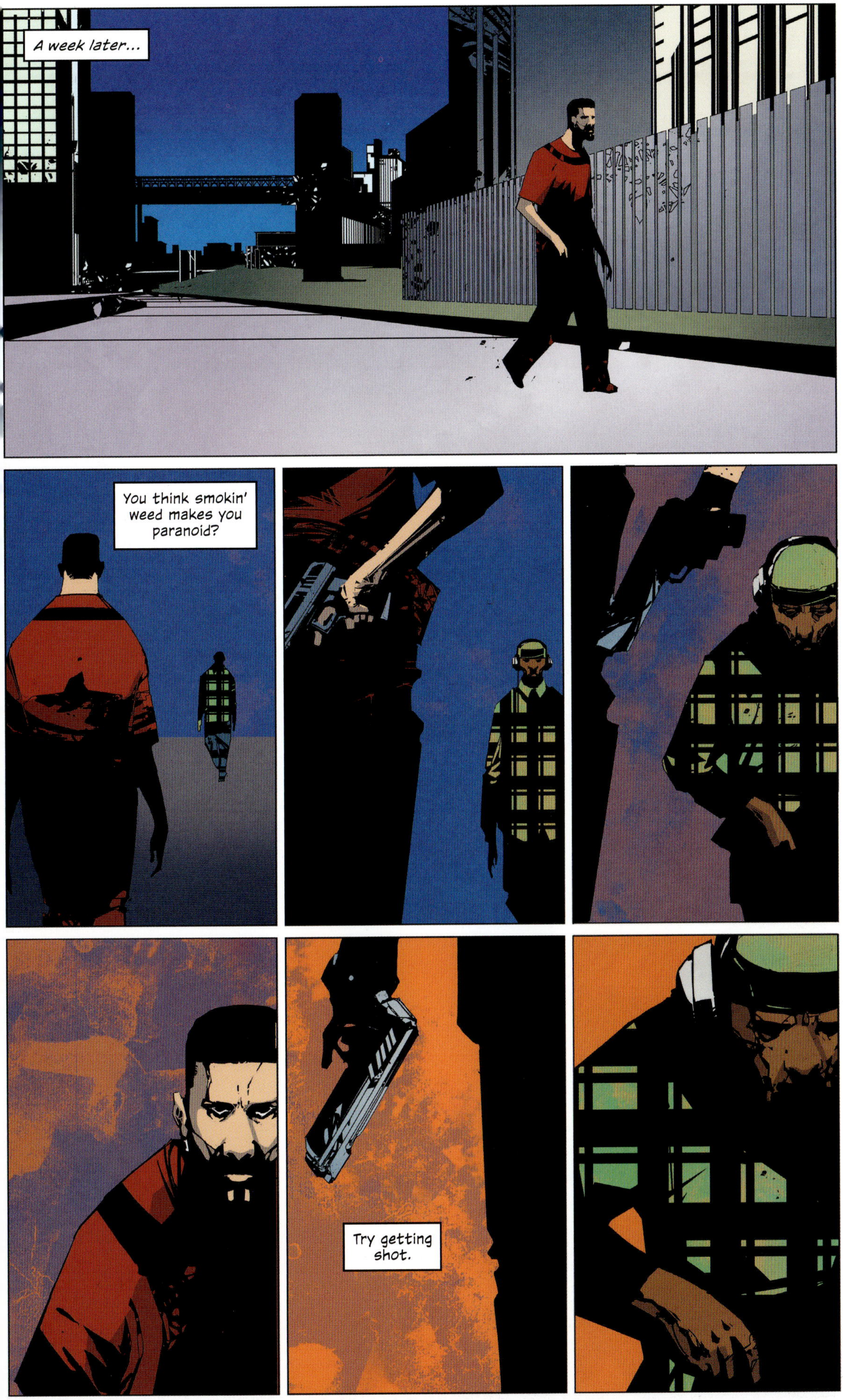
A week later...
You think smokin' weed makes you paranoid?
Try getting shot.

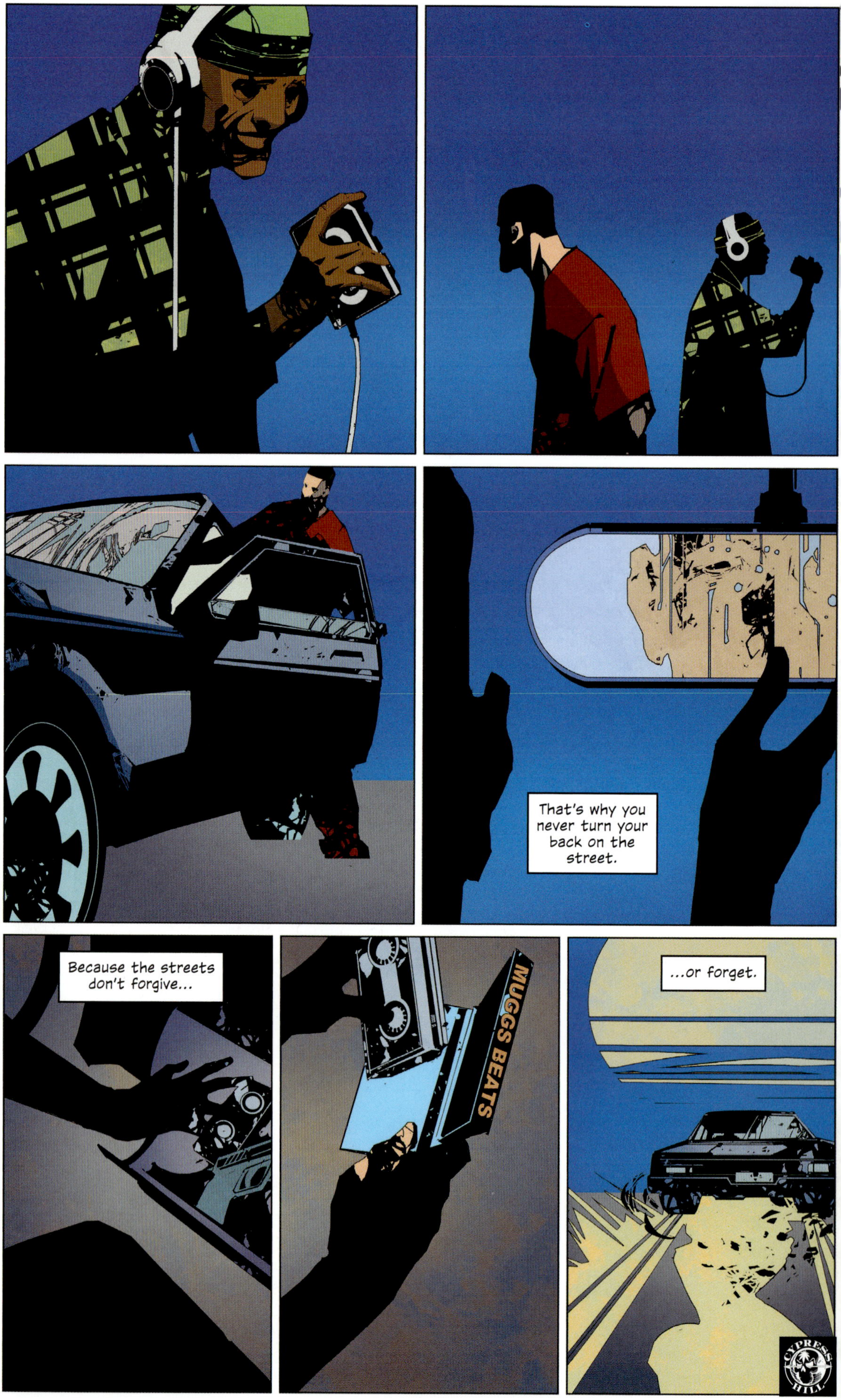
That's why you never turn your back on the street.
Because the streets don't forgive...
MUGGS BEATS
...or forget.

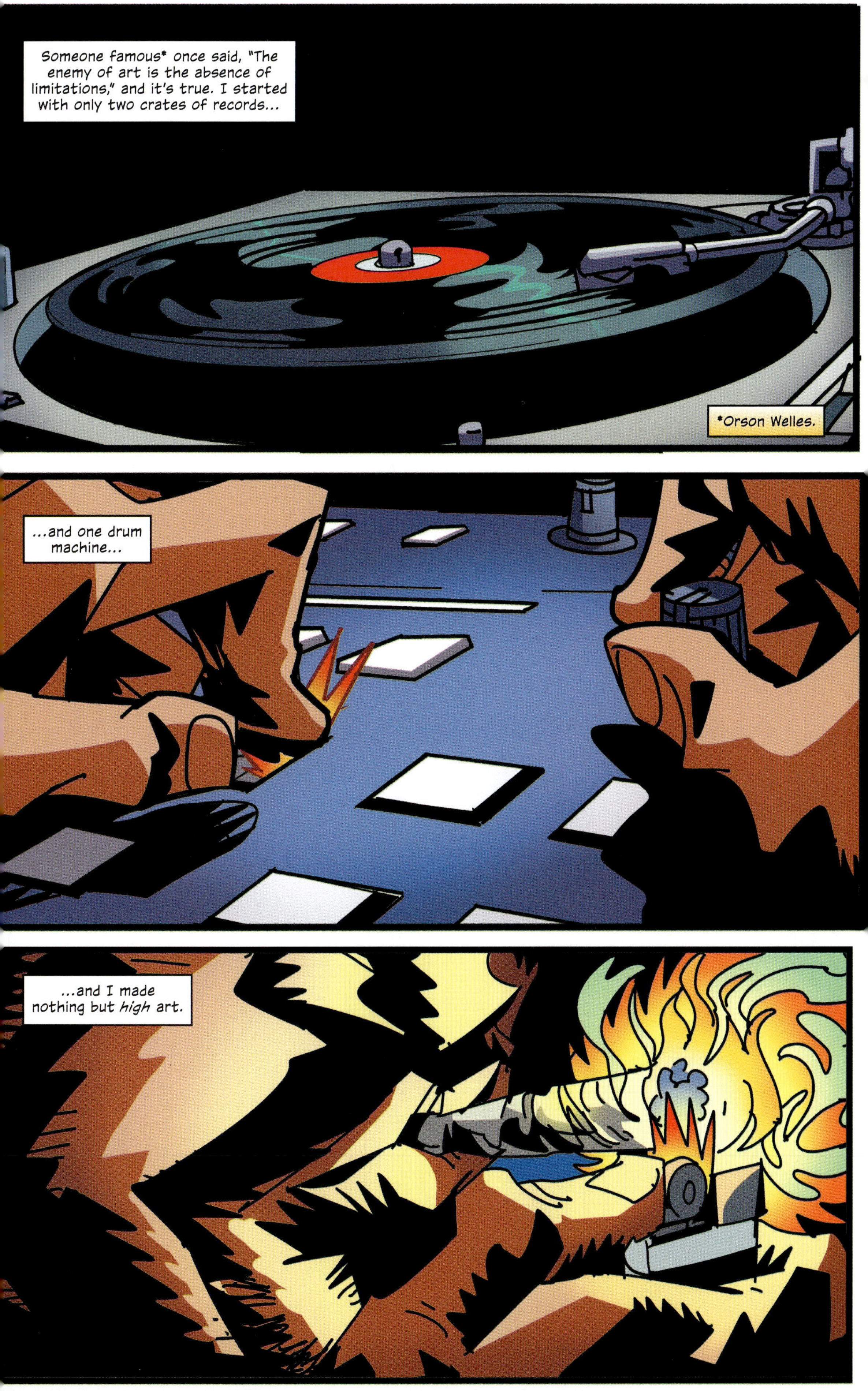
Someone famous* once said, "The enemy of art is the absence of limitations," and it's true. I started with only two crates of records...
*Orson Welles.
...and one drum machine...
...and I made nothing but *high* art.

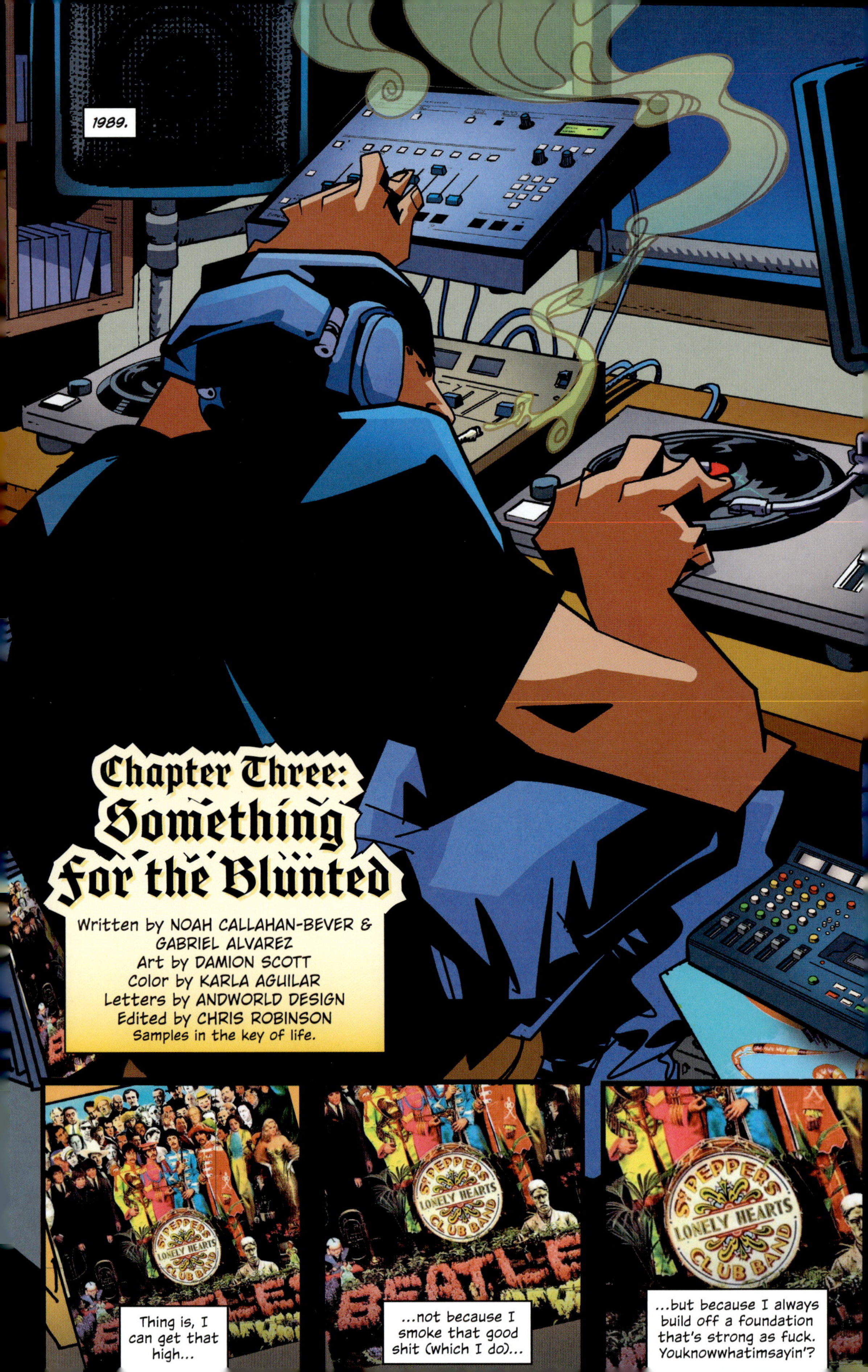
1989.
Chapter Three: Something For the Blünted
Written by NOAH CALLAHAN-BEVER & GABRIEL ALVAREZ
Art by DAMION SCOTT
Color by KARLA AGUILAR
Letters by ANDWORLD DESIGN
Edited by CHRIS ROBINSON
Samples in the key of life.
Thing is, I can get that high...
...not because I smoke that good shit (which I do)...
...but because I always build off a foundation that's strong as fuck. Youknowwhatimsayin'?

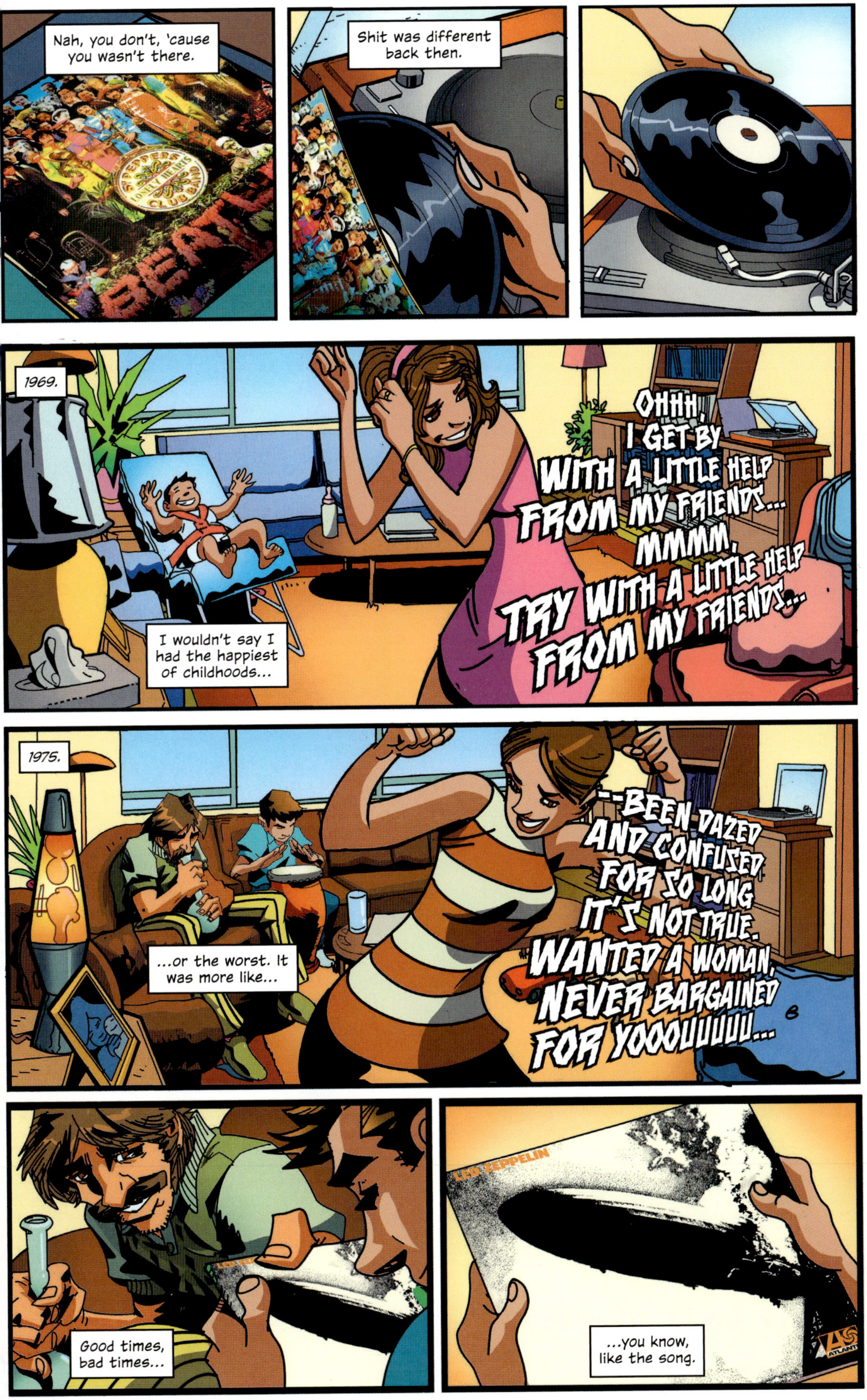

Nah, you don't, 'cause you wasn't there.
Shit was different back then.
1969.
OHHH, I GET BY WITH A LITTLE HELP FROM MY FRIENDS... MMMM, TRY WITH A LITTLE HELP FROM MY FRIENDS...
I wouldn't say I had the happiest of childhoods...
1975.
--BEEN DAZED AND CONFUSED FOR SO LONG IT'S NOT TRUE. WANTED A WOMAN, NEVER BARGAINED FOR YOOOUUUUU...
...or the worst. It was more like...
Good times, bad times...
LED ZEPPELIN
...you know, like the song.

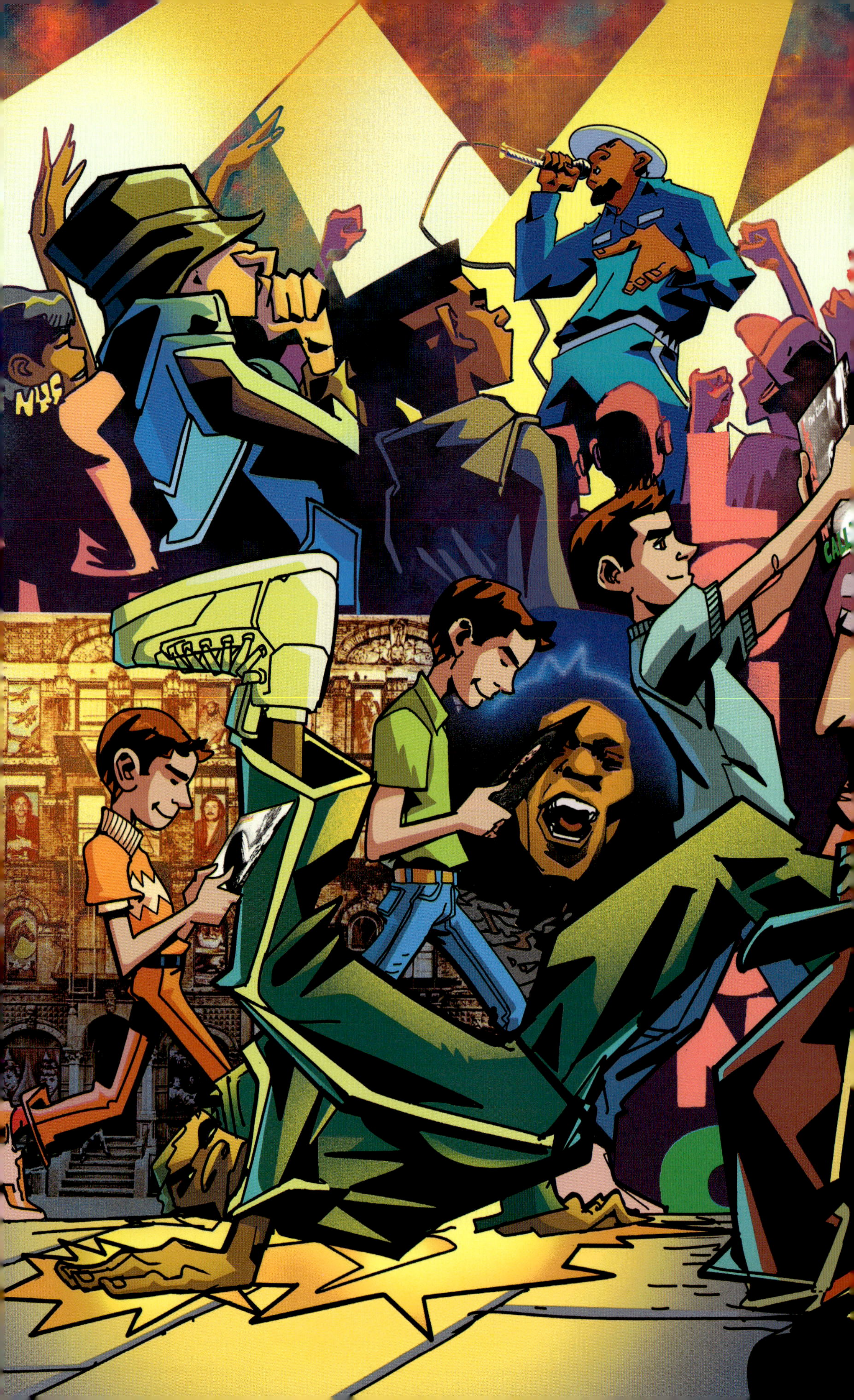
NYC

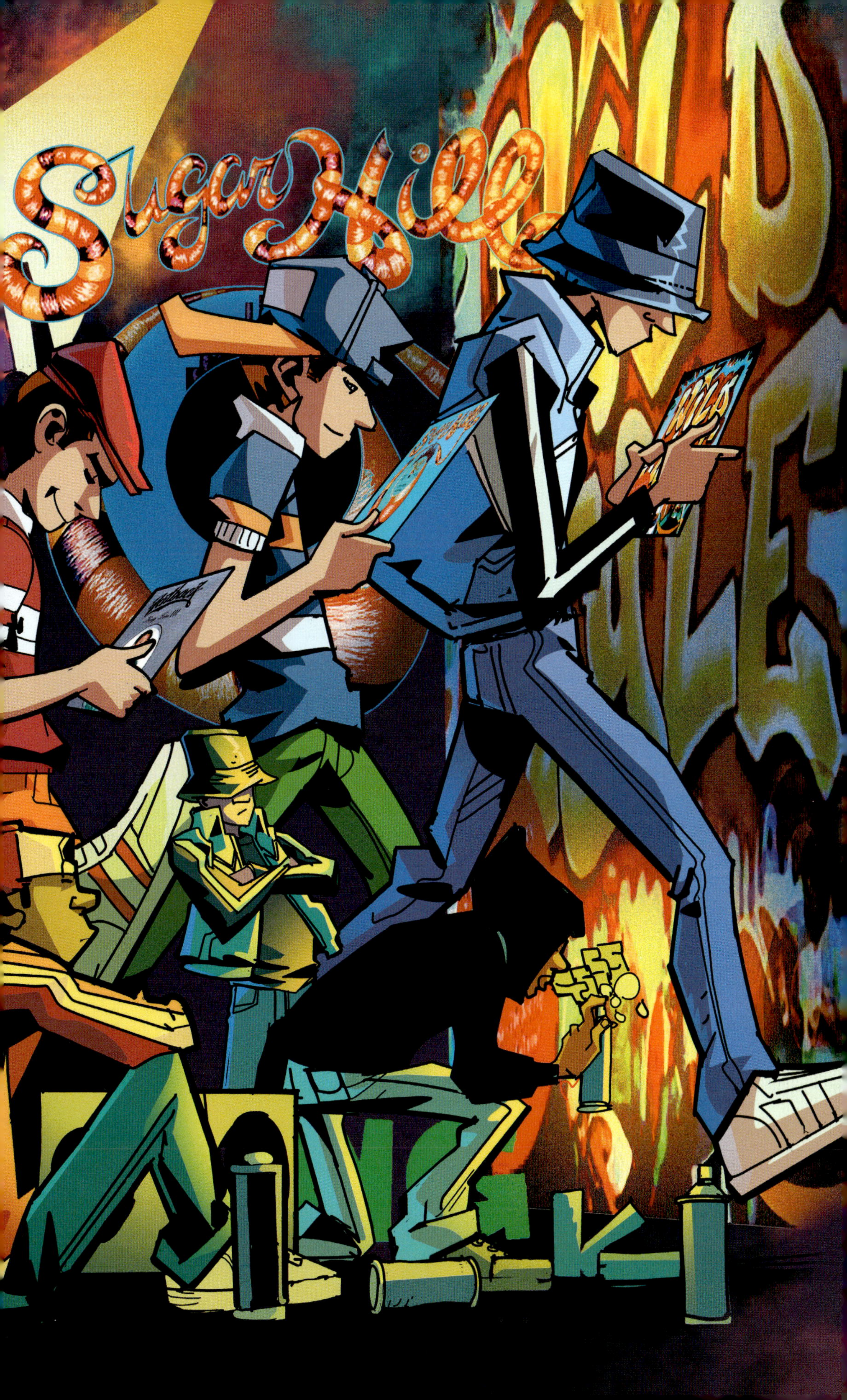
Sugar Hill

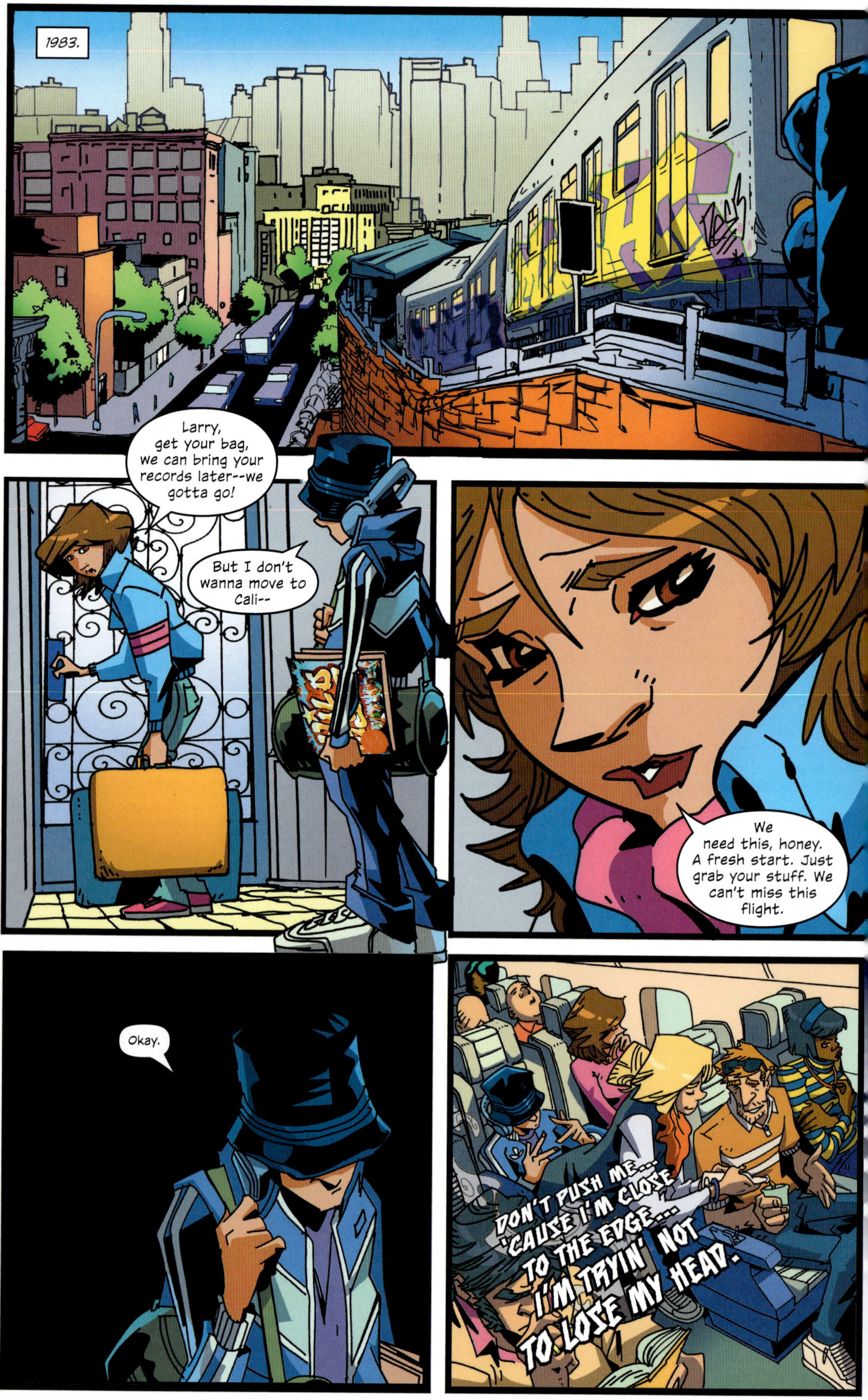
1983.
Larry, get your bag, we can bring your records later--we gotta go!
But I don't wanna move to Cali--
We need this, honey. A fresh start. Just grab your stuff. We can't miss this flight.
Okay.
DON'T PUSH ME... 'CAUSE I'M CLOSE TO THE EDGE... I'M TRYIN' NOT TO LOSE MY HEAD.

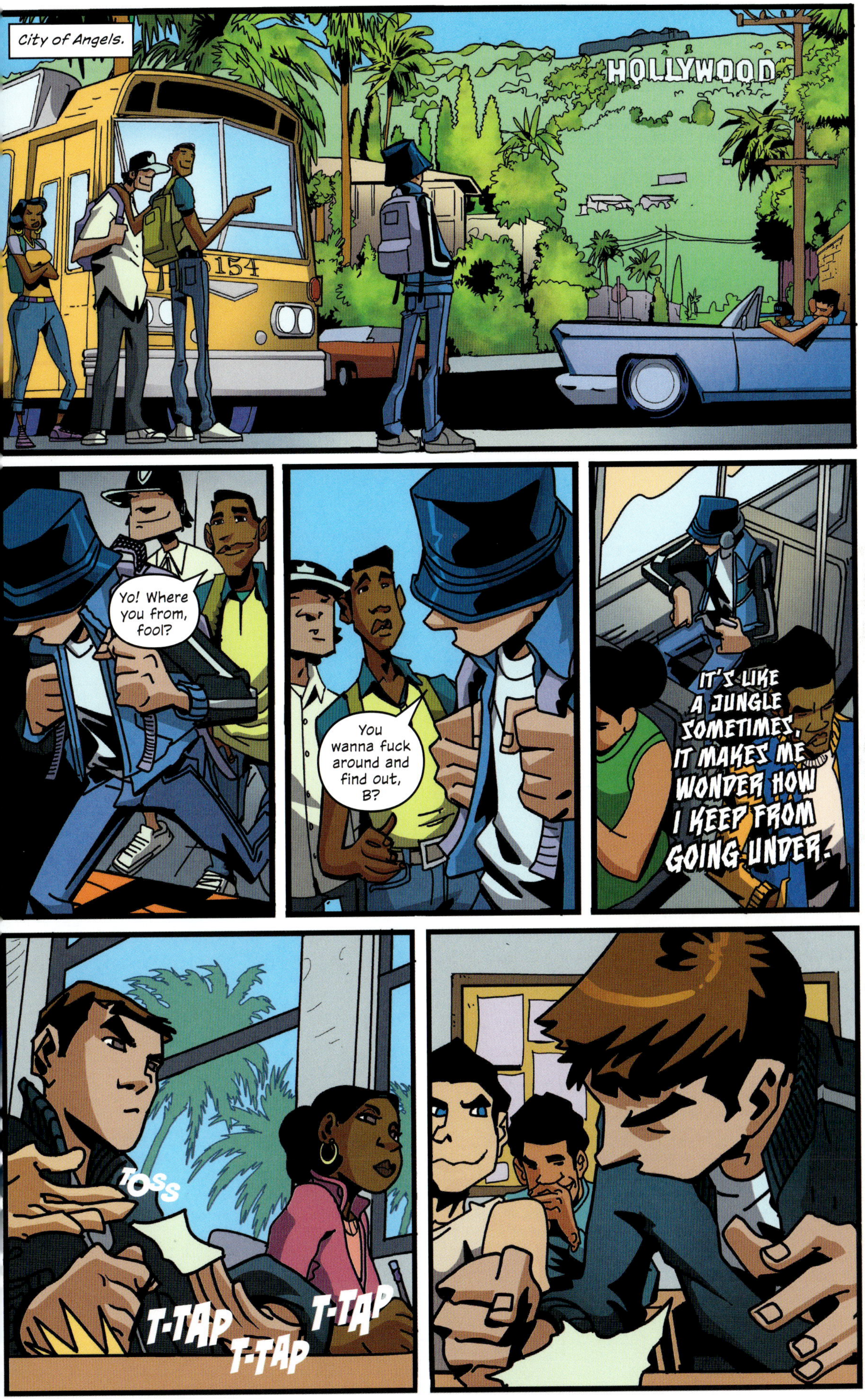
City of Angels.
HOLLYWOOD
154
Yo! Where you from, fool?
You wanna fuck around and find out, B?
IT'S LIKE A JUNGLE SOMETIMES, IT MAKES ME WONDER HOW I KEEP FROM GOING UNDER.
TOSS
T-TAP
T-TAP
T-TAP

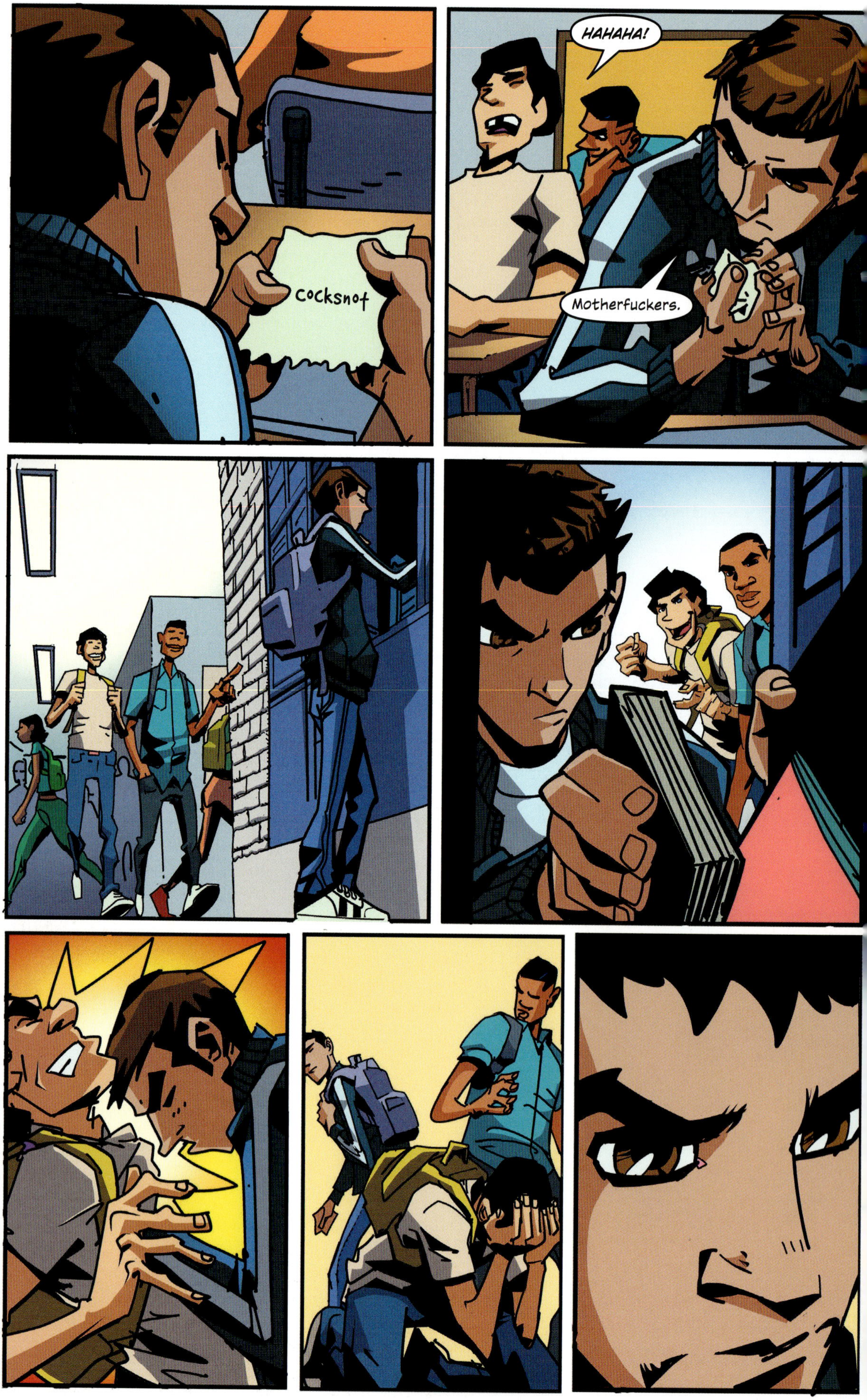
cocksnot
HAHAHA!
Motherfuckers.

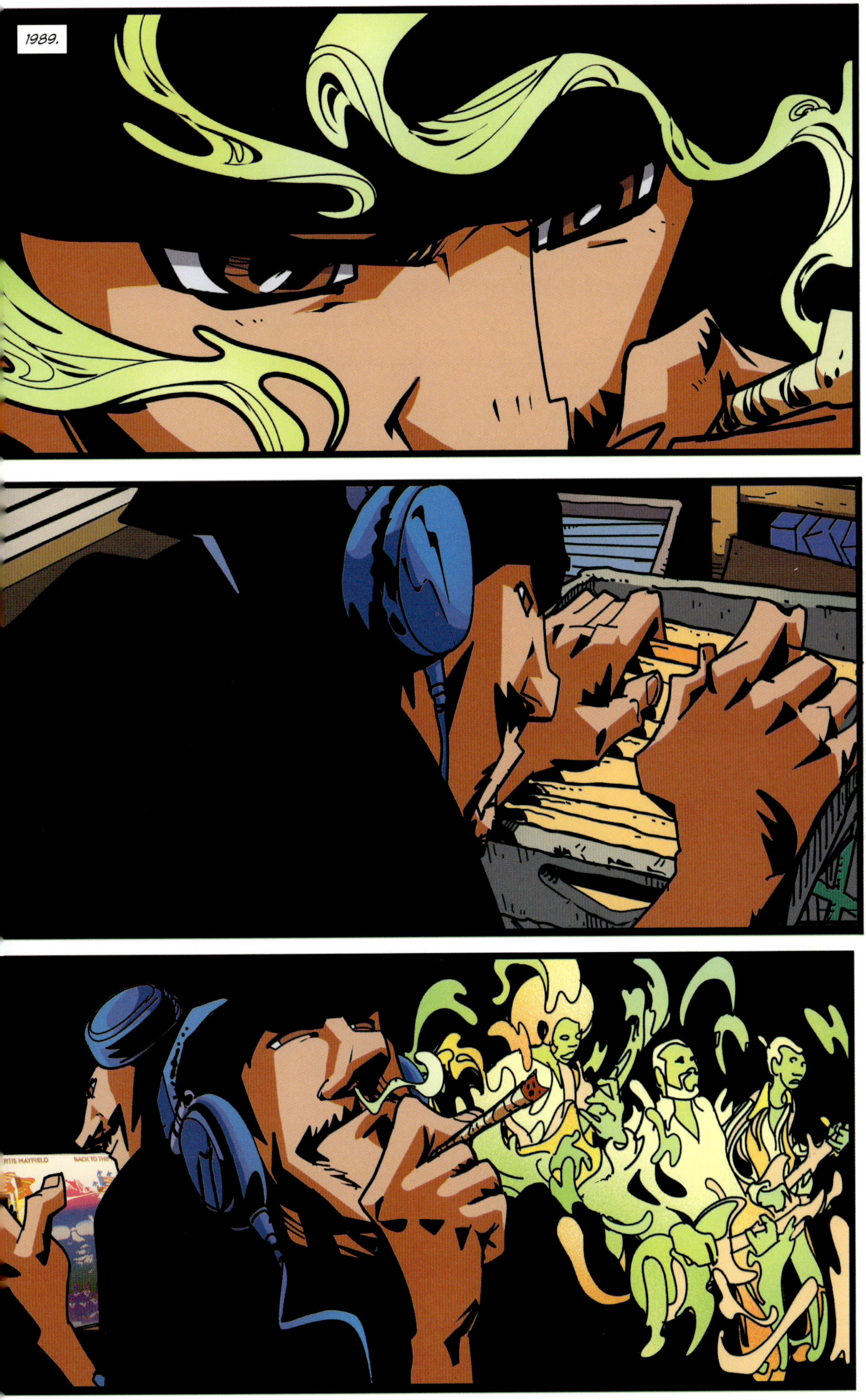
1989.
RTIS MAYFIELD
BACK TO THE

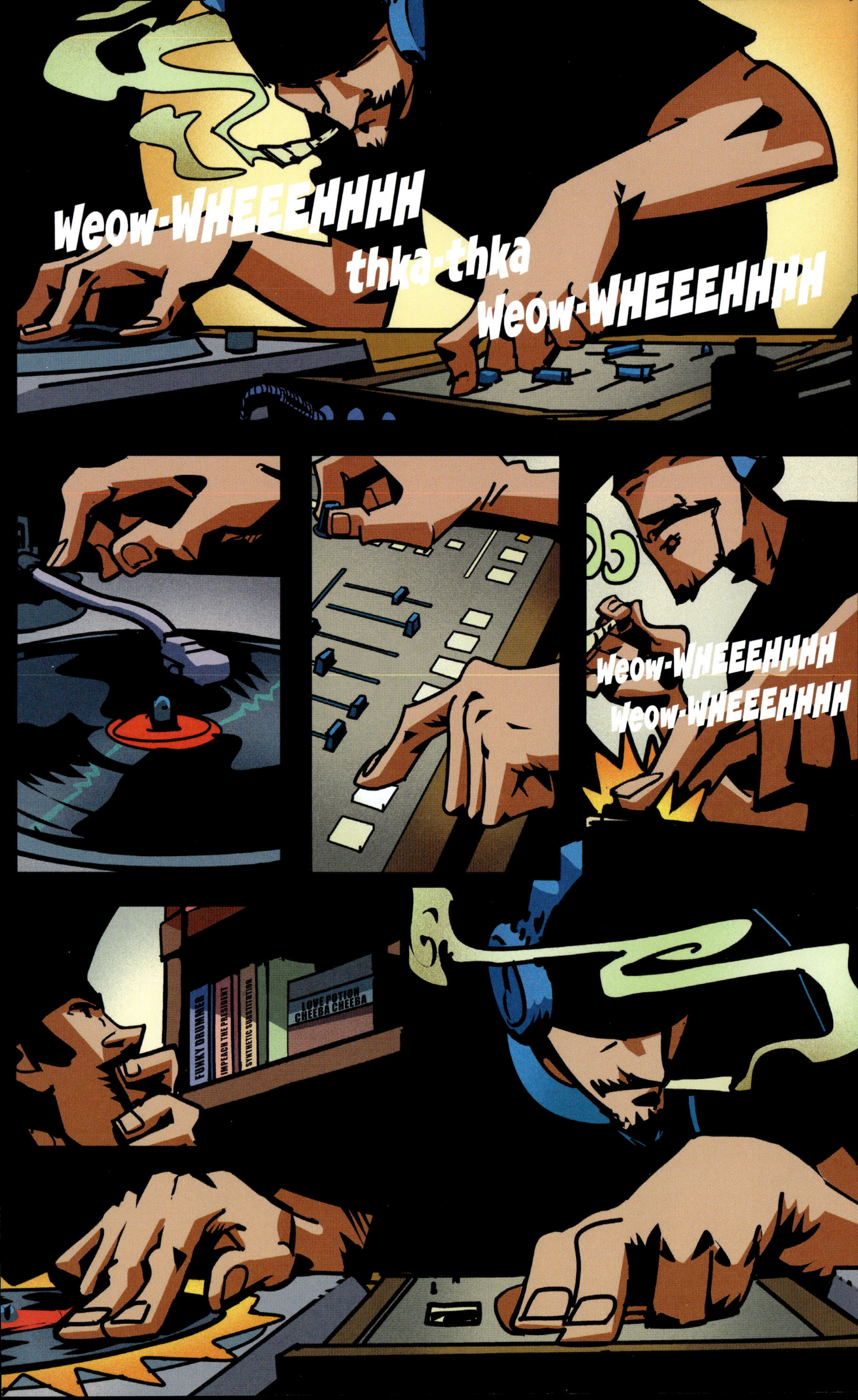
Weow-WHEEEHHHH
thka-thka
Weow-WHEEEHHHH
Weow-WHEEEHHHH
Weow-WHEEEHHHH
FUNKY DRUMMER
IMPEACH THE PRESIDENT
SYNTHETIC SUBSTITUTION
LOVE POTION
CHEEBA CHEEBA

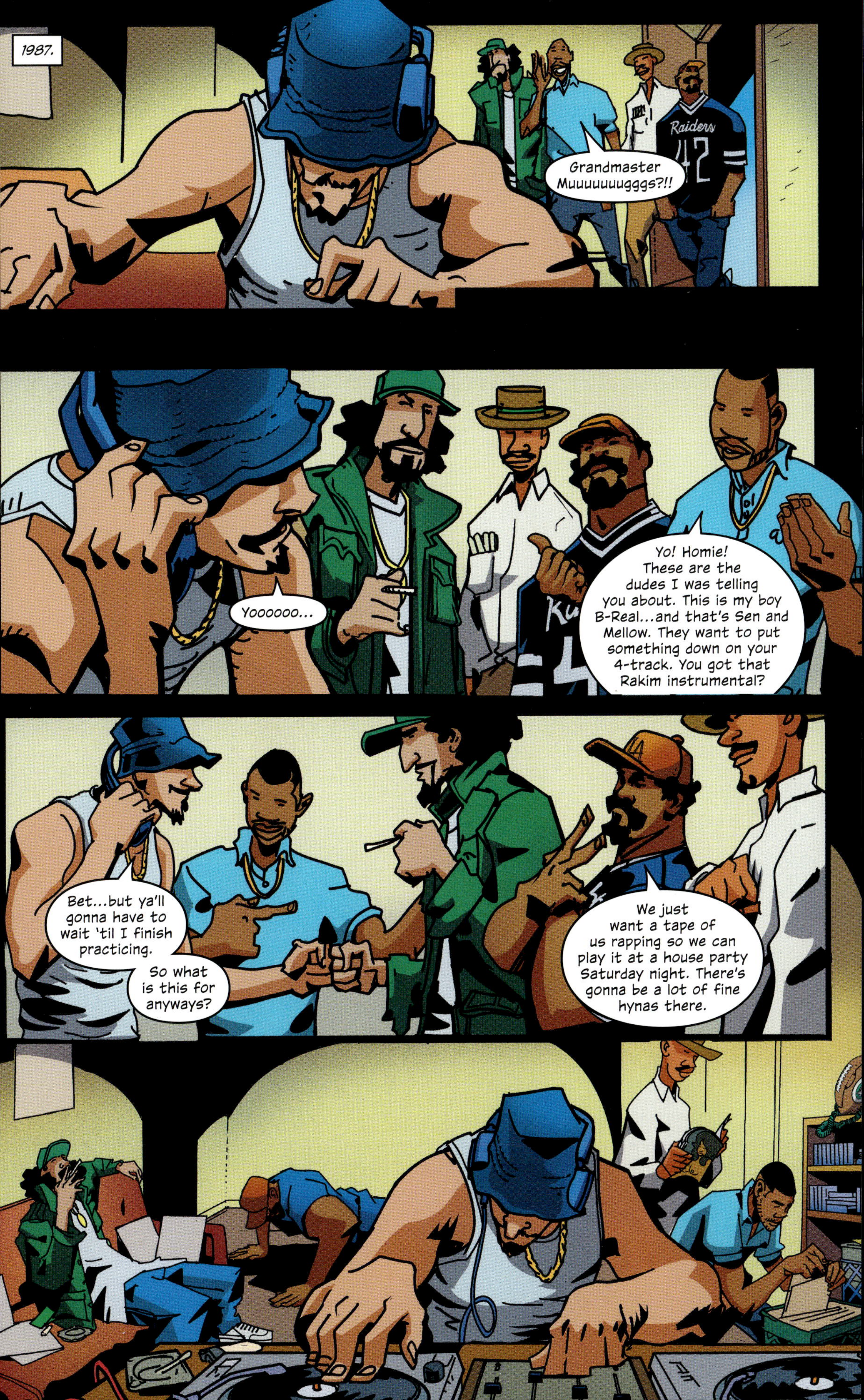
1987.
Grandmaster Muuuuuuugggs?!!
Yoooooo...
Yo! Homie! These are the dudes I was telling you about. This is my boy B-Real...and that's Sen and Mellow. They want to put something down on your 4-track. You got that Rakim instrumental?
Bet...but ya'll gonna have to wait 'til I finish practicing.
So what is this for anyways?
We just want a tape of us rapping so we can play it at a house party Saturday night. There's gonna be a lot of fine hynas there.

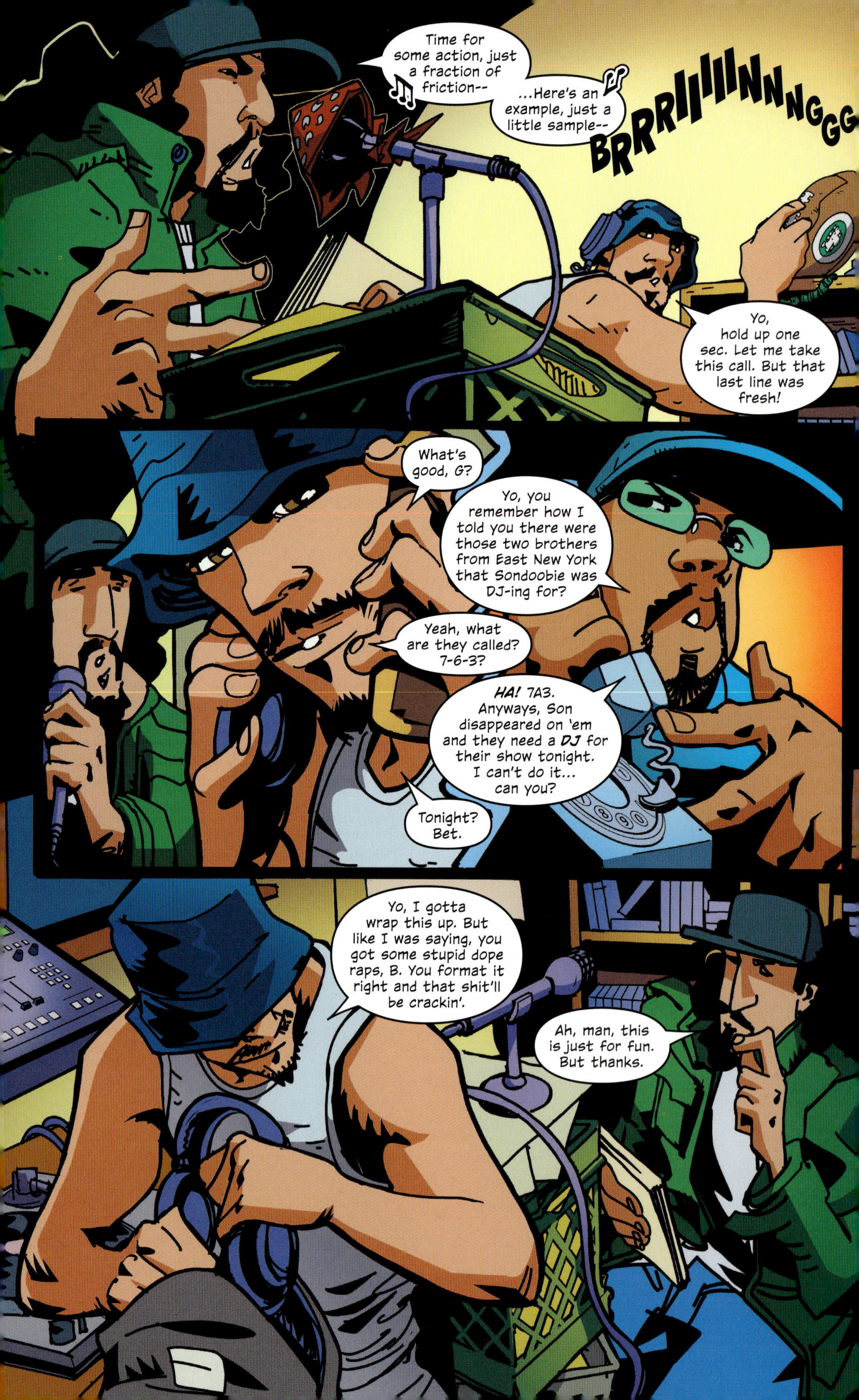

Time for some action, just a fraction of friction--
...Here's an example, just a little sample--
BRRRIIIIINNNGGG
Yo, hold up one sec. Let me take this call. But that last line was fresh!
What's good, G?
Yo, you remember how I told you there were those two brothers from East New York that Sondoobie was DJ-ing for?
Yeah, what are they called? 7-6-3?
HA! 7A3. Anyways, Son disappeared on 'em and they need a DJ for their show tonight. I can't do it... can you?
Tonight? Bet.
Yo, I gotta wrap this up. But like I was saying, you got some stupid dope raps, B. You format it right and that shit'll be crackin'.
Ah, man, this is just for fun. But thanks.

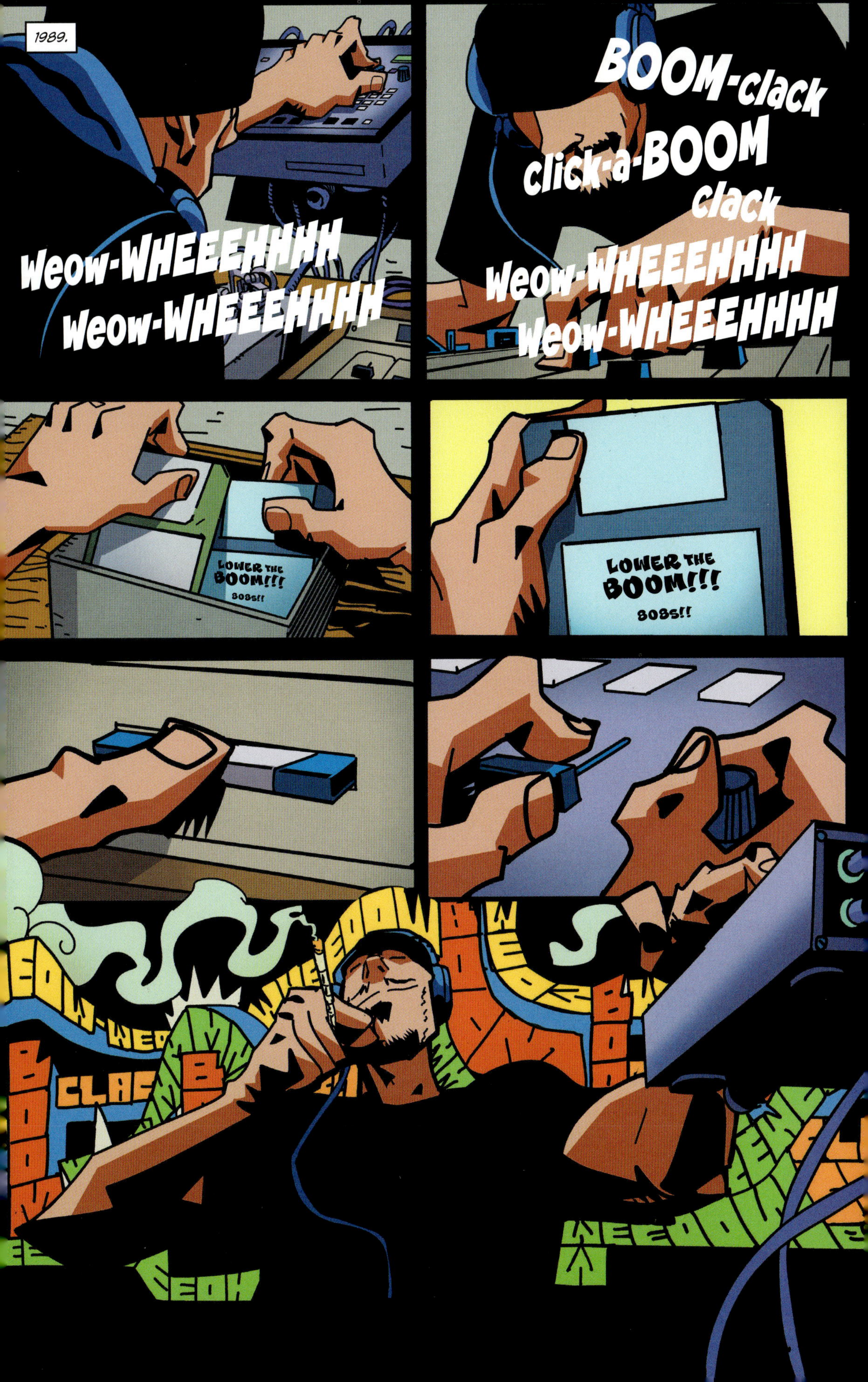
1989.
Weow-WHEEEHHHH
Weow-WHEEEHHHH
BOOM-clack
click-a-BOOM
clack
Weow-WHEEEHHHH
Weow-WHEEEHHHH
LOWER THE BOOM!!!
808S!!
LOWER THE BOOM!!!
808S!!

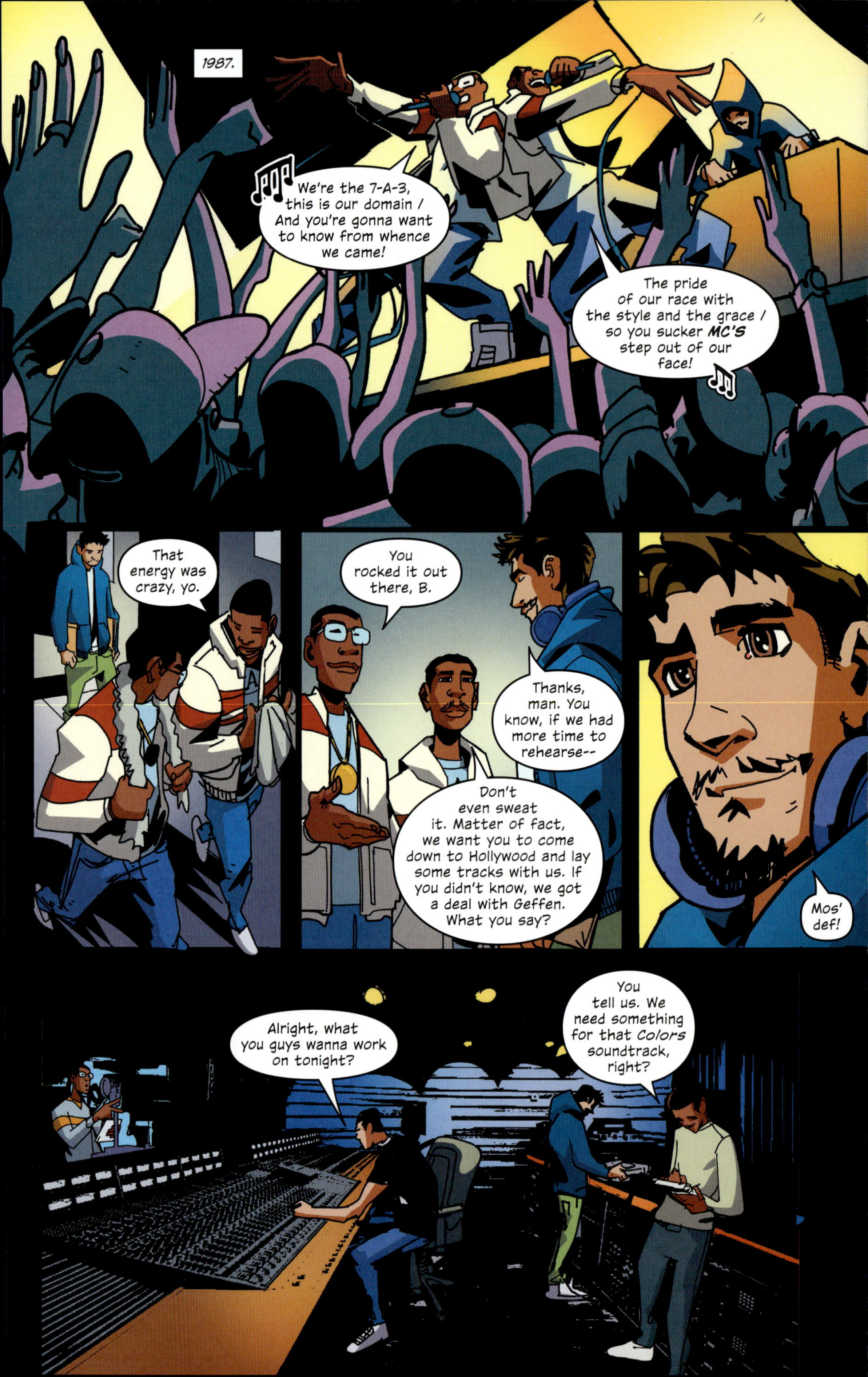
1987.
We're the 7-A-3, this is our domain / And you're gonna want to know from whence we came!
The pride of our race with the style and the grace / so you sucker **MC'S** step out of our face!
That energy was crazy, yo.
You rocked it out there, B.
Thanks, man. You know, if we had more time to rehearse--
Don't even sweat it. Matter of fact, we want you to come down to Hollywood and lay some tracks with us. If you didn't know, we got a deal with Geffen. What you say?
Mos' def!
Alright, what you guys wanna work on tonight?
You tell us. We need something for that *Colors* soundtrack, right?

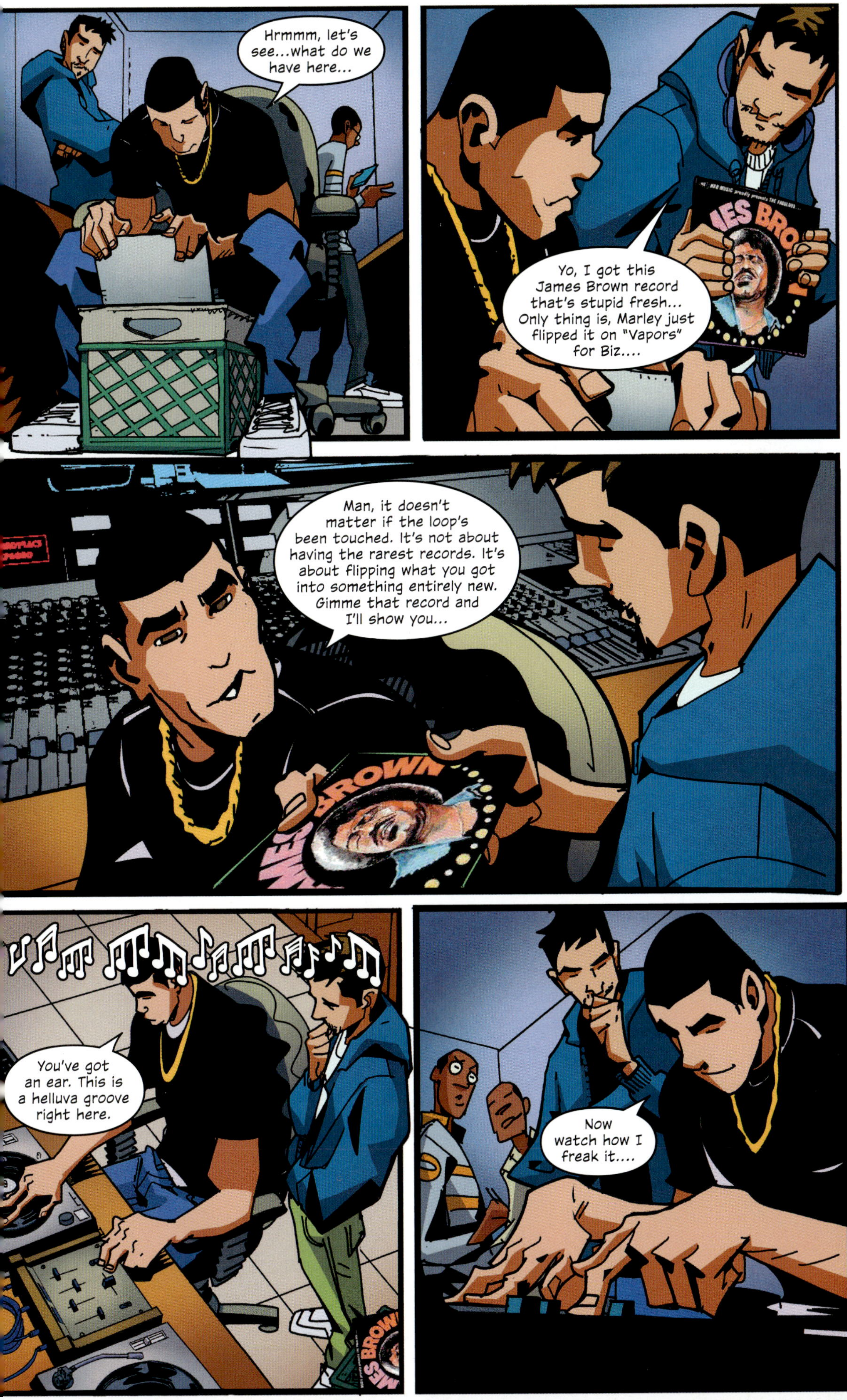
Hrmmm, let's see...what do we have here...
Yo, I got this James Brown record that's stupid fresh... Only thing is, Marley just flipped it on "Vapors" for Biz....
Man, it doesn't matter if the loop's been touched. It's not about having the rarest records. It's about flipping what you got into something entirely new. Gimme that record and I'll show you...
You've got an ear. This is a helluva groove right here.
Now watch how I freak it....

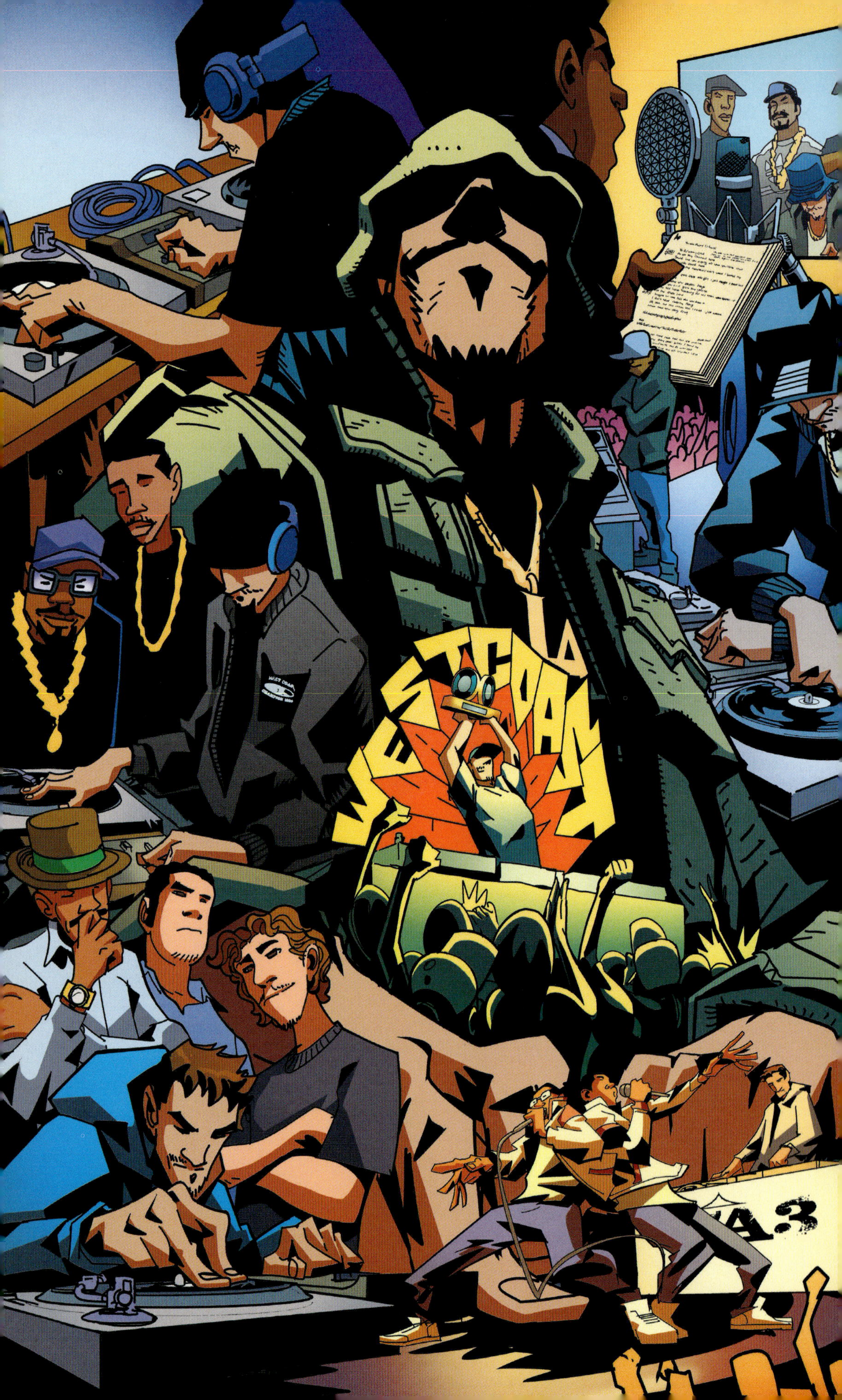

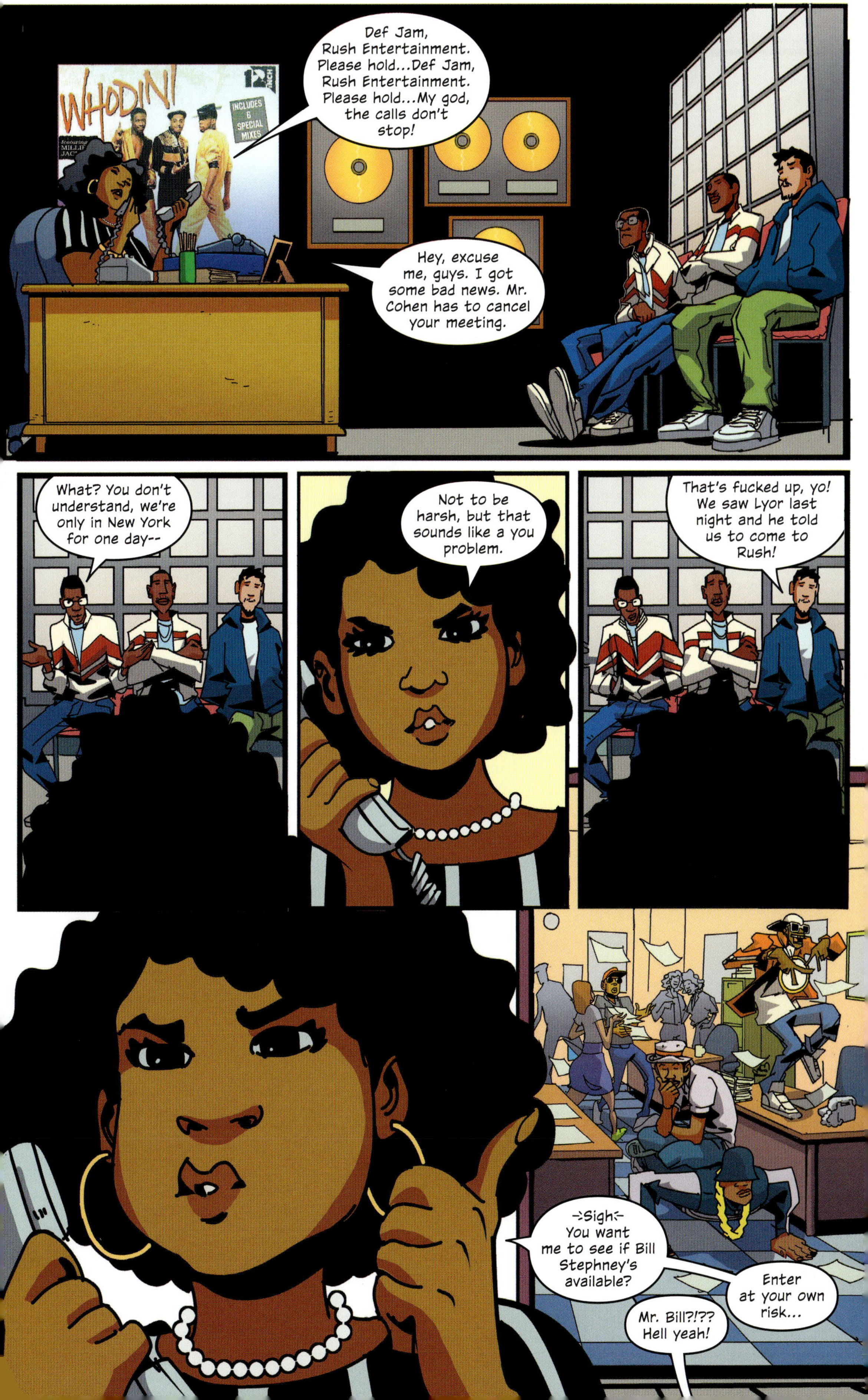

WHODINI
INCLUDES 6 SPECIAL MIXES
Def Jam, Rush Entertainment. Please hold...Def Jam, Rush Entertainment. Please hold...My god, the calls don't stop!
Hey, excuse me, guys. I got some bad news. Mr. Cohen has to cancel your meeting.
What? You don't understand, we're only in New York for one day--
Not to be harsh, but that sounds like a you problem.
That's fucked up, yo! We saw Lyor last night and he told us to come to Rush!
-Sigh- You want me to see if Bill Stephney's available?
Mr. Bill?!?? Hell yeah!
Enter at your own risk...

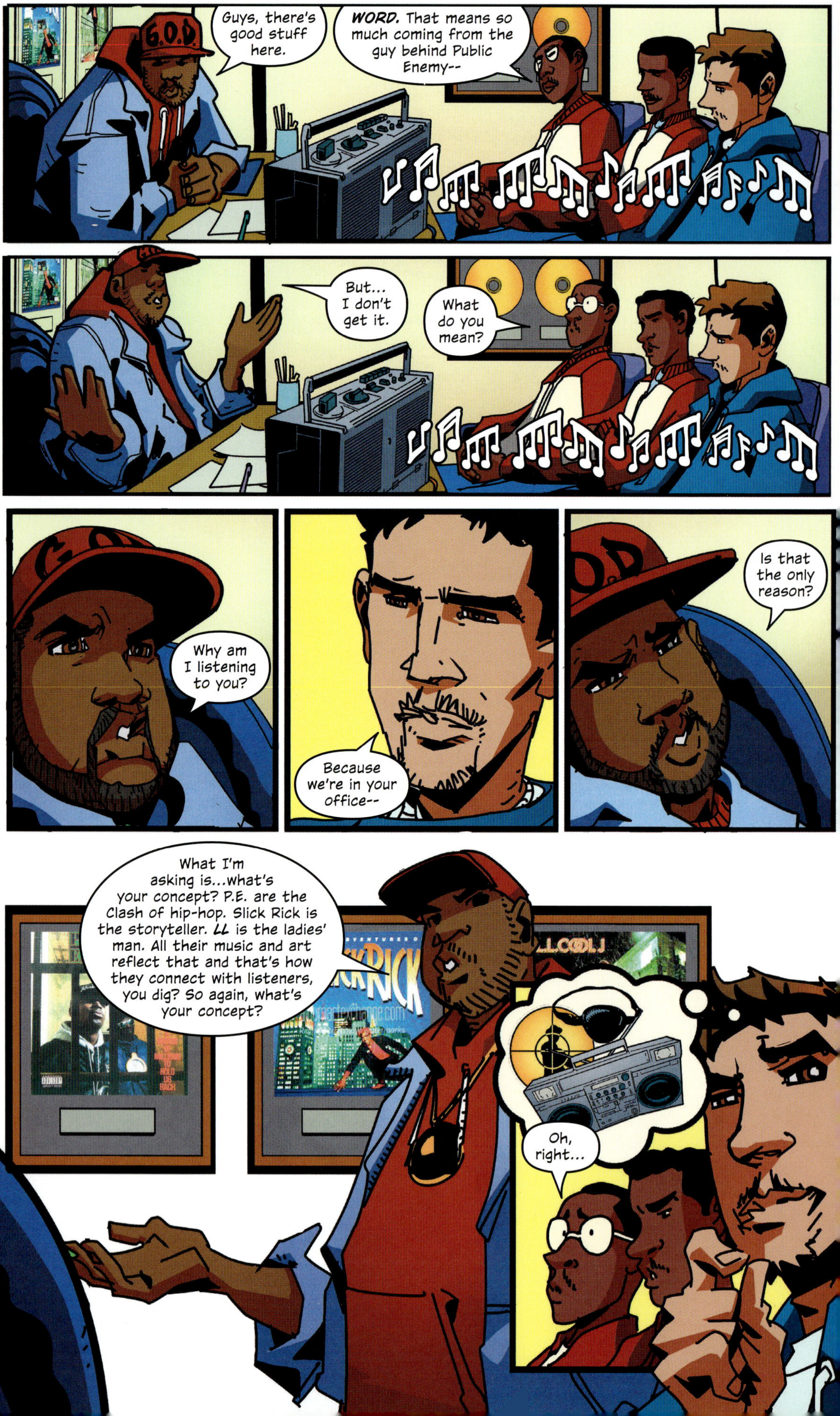
Guys, there's good stuff here.
WORD. That means so much coming from the guy behind Public Enemy--
But... I don't get it.
What do you mean?
Why am I listening to you?
Because we're in your office--
Is that the only reason?
What I'm asking is...what's your concept? P.E. are the Clash of hip-hop. Slick Rick is the storyteller. LL is the ladies' man. All their music and art reflect that and that's how they connect with listeners, you dig? So again, what's your concept?
Oh, right...

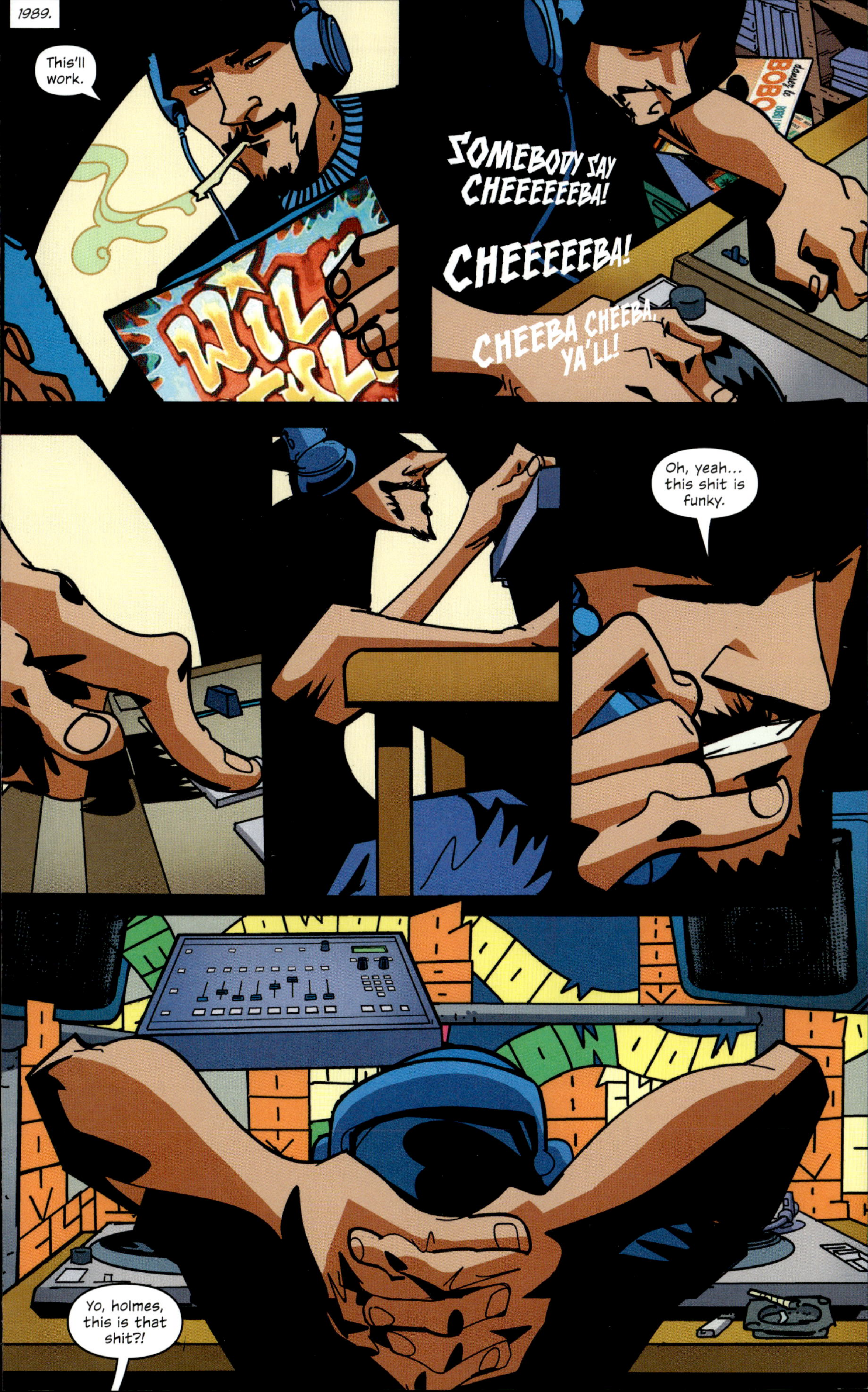
1989.
This'll work.
SOMEBODY SAY CHEEEEEEBA!
CHEEEEEEBA!
CHEEBA CHEEBA, YA'LL!
Oh, yeah... this shit is funky.
Yo, holmes, this is that shit?!

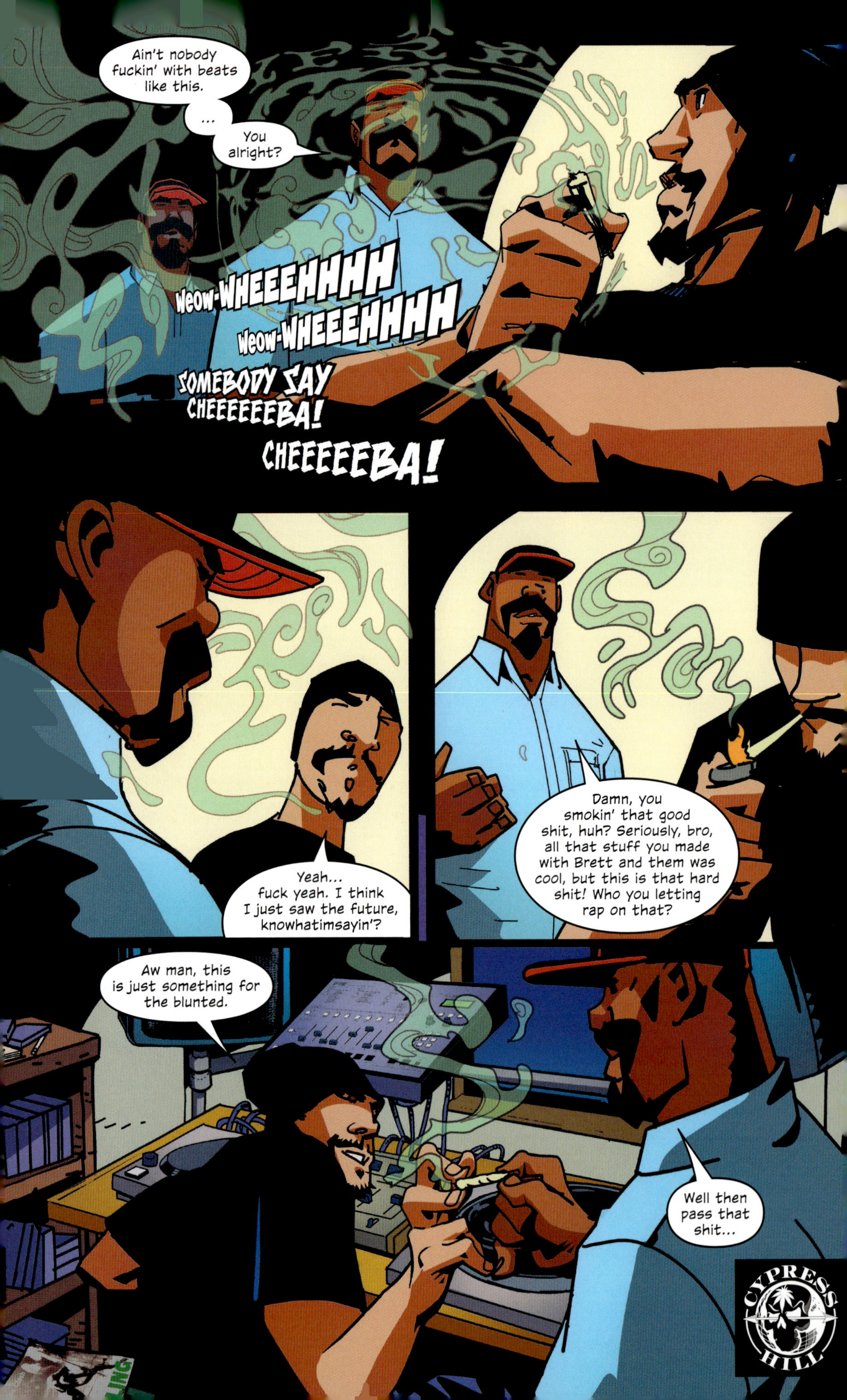
Ain't nobody fuckin' with beats like this.
...
You alright?
Weow-WHEEEHHHH
Weow-WHEEEHHHH
SOMEBODY SAY CHEEEEEEBA!
CHEEEEEBA!
Yeah... fuck yeah. I think I just saw the future, knowhatimsayin'?
Damn, you smokin' that good shit, huh? Seriously, bro, all that stuff you made with Brett and them was cool, but this is that hard shit! Who you letting rap on that?
Aw man, this is just something for the blunted.
Well then pass that shit...

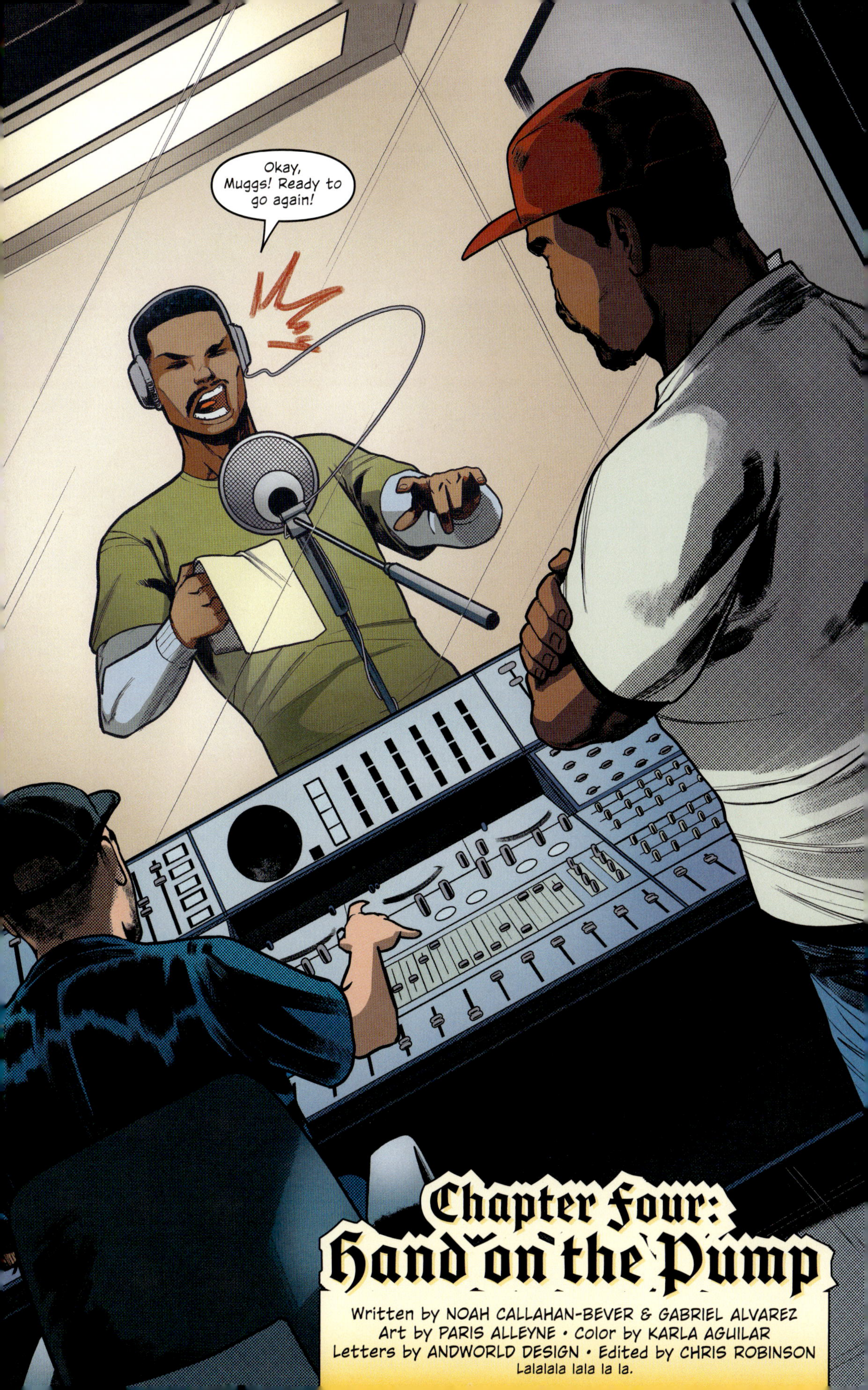
Okay, Muggs! Ready to go again!
Chapter Four:
Hand on the Pump
Written by NOAH CALLAHAN-BEVER & GABRIEL ALVAREZ
Art by PARIS ALLEYNE • Color by KARLA AGUILAR
Letters by ANDWORLD DESIGN • Edited by CHRIS ROBINSON
Lalalala lala la la.

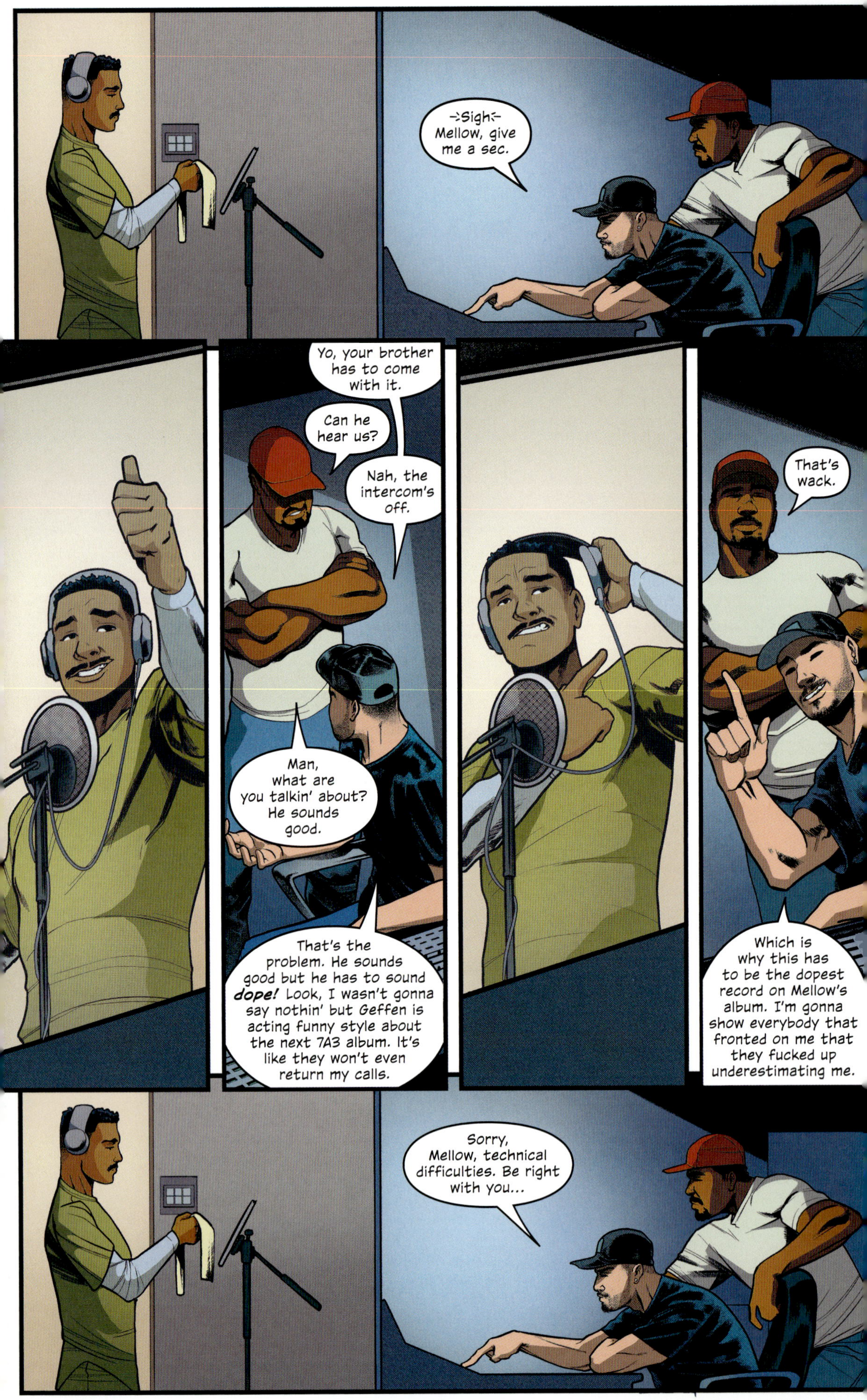
-Sigh-
Mellow, give me a sec.
Yo, your brother has to come with it.
Can he hear us?
Nah, the intercom's off.
Man, what are you talkin' about? He sounds good.
That's the problem. He sounds good but he has to sound *dope!* Look, I wasn't gonna say nothin' but Geffen is acting funny style about the next 7A3 album. It's like they won't even return my calls.
That's wack.
Which is why this has to be the dopest record on Mellow's album. I'm gonna show everybody that fronted on me that they fucked up underestimating me.
Sorry, Mellow, technical difficulties. Be right with you...

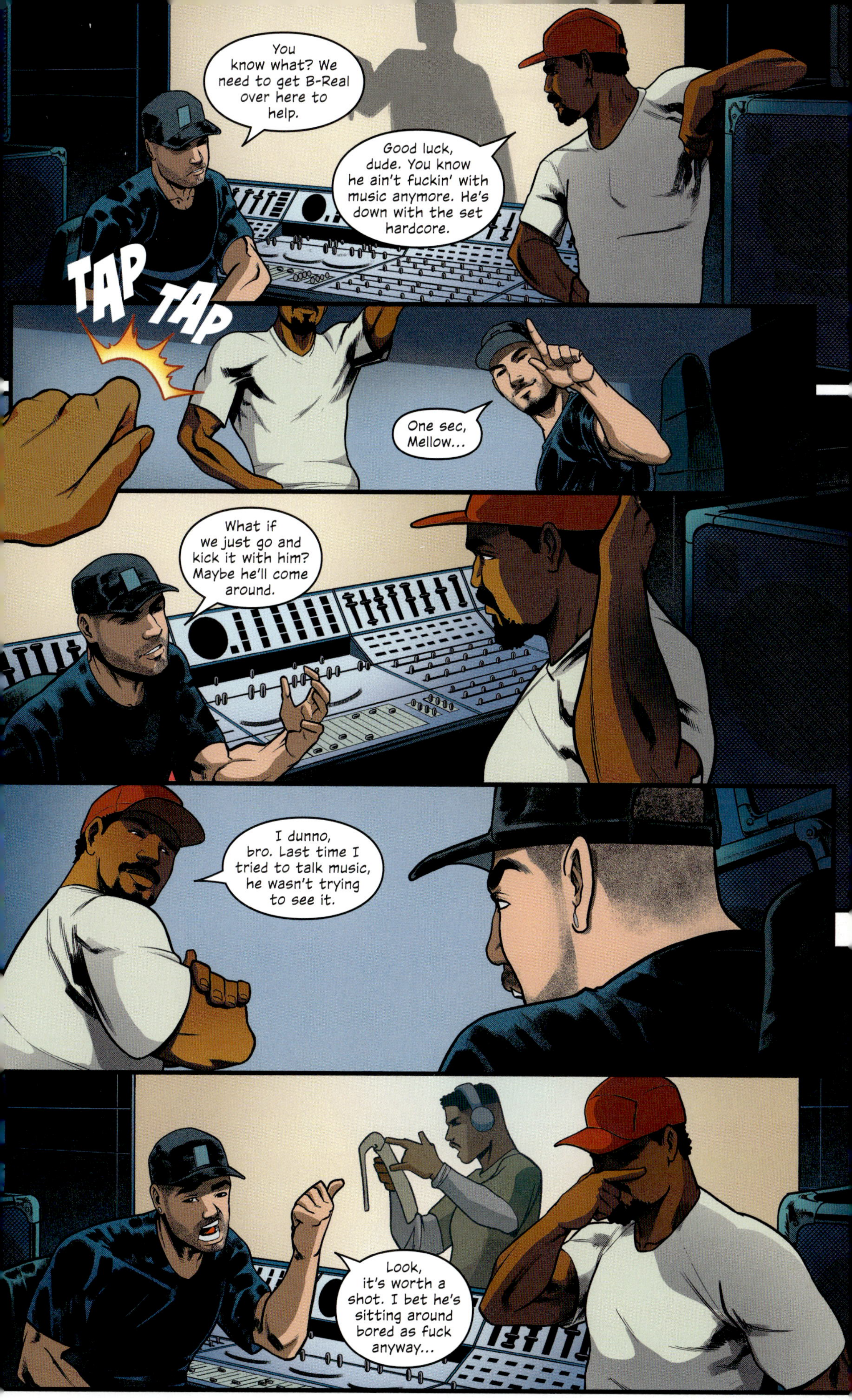
You know what? We need to get B-Real over here to help.
Good luck, dude. You know he ain't fuckin' with music anymore. He's down with the set hardcore.
TAP TAP
One sec, Mellow...
What if we just go and kick it with him? Maybe he'll come around.
I dunno, bro. Last time I tried to talk music, he wasn't trying to see it.
Look, it's worth a shot. I bet he's sitting around bored as fuck anyway...

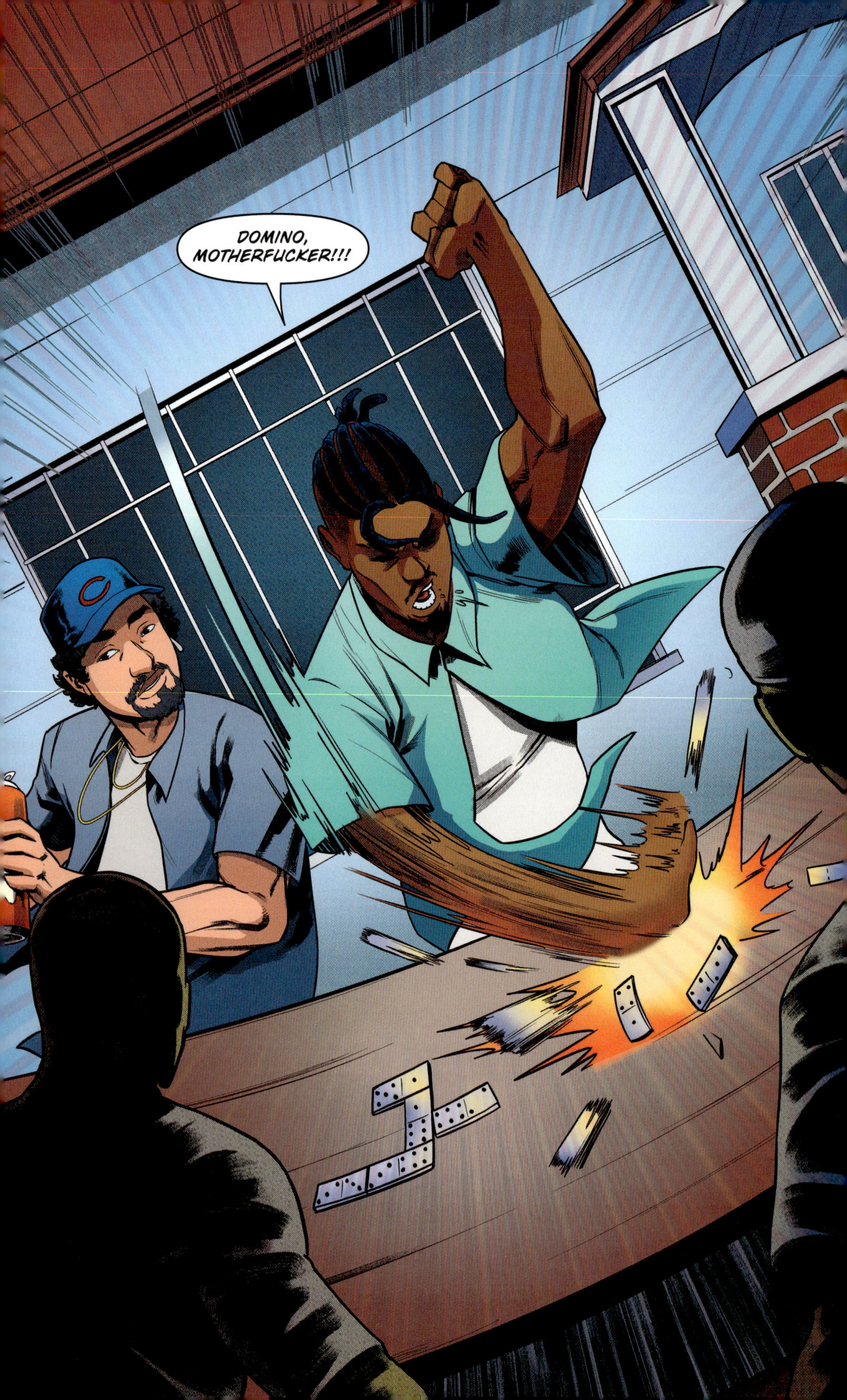
DOMINO, MOTHERFUCKER!!!

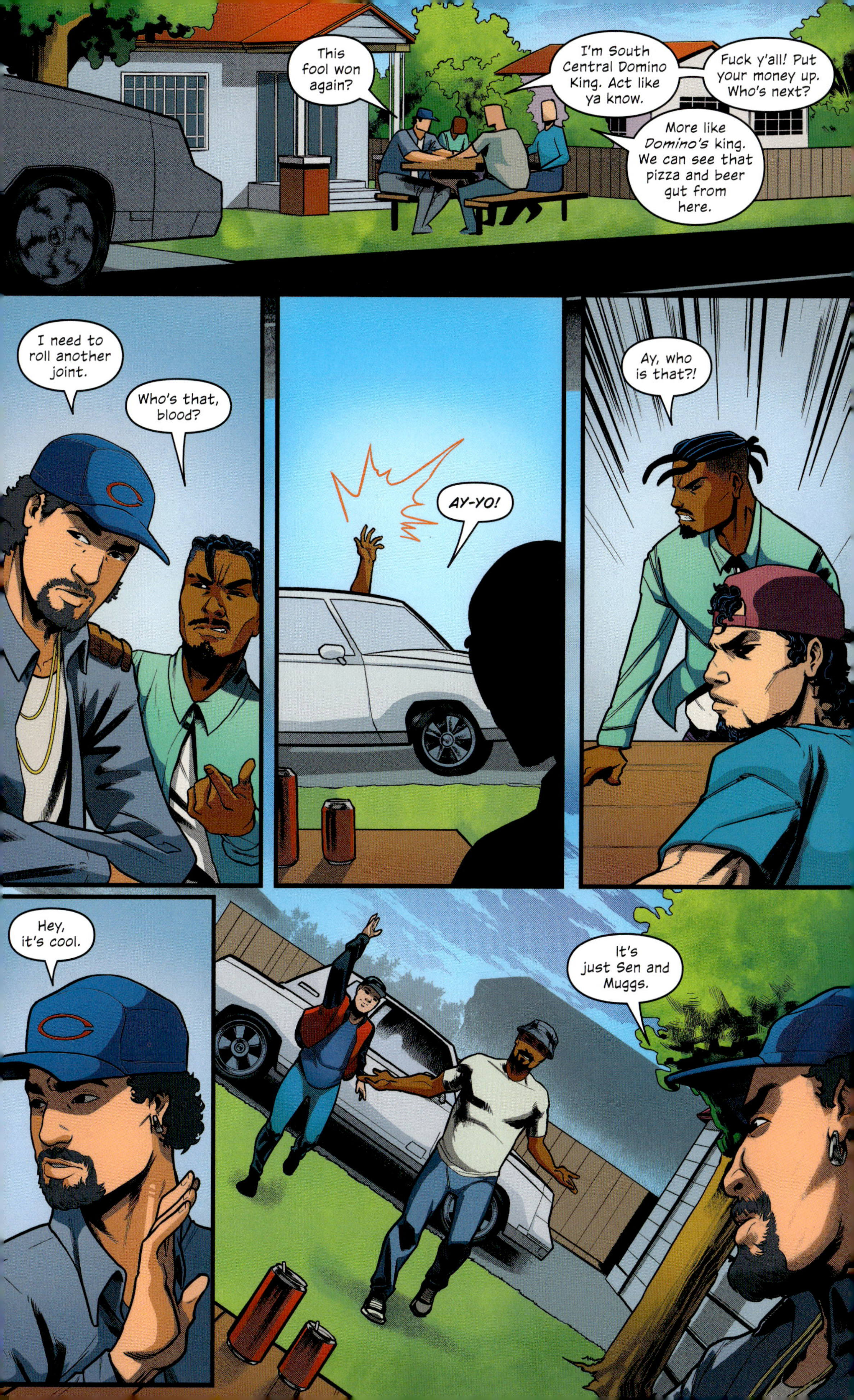
This fool won again?
I'm South Central Domino King. Act like ya know.
Fuck y'all! Put your money up. Who's next?
More like *Domino's* king. We can see that pizza and beer gut from here.
I need to roll another joint.
Who's that, blood?
AY-YO!
Ay, who is that?!
Hey, it's cool.
It's just Sen and Muggs.

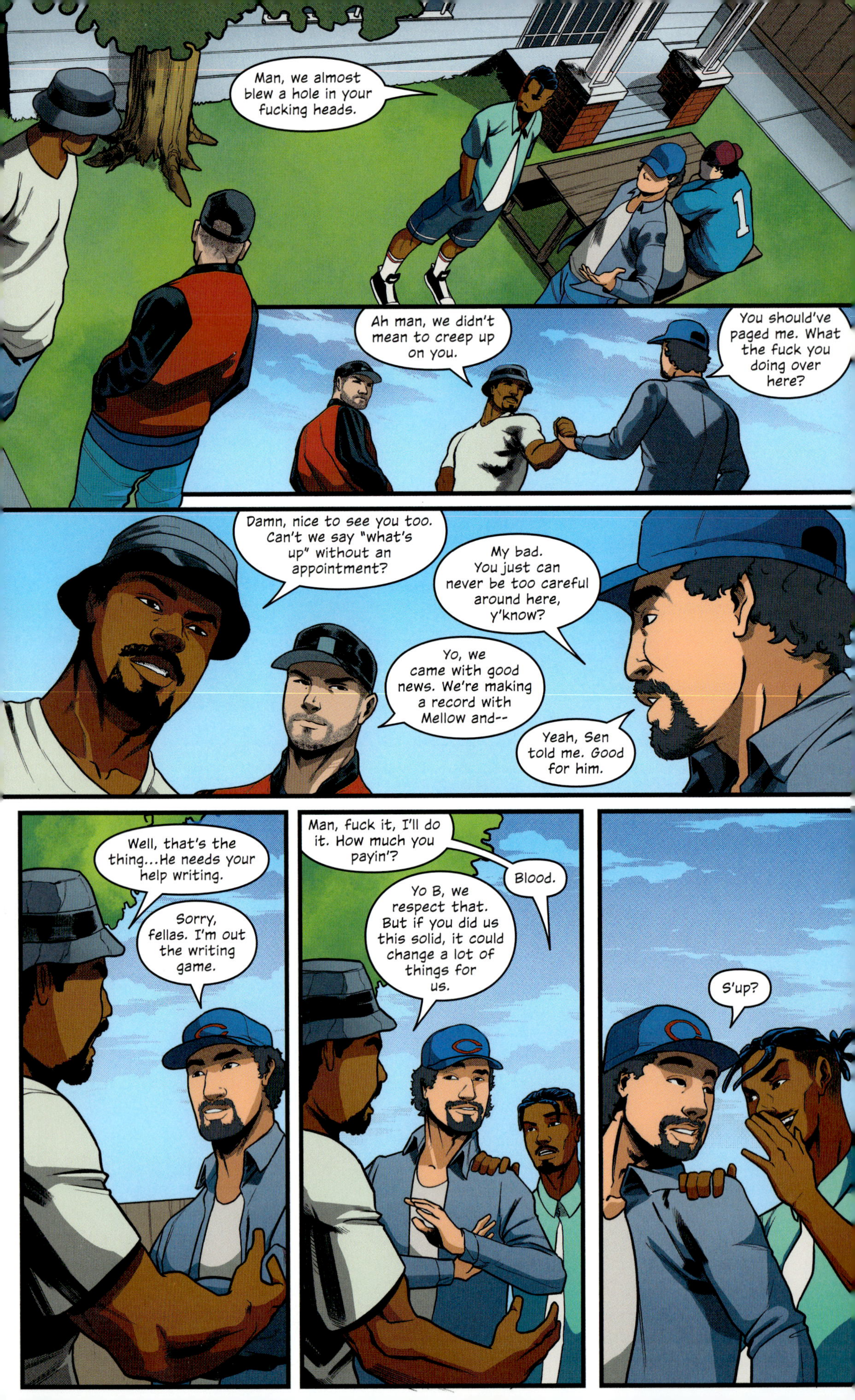
Man, we almost blew a hole in your fucking heads.
Ah man, we didn't mean to creep up on you.
You should've paged me. What the fuck you doing over here?
Damn, nice to see you too. Can't we say "what's up" without an appointment?
My bad. You just can never be too careful around here, y'know?
Yo, we came with good news. We're making a record with Mellow and--
Yeah, Sen told me. Good for him.
Well, that's the thing...He needs your help writing.
Sorry, fellas. I'm out the writing game.
Yo B, we respect that. But if you did us this solid, it could change a lot of things for us.
Blood.
Man, fuck it, I'll do it. How much you payin'?
S'up?

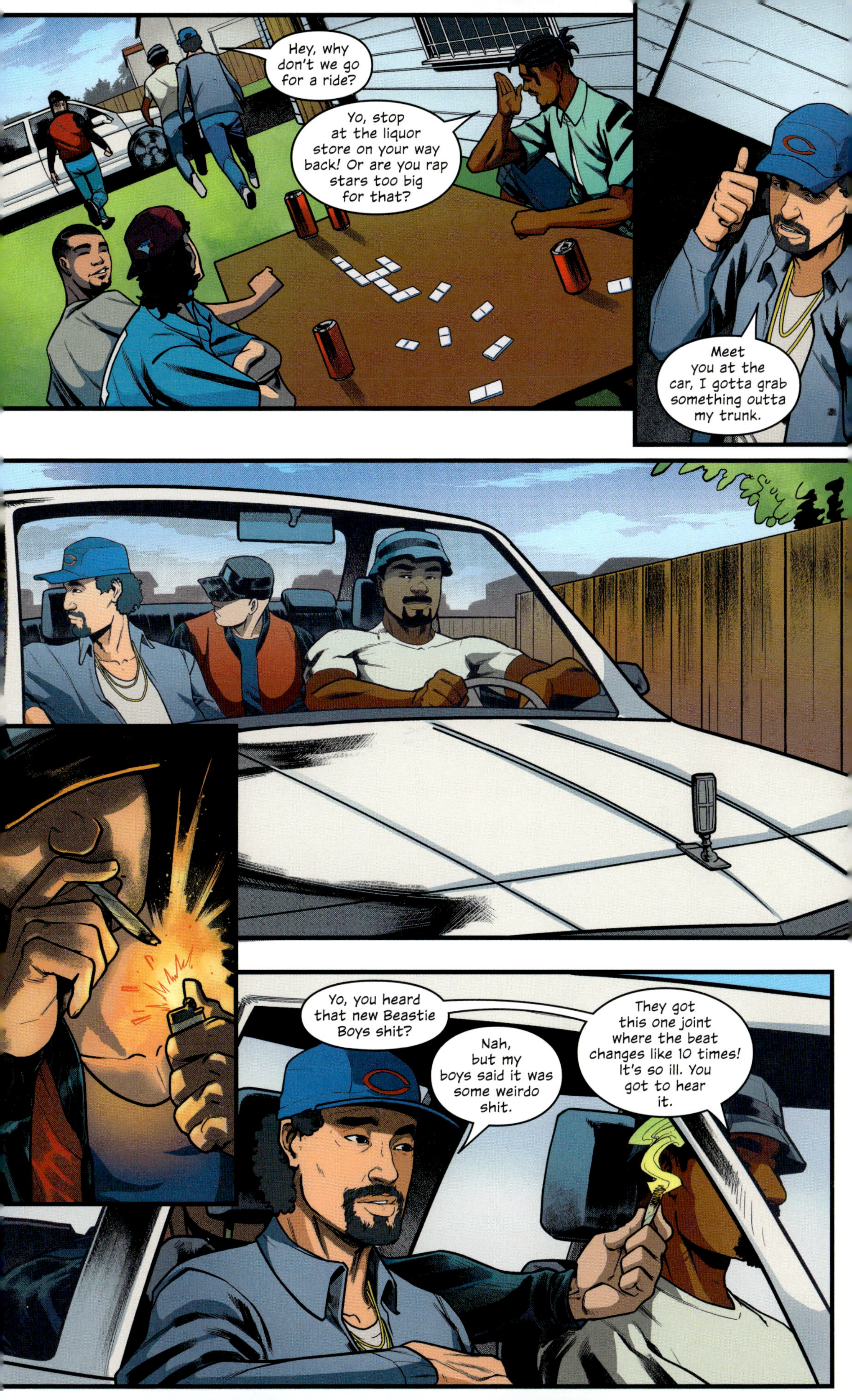
Hey, why don't we go for a ride?
Yo, stop at the liquor store on your way back! Or are you rap stars too big for that?
Meet you at the car, I gotta grab something outta my trunk.
Yo, you heard that new Beastie Boys shit?
Nah, but my boys said it was some weirdo shit.
They got this one joint where the beat changes like 10 times! It's so ill. You got to hear it.

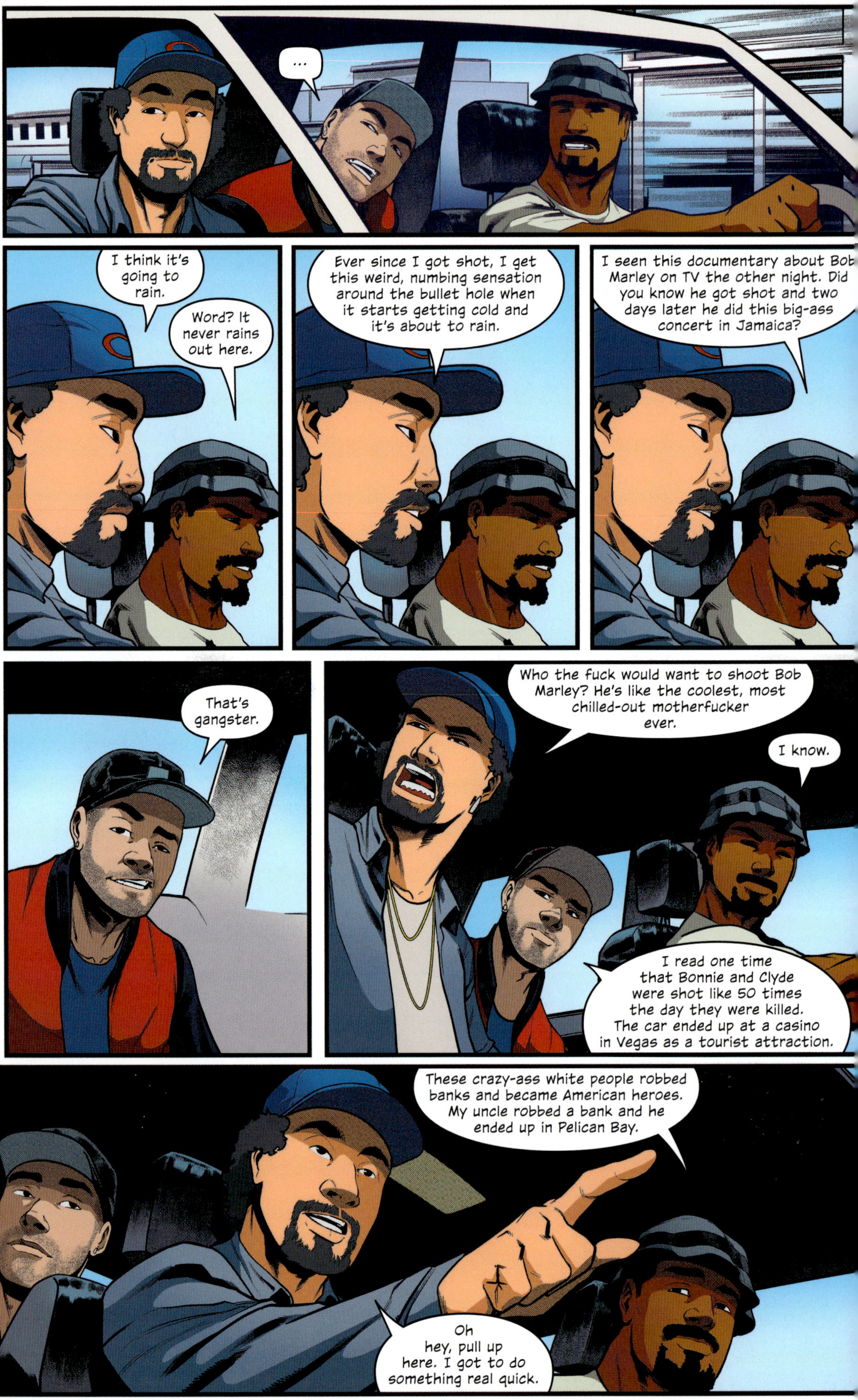
...
I think it's going to rain.
Word? It never rains out here.
Ever since I got shot, I get this weird, numbing sensation around the bullet hole when it starts getting cold and it's about to rain.
I seen this documentary about Bob Marley on TV the other night. Did you know he got shot and two days later he did this big-ass concert in Jamaica?
That's gangster.
Who the fuck would want to shoot Bob Marley? He's like the coolest, most chilled-out motherfucker ever.
I know.
I read one time that Bonnie and Clyde were shot like 50 times the day they were killed. The car ended up at a casino in Vegas as a tourist attraction.
These crazy-ass white people robbed banks and became American heroes. My uncle robbed a bank and he ended up in Pelican Bay.
Oh hey, pull up here. I got to do something real quick.

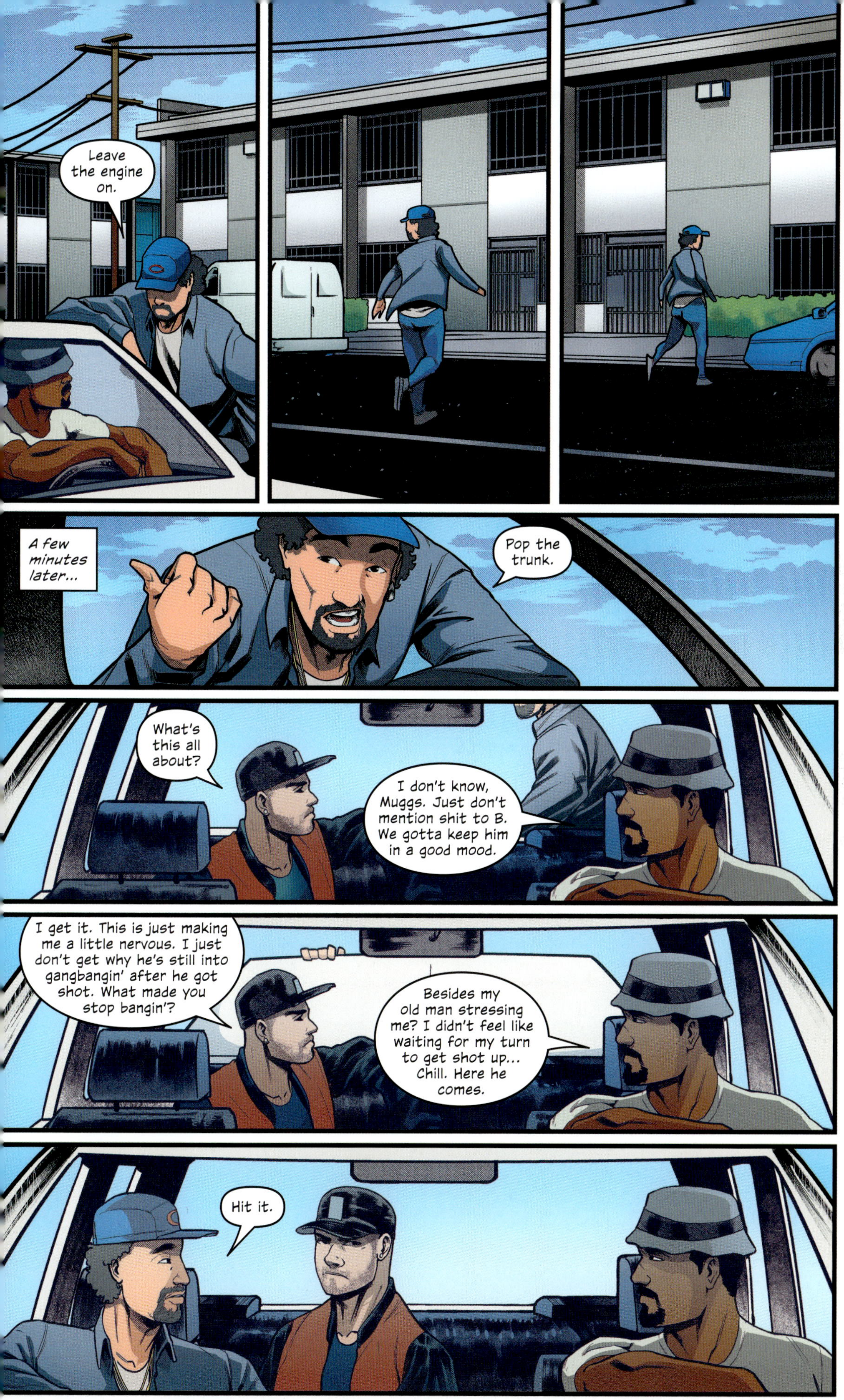
Leave the engine on.
A few minutes later...
Pop the trunk.
What's this all about?
I don't know, Muggs. Just don't mention shit to B. We gotta keep him in a good mood.
I get it. This is just making me a little nervous. I just don't get why he's still into gangbangin' after he got shot. What made you stop bangin'?
Besides my old man stressing me? I didn't feel like waiting for my turn to get shot up... Chill. Here he comes.
Hit it.

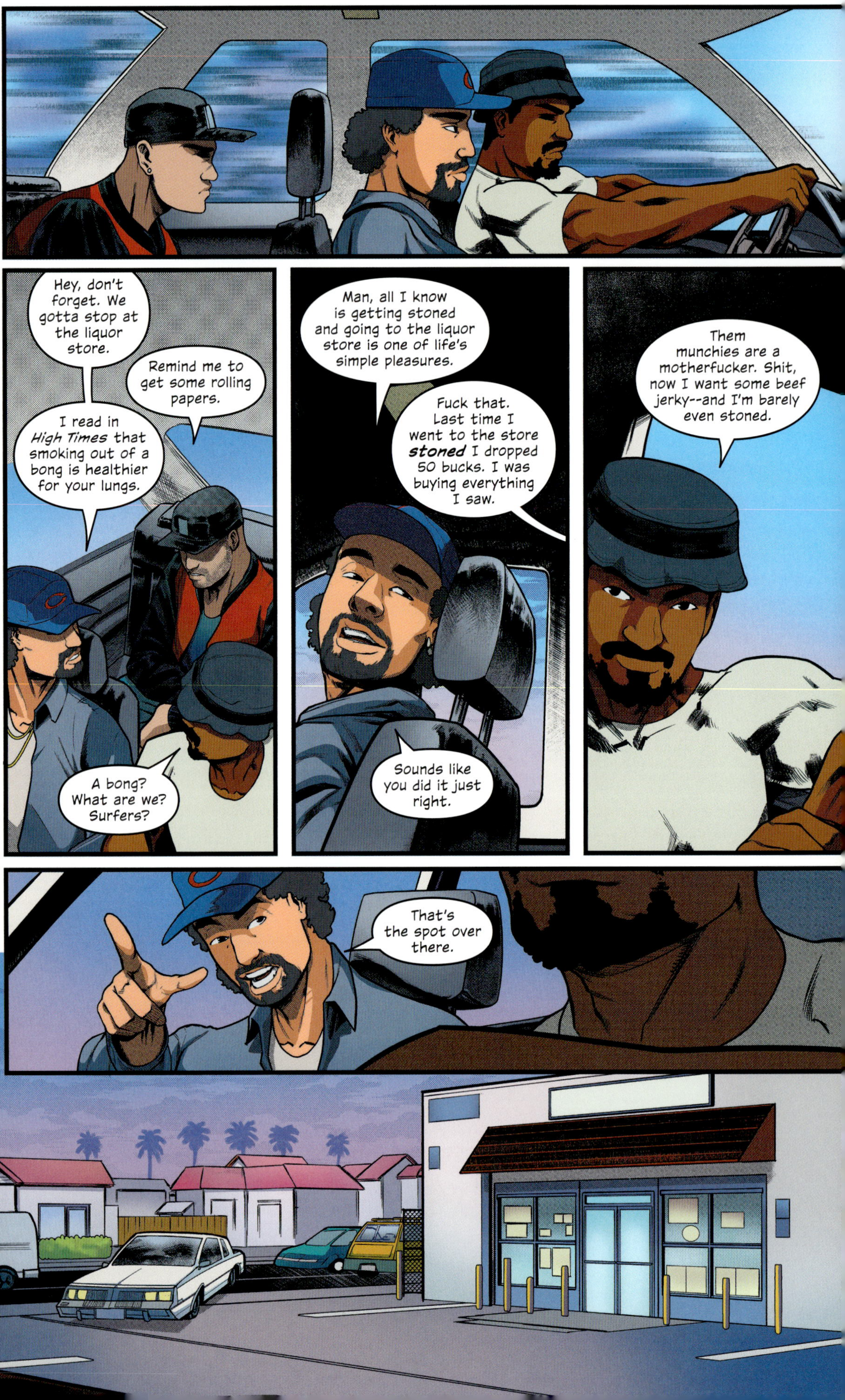

Hey, don't forget. We gotta stop at the liquor store.
Remind me to get some rolling papers.
I read in *High Times* that smoking out of a bong is healthier for your lungs.
A bong? What are we? Surfers?
Man, all I know is getting stoned and going to the liquor store is one of life's simple pleasures.
Fuck that. Last time I went to the store ***stoned*** I dropped 50 bucks. I was buying everything I saw.
Sounds like you did it just right.
Them munchies are a motherfucker. Shit, now I want some beef jerky--and I'm barely even stoned.
That's the spot over there.

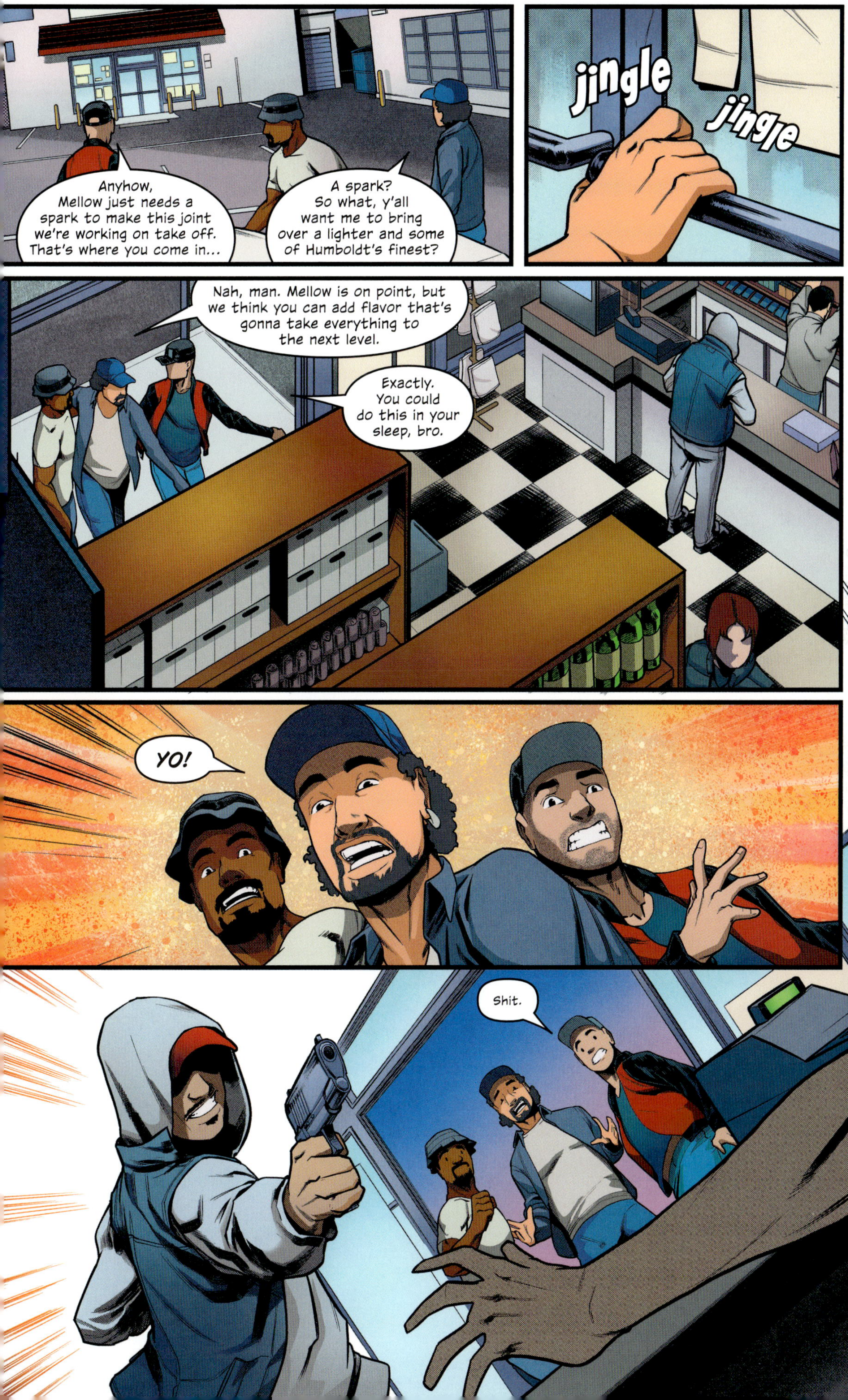

Anyhow, Mellow just needs a spark to make this joint we're working on take off. That's where you come in...
A spark? So what, y'all want me to bring over a lighter and some of Humboldt's finest?
jingle
jingle
Nah, man. Mellow is on point, but we think you can add flavor that's gonna take everything to the next level.
Exactly. You could do this in your sleep, bro.
YO!
Shit.

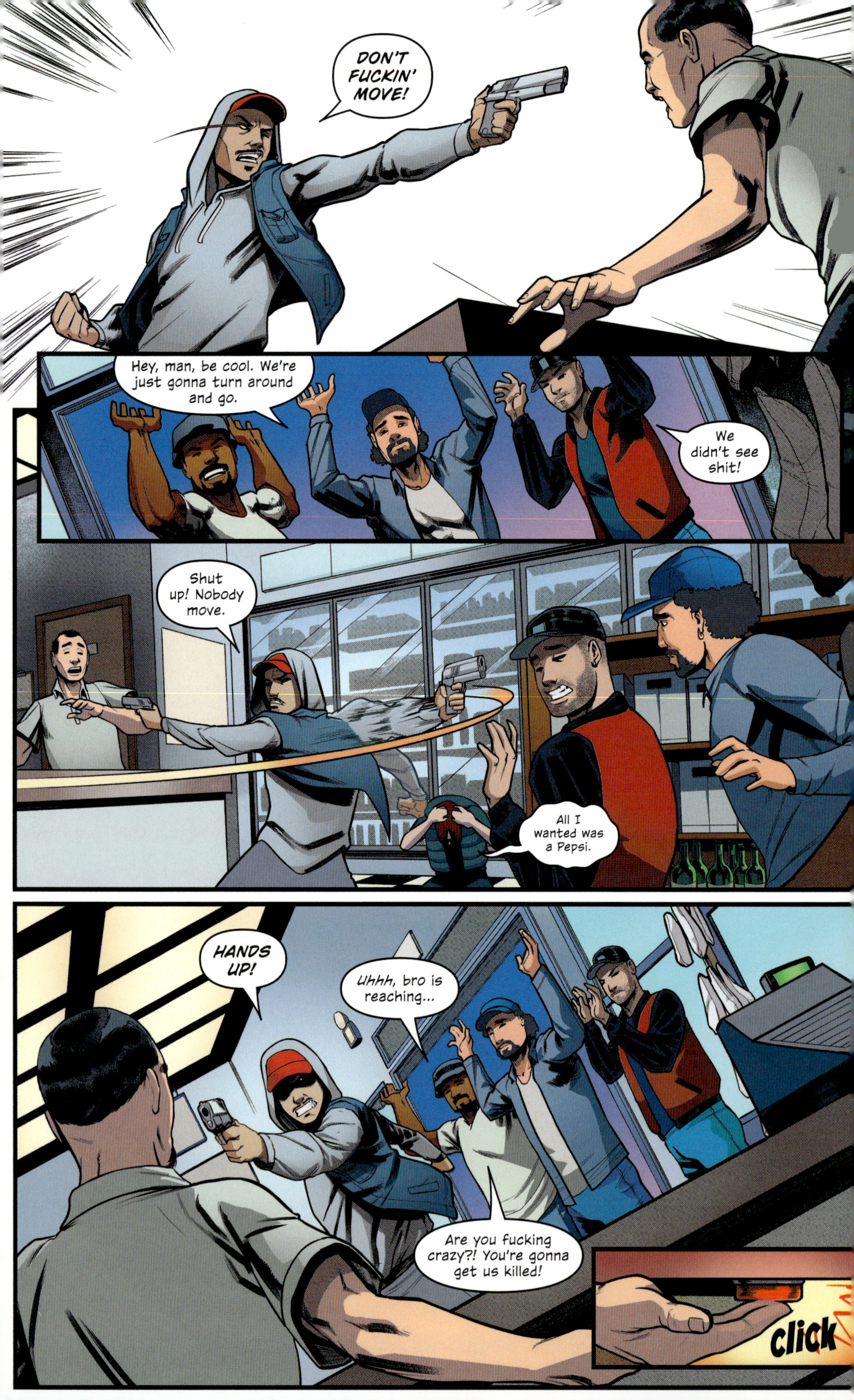
DON'T FUCKIN' MOVE!
Hey, man, be cool. We're just gonna turn around and go.
We didn't see shit!
Shut up! Nobody move.
All I wanted was a Pepsi.
HANDS UP!
Uhhh, bro is reaching...
Are you fucking crazy?! You're gonna get us killed!
CLICK

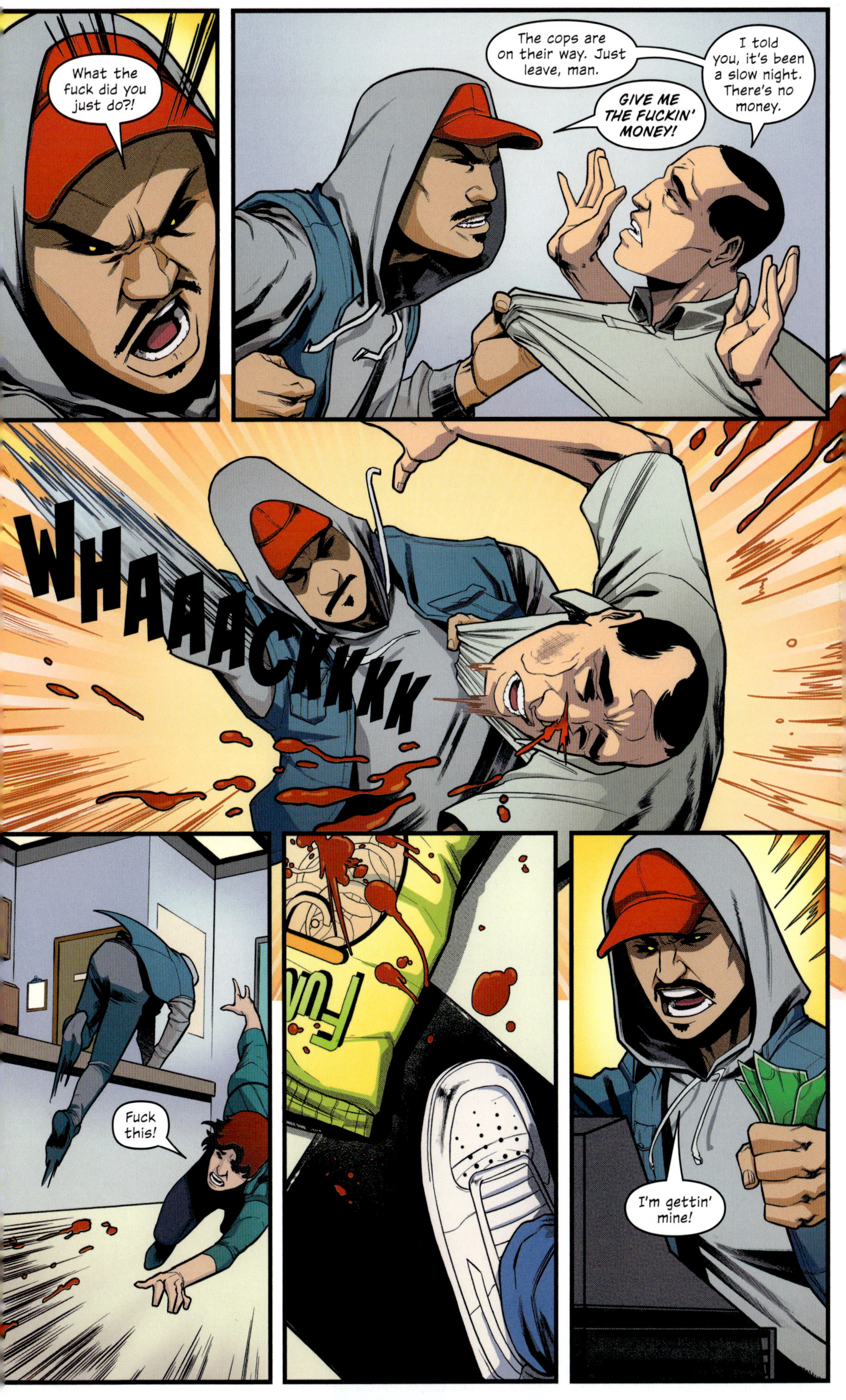
What the fuck did you just do?!
The cops are on their way. Just leave, man.
I told you, it's been a slow night. There's no money.
GIVE ME THE FUCKIN' MONEY!
WHAAAACKKKK
Fuck this!
I'm gettin' mine!

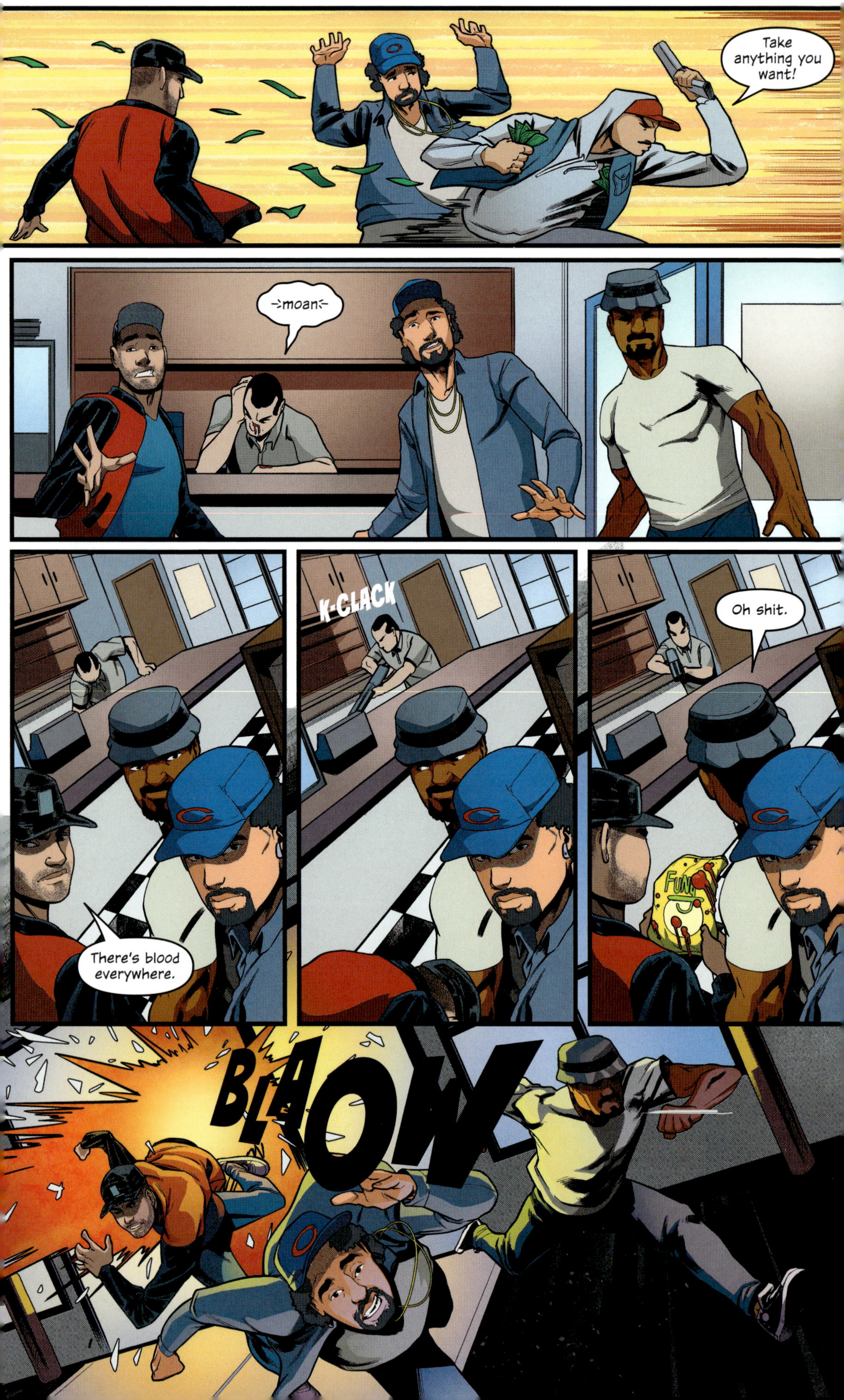
Take anything you want!
-moan-
K-CLACK
There's blood everywhere.
Oh shit.
BLAOW

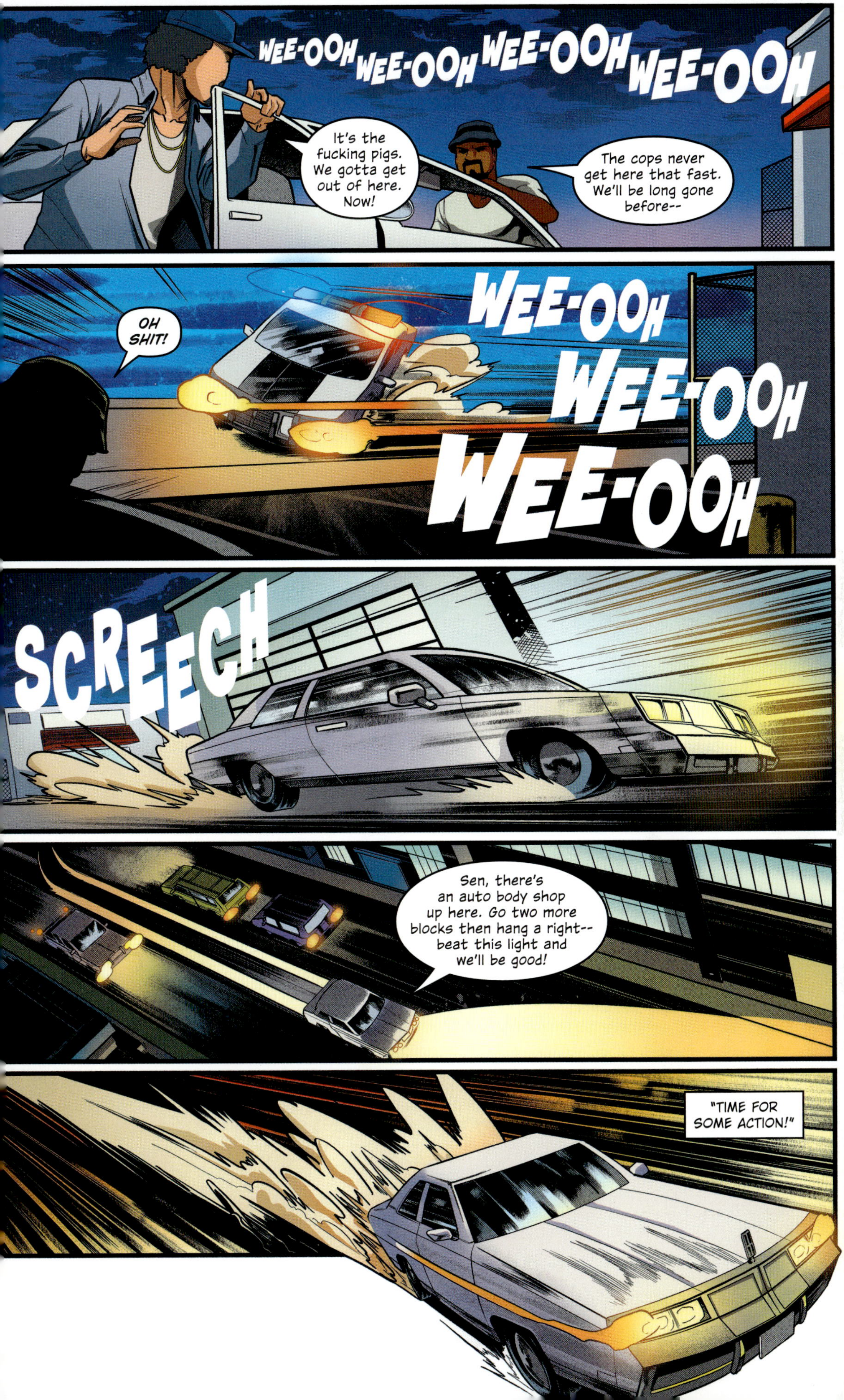
WEE-OOH WEE-OOH WEE-OOH WEE-OOH
It's the fucking pigs. We gotta get out of here. Now!
The cops never get here that fast. We'll be long gone before--
OH SHIT!
WEE-OOH
WEE-OOH
WEE-OOH
SCREECH
Sen, there's an auto body shop up here. Go two more blocks then hang a right-- beat this light and we'll be good!
"TIME FOR SOME ACTION!"

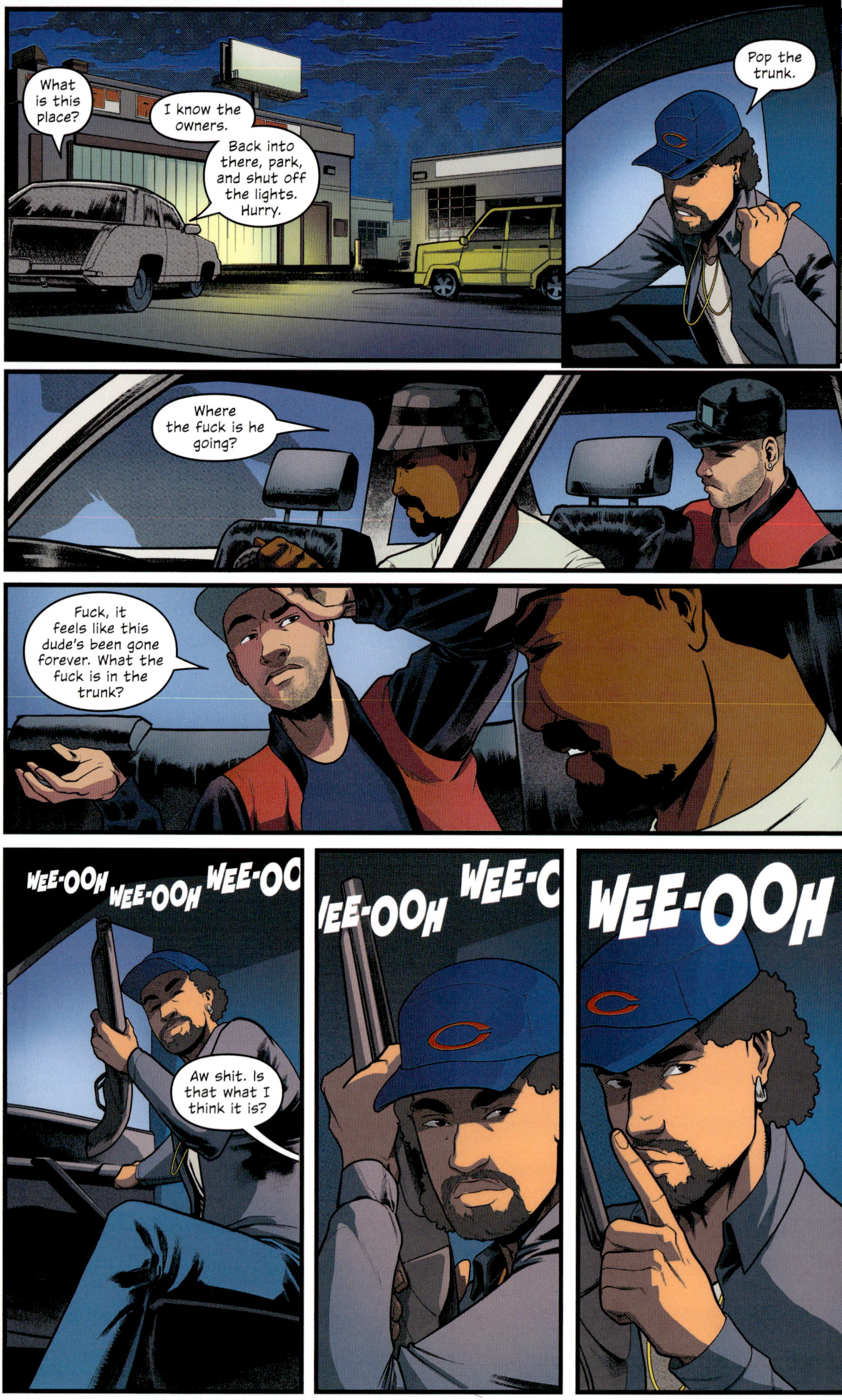
What is this place?
I know the owners.
Back into there, park, and shut off the lights. Hurry.
Pop the trunk.
Where the fuck is he going?
Fuck, it feels like this dude's been gone forever. What the fuck is in the trunk?
WEE-OOH WEE-OOH WEE-OO
Aw shit. Is that what I think it is?
EE-OOH WEE-C
WEE-OOH

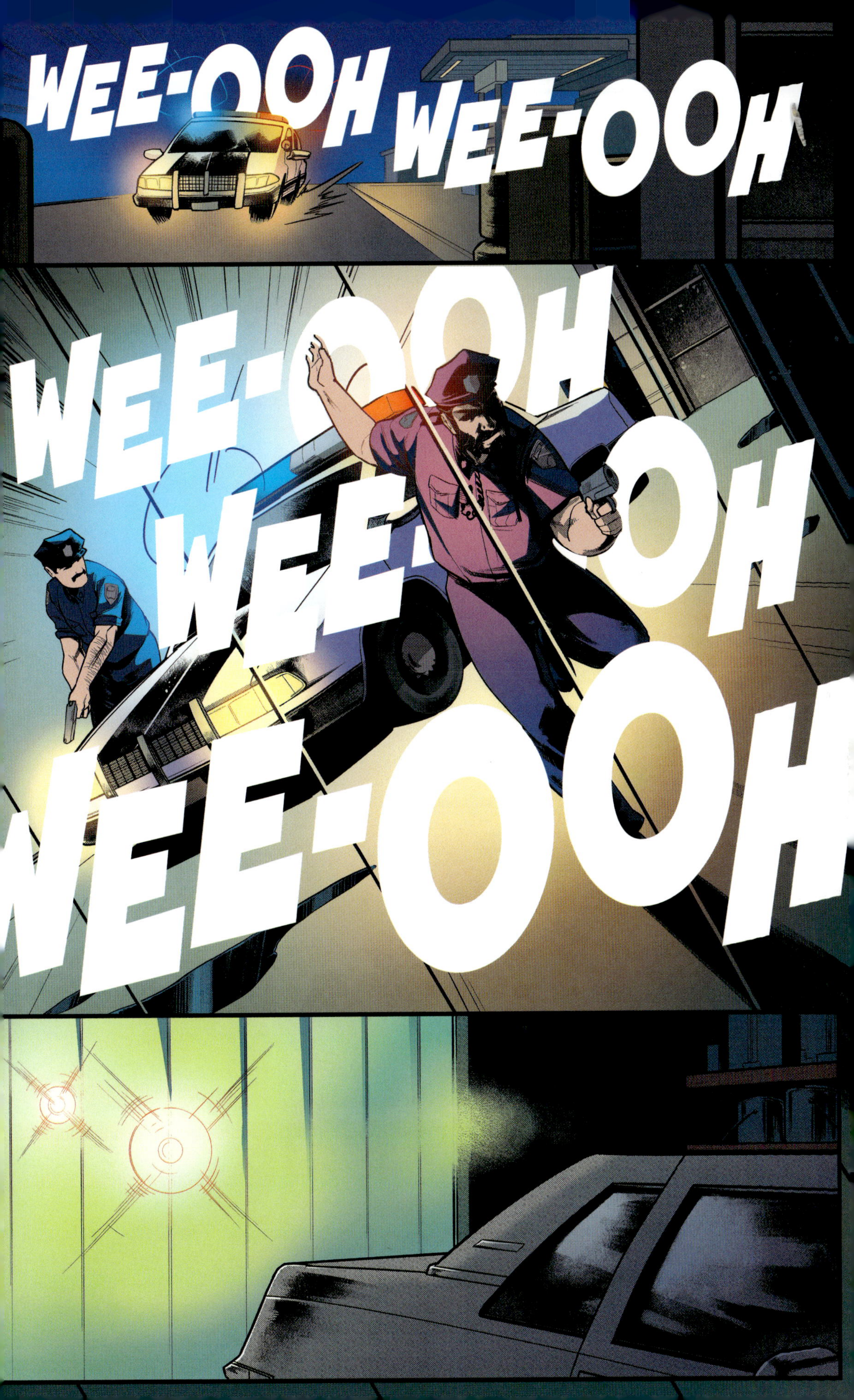
WEE-OOH WEE-OOH
WEE-OOH
WEE-OOH
WEE-OOH

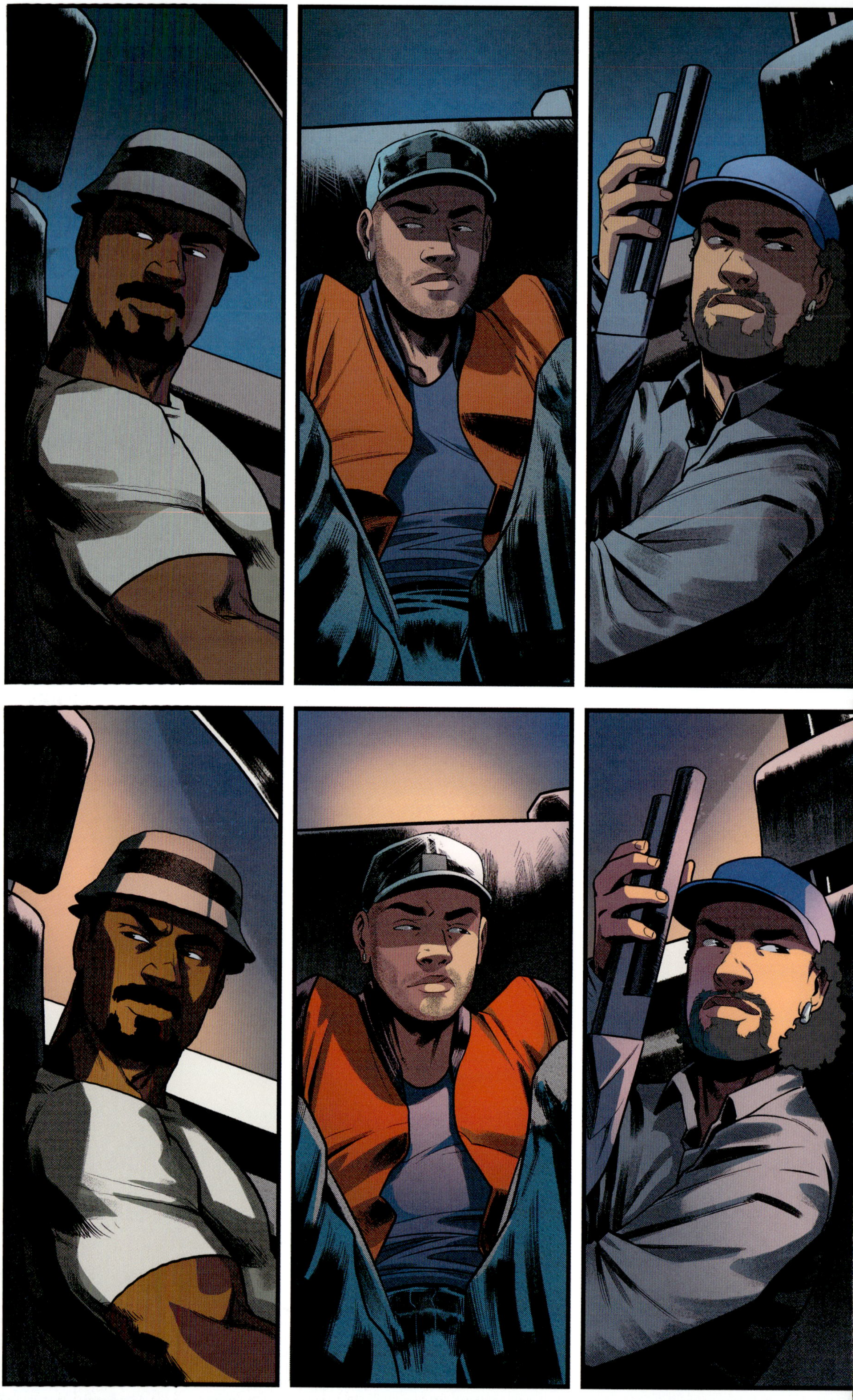

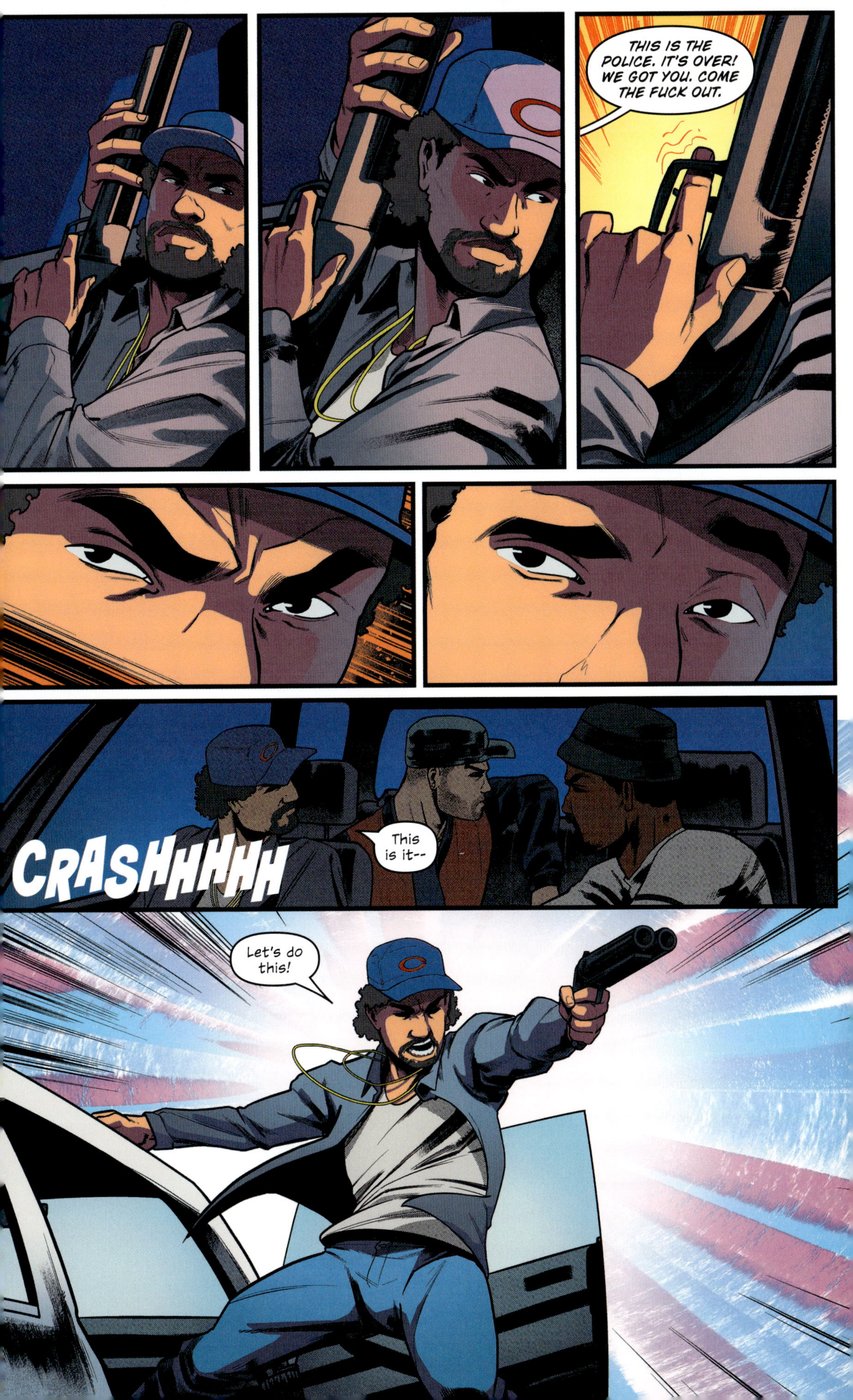
THIS IS THE POLICE. IT'S OVER! WE GOT YOU. COME THE FUCK OUT.
CRASHHHHHH
This is it--
Let's do this!

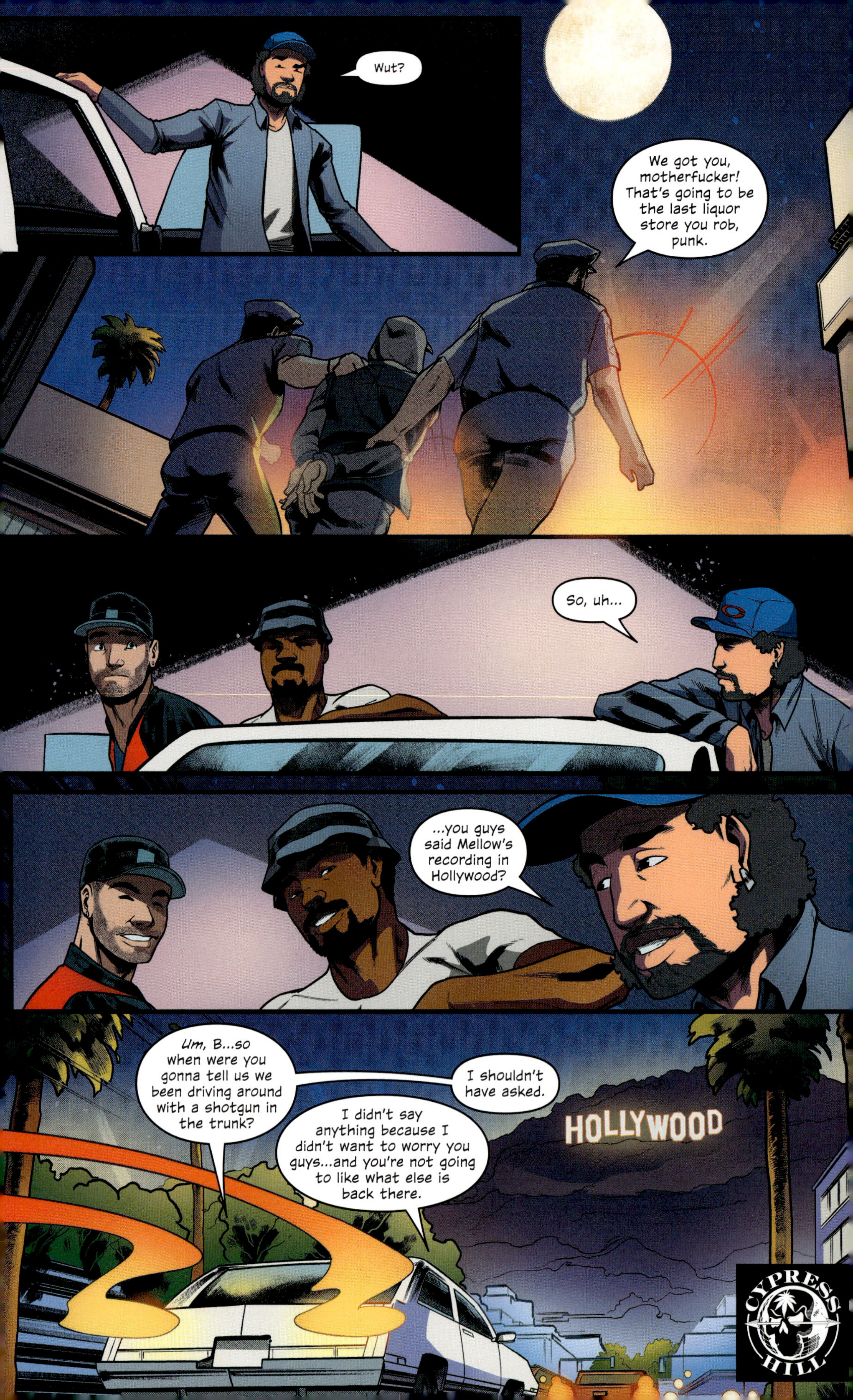
Wut?
We got you, motherfucker! That's going to be the last liquor store you rob, punk.
So, uh...
...you guys said Mellow's recording in Hollywood?
Um, B...so when were you gonna tell us we been driving around with a shotgun in the trunk?
I shouldn't have asked.
I didn't say anything because I didn't want to worry you guys...and you're not going to like what else is back there.
HOLLYWOOD
CYPRESS HILL

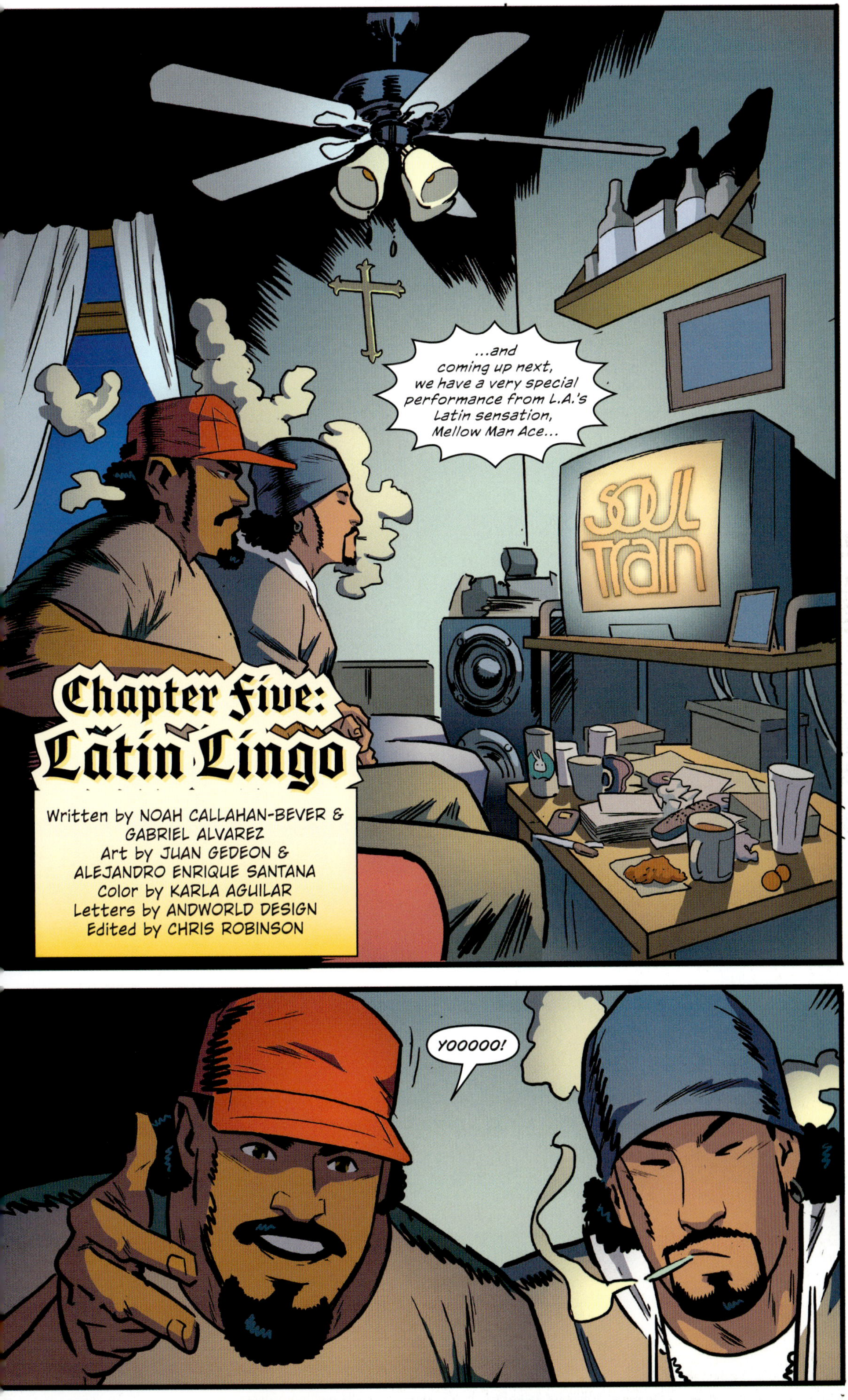
...and coming up next, we have a very special performance from L.A.'s Latin sensation, Mellow Man Ace...
SOUL TRAIN
Chapter Five:
Latin Lingo
Written by NOAH CALLAHAN-BEVER &
GABRIEL ALVAREZ
Art by JUAN GEDEON &
ALEJANDRO ENRIQUE SANTANA
Color by KARLA AGUILAR
Letters by ANDWORLD DESIGN
Edited by CHRIS ROBINSON
YOOOOO!

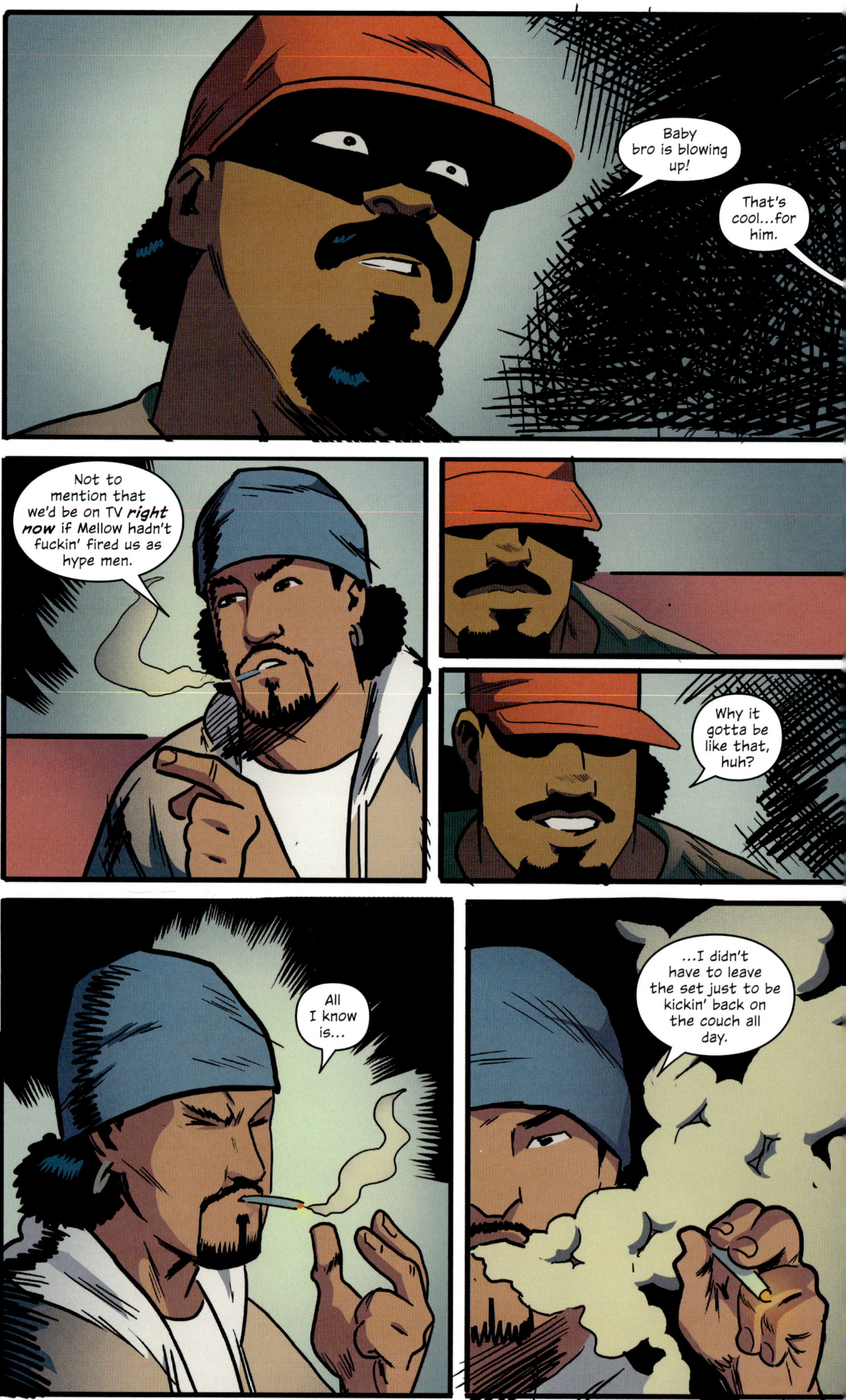
Baby bro is blowing up!
That's cool...for him.
Not to mention that we'd be on TV ***right now*** if Mellow hadn't fuckin' fired us as hype men.
Why it gotta be like that, huh?
All I know is...
...I didn't have to leave the set just to be kickin' back on the couch all day.

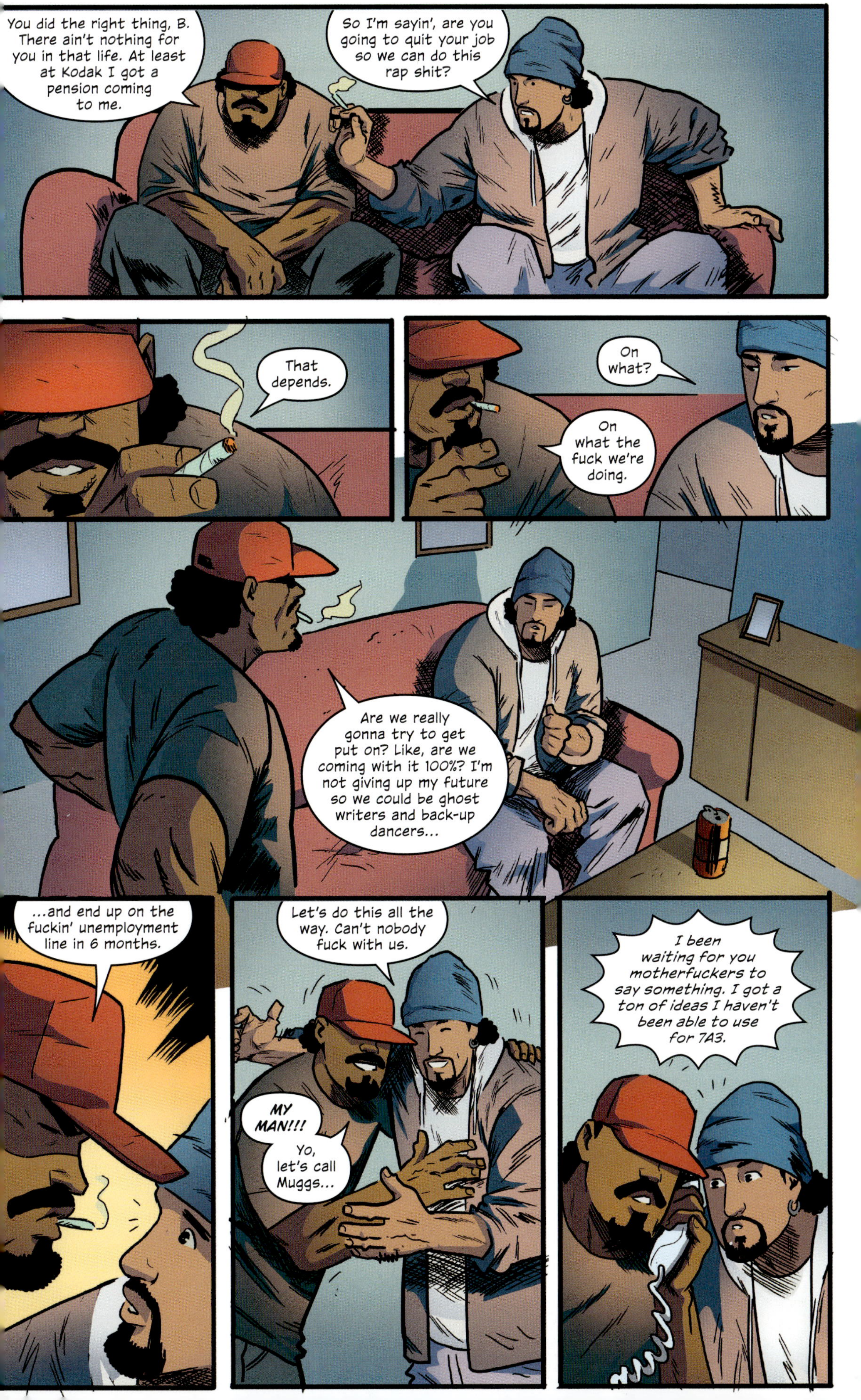
You did the right thing, B. There ain't nothing for you in that life. At least at Kodak I got a pension coming to me.
So I'm sayin', are you going to quit your job so we can do this rap shit?
That depends.
On what?
On what the fuck we're doing.
Are we really gonna try to get put on? Like, are we coming with it 100%? I'm not giving up my future so we could be ghost writers and back-up dancers...
...and end up on the fuckin' unemployment line in 6 months.
Let's do this all the way. Can't nobody fuck with us.
MY MAN!!!
Yo, let's call Muggs...
I been waiting for you motherfuckers to say something. I got a ton of ideas I haven't been able to use for 7A3.

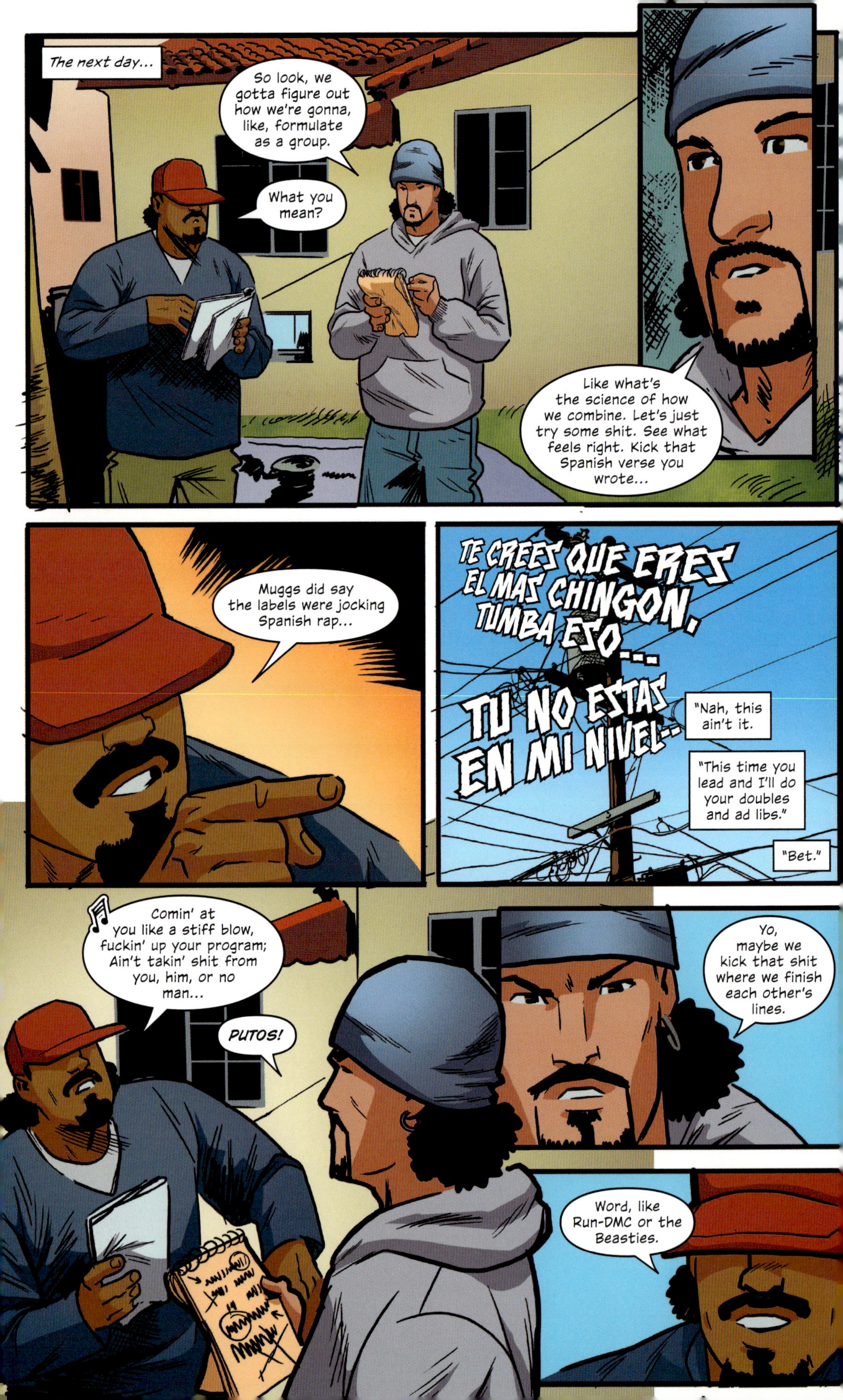
The next day...
So look, we gotta figure out how we're gonna, like, formulate as a group.
What you mean?
Like what's the science of how we combine. Let's just try some shit. See what feels right. Kick that Spanish verse you wrote...
Muggs did say the labels were jocking Spanish rap...
TE CREES QUE ERES EL MAS CHINGON, TUMBA ESO...
TU NO ESTAS EN MI NIVEL...
"Nah, this ain't it.
"This time you lead and I'll do your doubles and ad libs."
"Bet."
Comin' at you like a stiff blow, fuckin' up your program; Ain't takin' shit from you, him, or no man...
PUTOS!
Yo, maybe we kick that shit where we finish each other's lines.
Word, like Run-DMC or the Beasties.

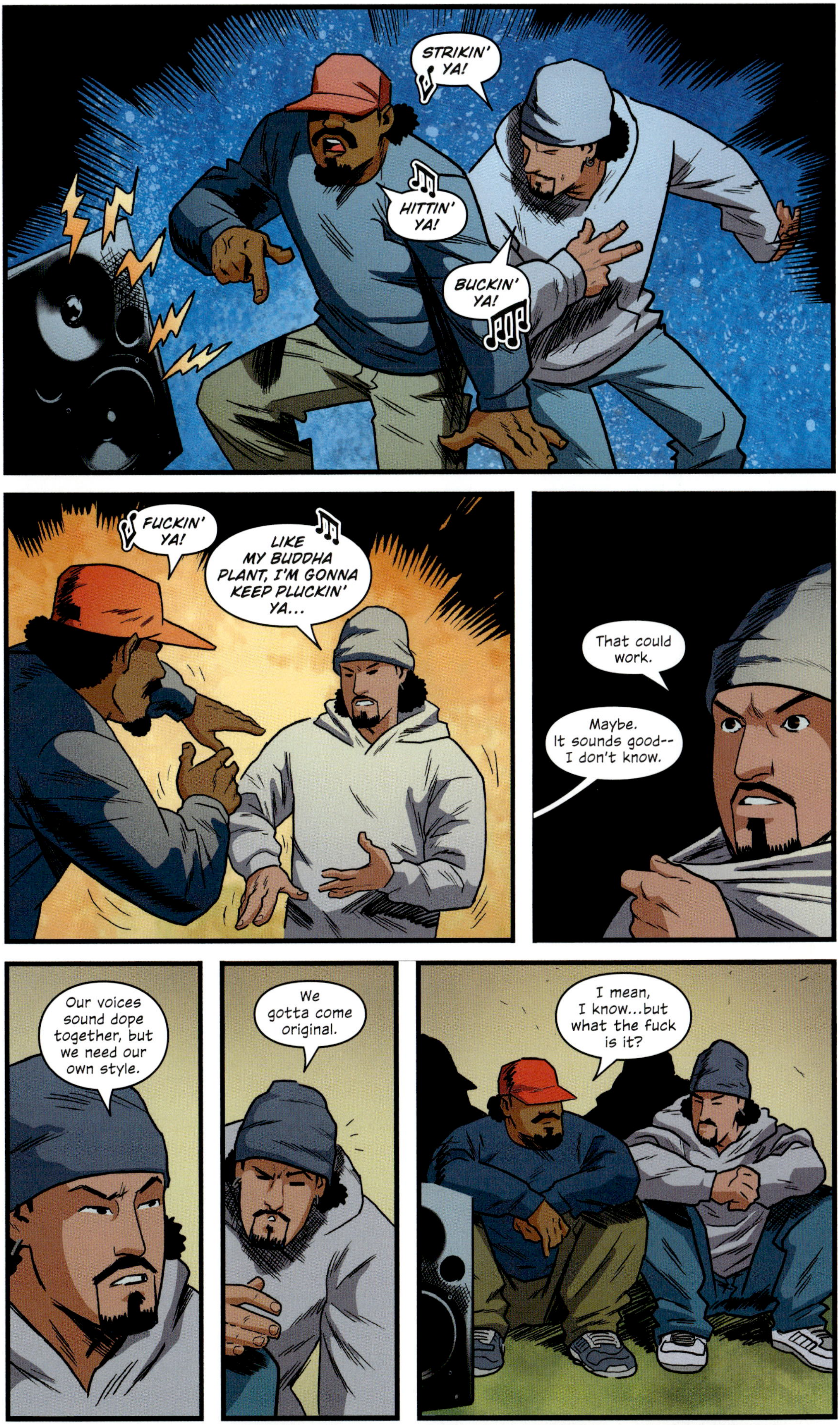
STRIKIN' YA!
HITTIN' YA!
BUCKIN' YA!
POP
FUCKIN' YA!
LIKE MY BUDDHA PLANT, I'M GONNA KEEP PLUCKIN' YA...
That could work.
Maybe. It sounds good-- I don't know.
Our voices sound dope together, but we need our own style.
We gotta come original.
I mean, I know...but what the fuck is it?

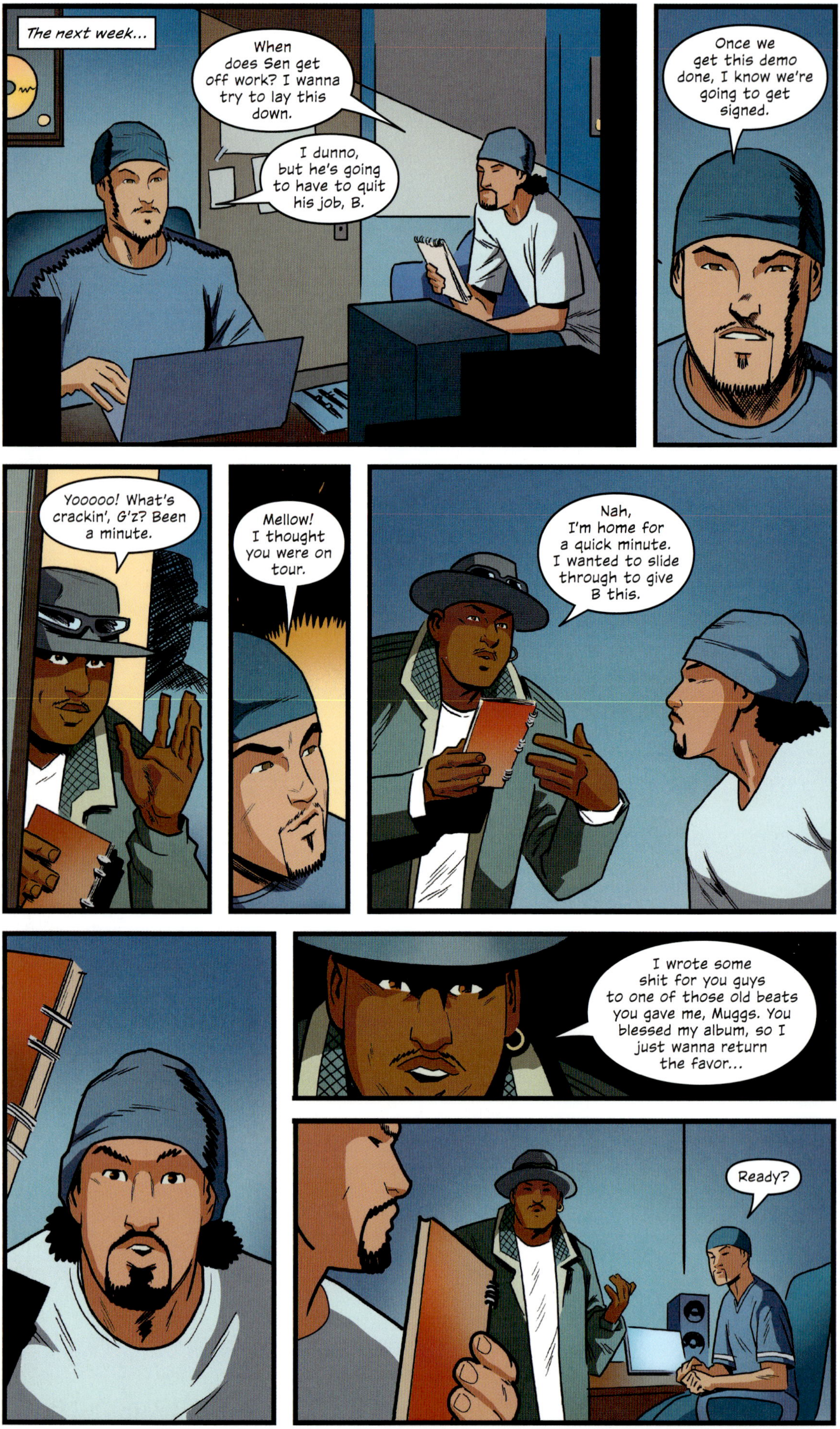
The next week...
When does Sen get off work? I wanna try to lay this down.
I dunno, but he's going to have to quit his job, B.
Once we get this demo done, I know we're going to get signed.
Yooooo! What's crackin', G'z? Been a minute.
Mellow! I thought you were on tour.
Nah, I'm home for a quick minute. I wanted to slide through to give B this.
I wrote some shit for you guys to one of those old beats you gave me, Muggs. You blessed my album, so I just wanna return the favor...
Ready?

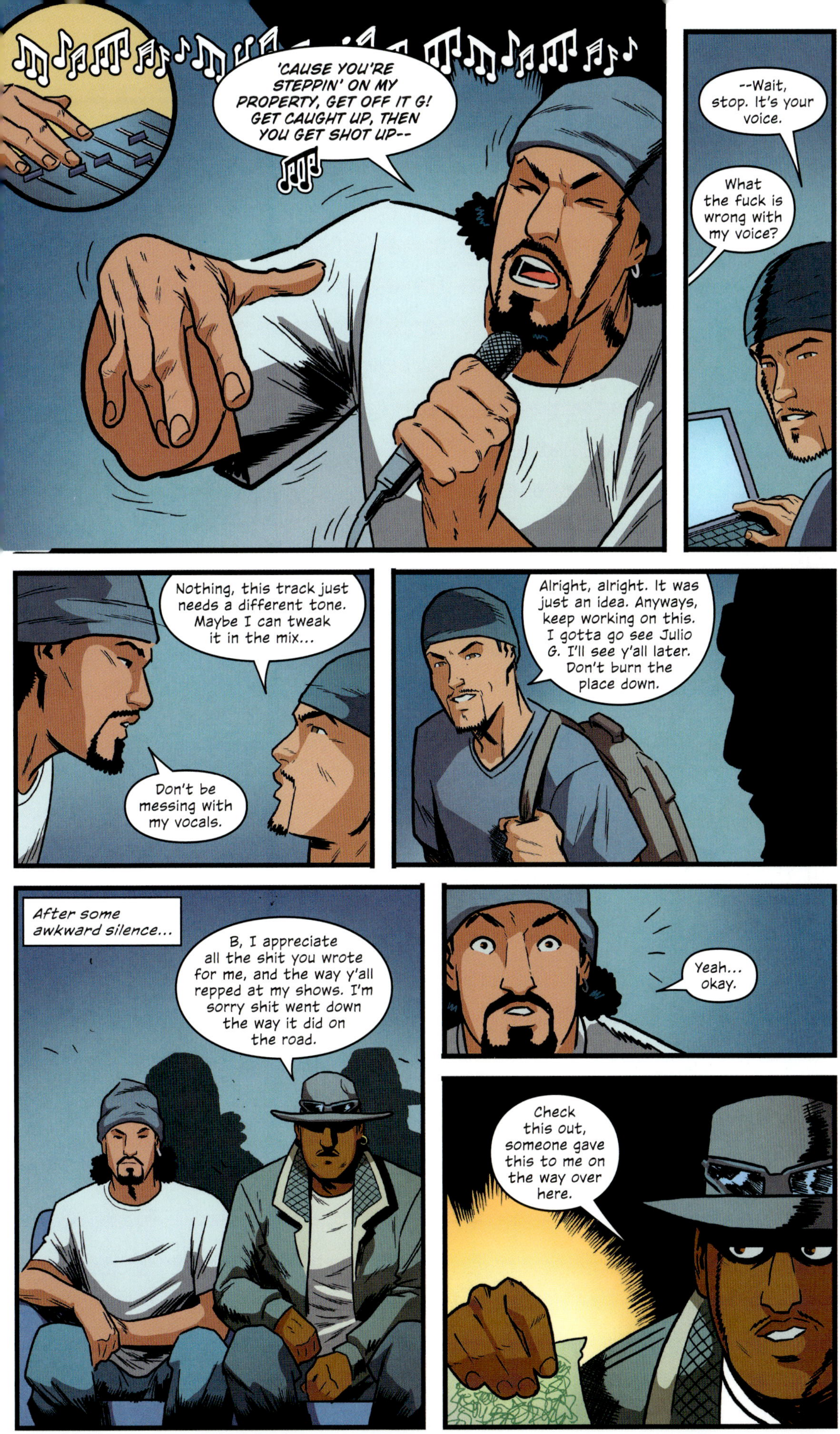
'CAUSE YOU'RE STEPPIN' ON MY PROPERTY, GET OFF IT G! GET CAUGHT UP, THEN YOU GET SHOT UP--
--Wait, stop. It's your voice.
What the fuck is wrong with my voice?
Nothing, this track just needs a different tone. Maybe I can tweak it in the mix...
Don't be messing with my vocals.
Alright, alright. It was just an idea. Anyways, keep working on this. I gotta go see Julio G. I'll see y'all later. Don't burn the place down.
After some awkward silence...
B, I appreciate all the shit you wrote for me, and the way y'all repped at my shows. I'm sorry shit went down the way it did on the road.
Yeah... okay.
Check this out, someone gave this to me on the way over here.

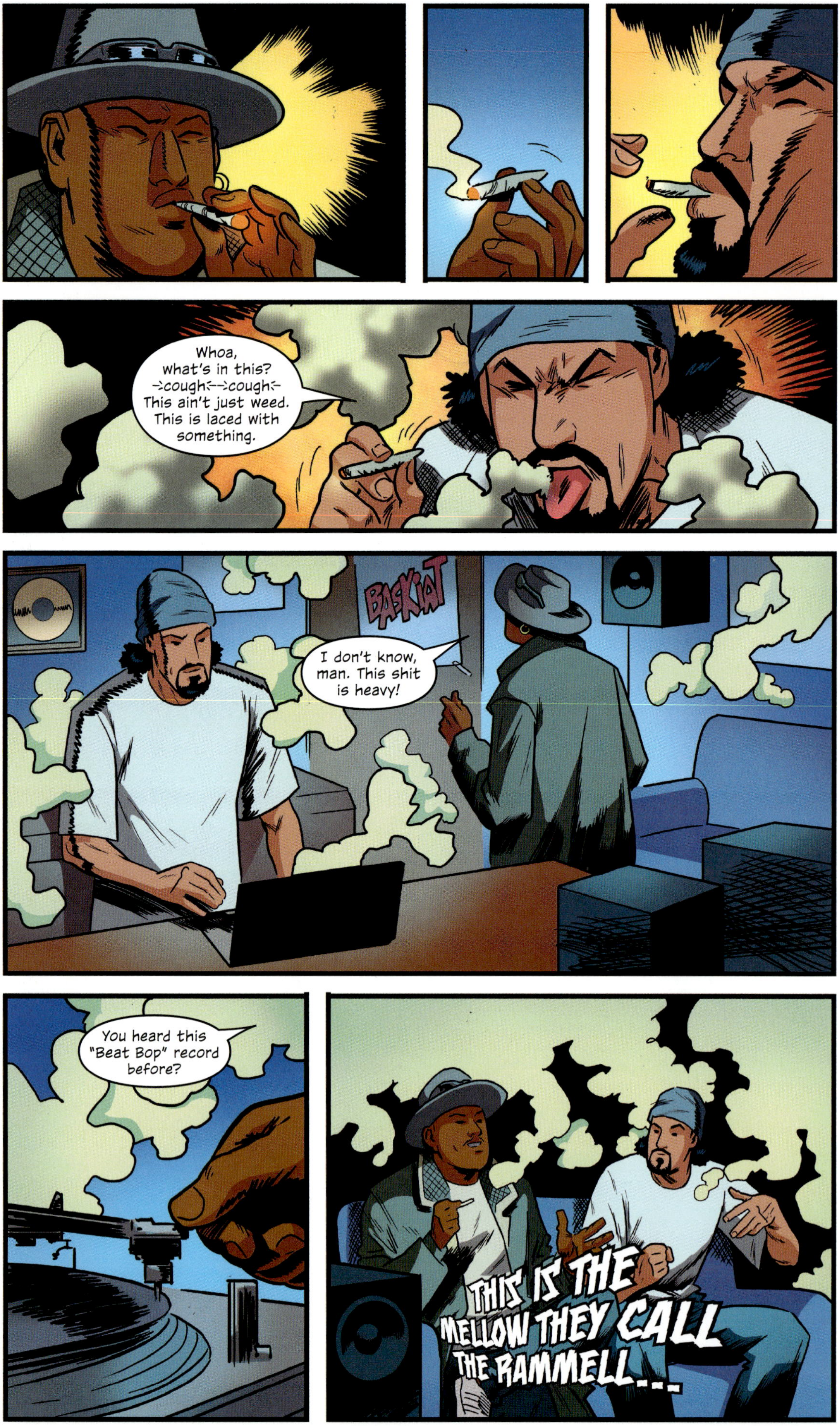
Whoa,
what's in this?
-cough- -cough-
This ain't just weed.
This is laced with
something.
BASKIAT
I don't know,
man. This shit
is heavy!
You heard this
"Beat Bop" record
before?
THIS IS THE
MELLOW THEY CALL
THE RAMMELL...

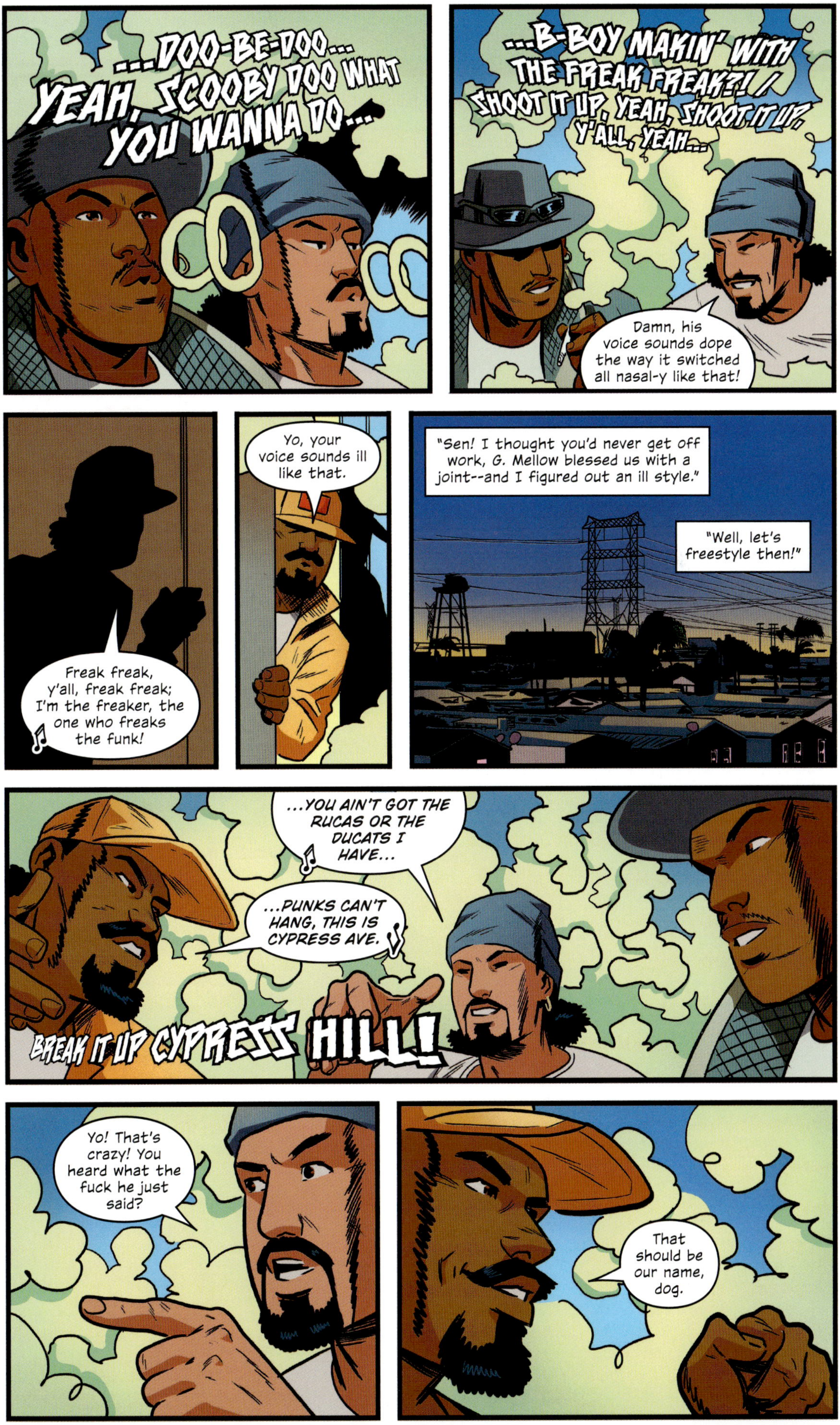
...DOO-BE-DOO...
YEAH, SCOOBY DOO WHAT YOU WANNA DO...
...B-BOY MAKIN' WITH THE FREAK FREAK?! / SHOOT IT UP, YEAH, SHOOT IT UP, Y'ALL, YEAH...
Damn, his voice sounds dope the way it switched all nasal-y like that!
Freak freak, y'all, freak freak; I'm the freaker, the one who freaks the funk!
Yo, your voice sounds ill like that.
"Sen! I thought you'd never get off work, G. Mellow blessed us with a joint--and I figured out an ill style."
"Well, let's freestyle then!"
...YOU AIN'T GOT THE RUCAS OR THE DUCATS I HAVE...
...PUNKS CAN'T HANG, THIS IS CYPRESS AVE.
BREAK IT UP CYPRESS HILL!
Yo! That's crazy! You heard what the fuck he just said?
That should be our name, dog.

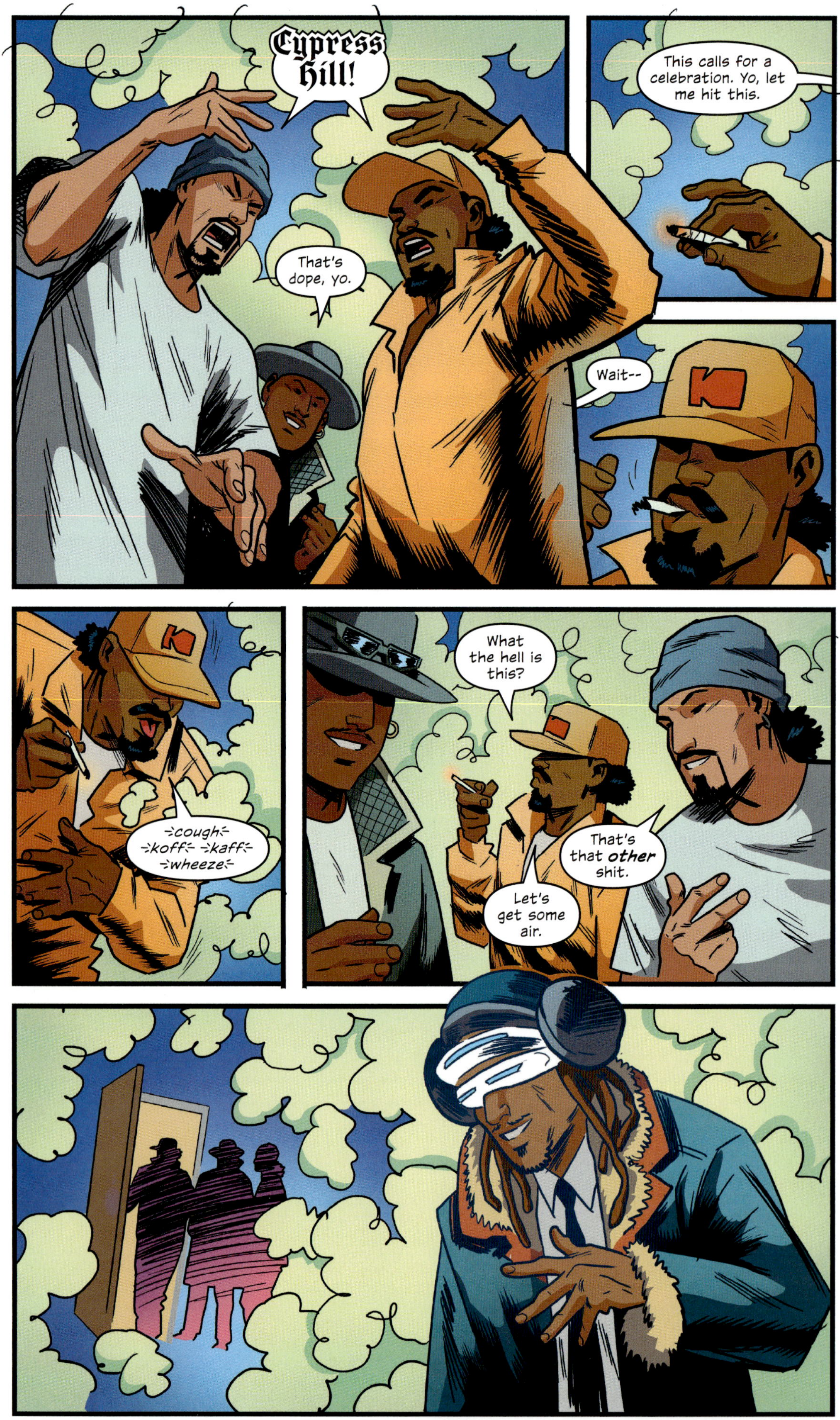
Cypress Hill!
That's dope, yo.
This calls for a celebration. Yo, let me hit this.
Wait--
-cough- -koff- -kaff- -wheeze-
What the hell is this?
That's that *other* shit.
Let's get some air.

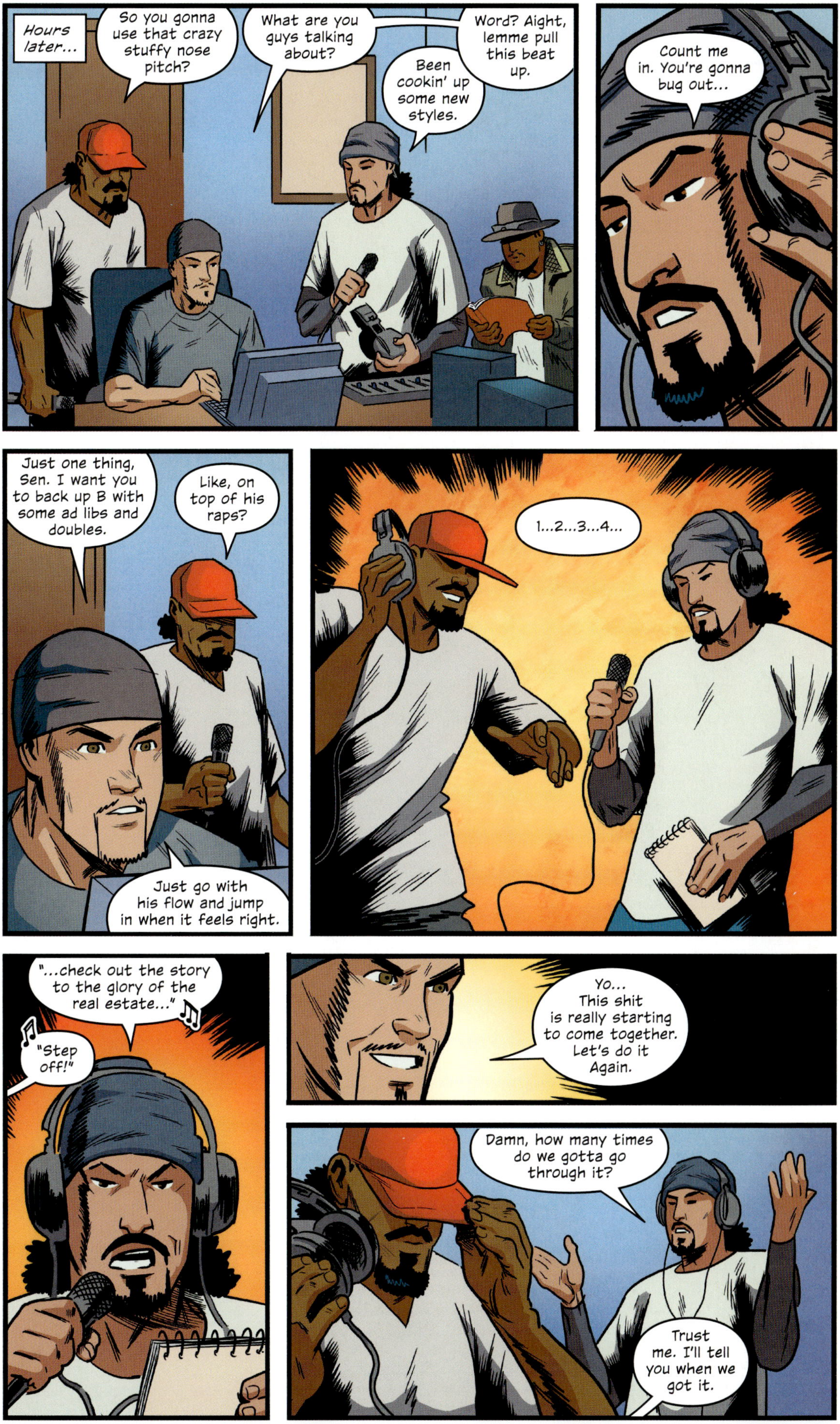
Hours later...
So you gonna use that crazy stuffy nose pitch?
What are you guys talking about?
Word? Aight, lemme pull this beat up.
Been cookin' up some new styles.
Count me in. You're gonna bug out...
Just one thing, Sen. I want you to back up B with some ad libs and doubles.
Like, on top of his raps?
Just go with his flow and jump in when it feels right.
1...2...3...4...
"...check out the story to the glory of the real estate..."
"Step off!"
Yo... This shit is really starting to come together. Let's do it Again.
Damn, how many times do we gotta go through it?
Trust me. I'll tell you when we got it.

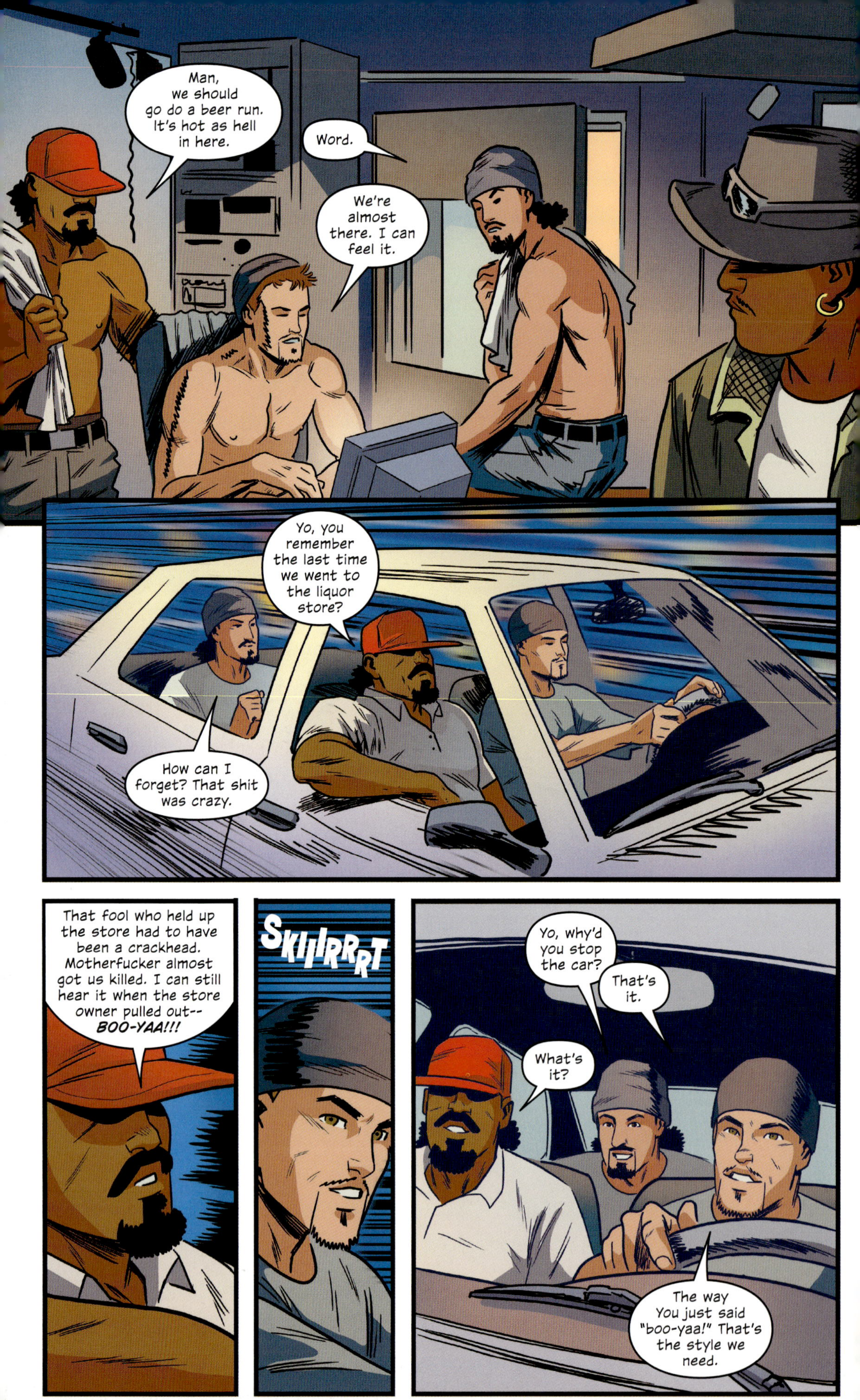

Man, we should go do a beer run. It's hot as hell in here.
Word.
We're almost there. I can feel it.
Yo, you remember the last time we went to the liquor store?
How can I forget? That shit was crazy.
That fool who held up the store had to have been a crackhead. Motherfucker almost got us killed. I can still hear it when the store owner pulled out-- BOO-YAA!!!
SKIIIRRRT
Yo, why'd you stop the car?
That's it.
What's it?
The way You just said "boo-yaa!" That's the style we need.

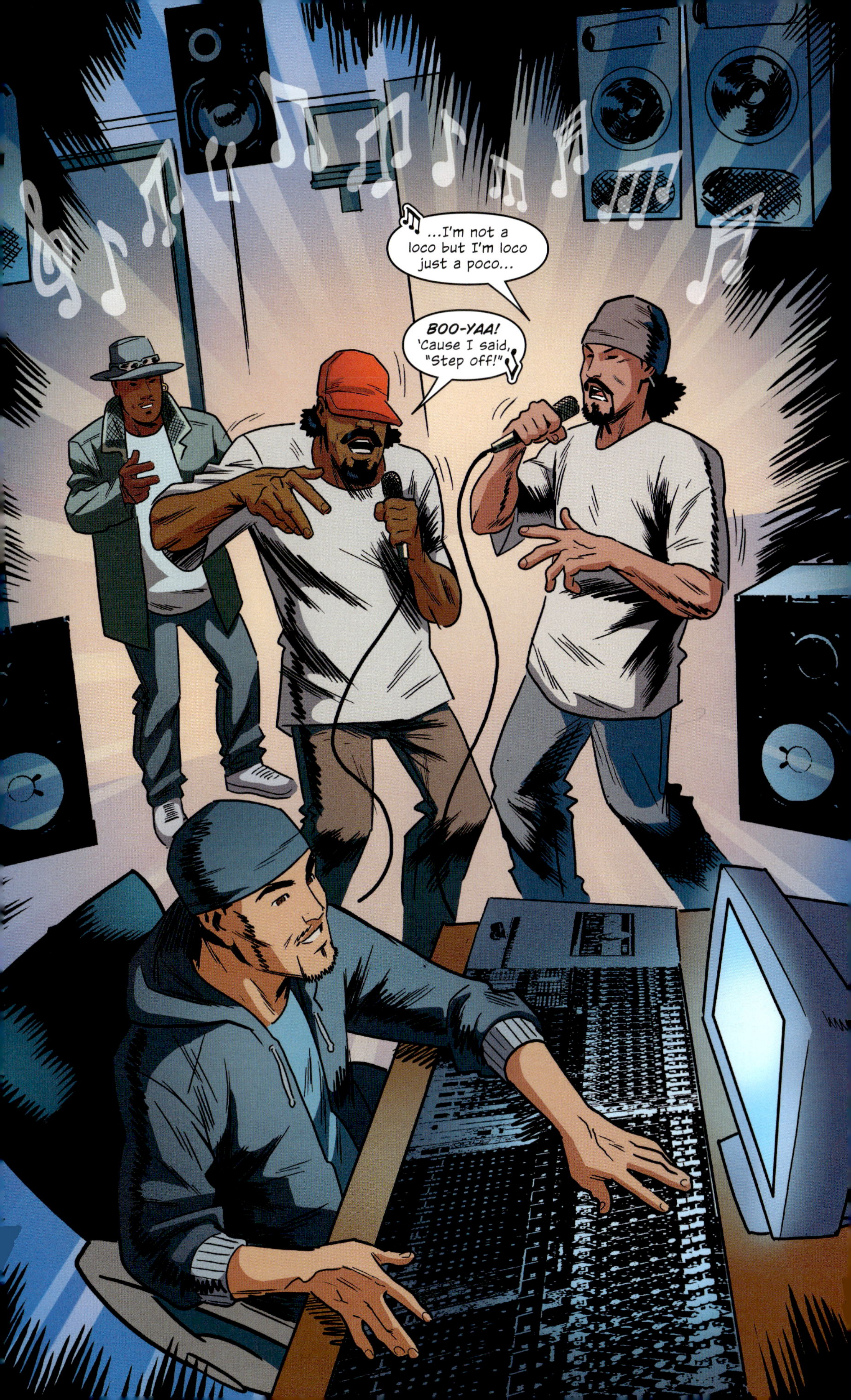
...I'm not a loco but I'm loco just a poco...
BOO-YAA! 'Cause I said, "Step off!"

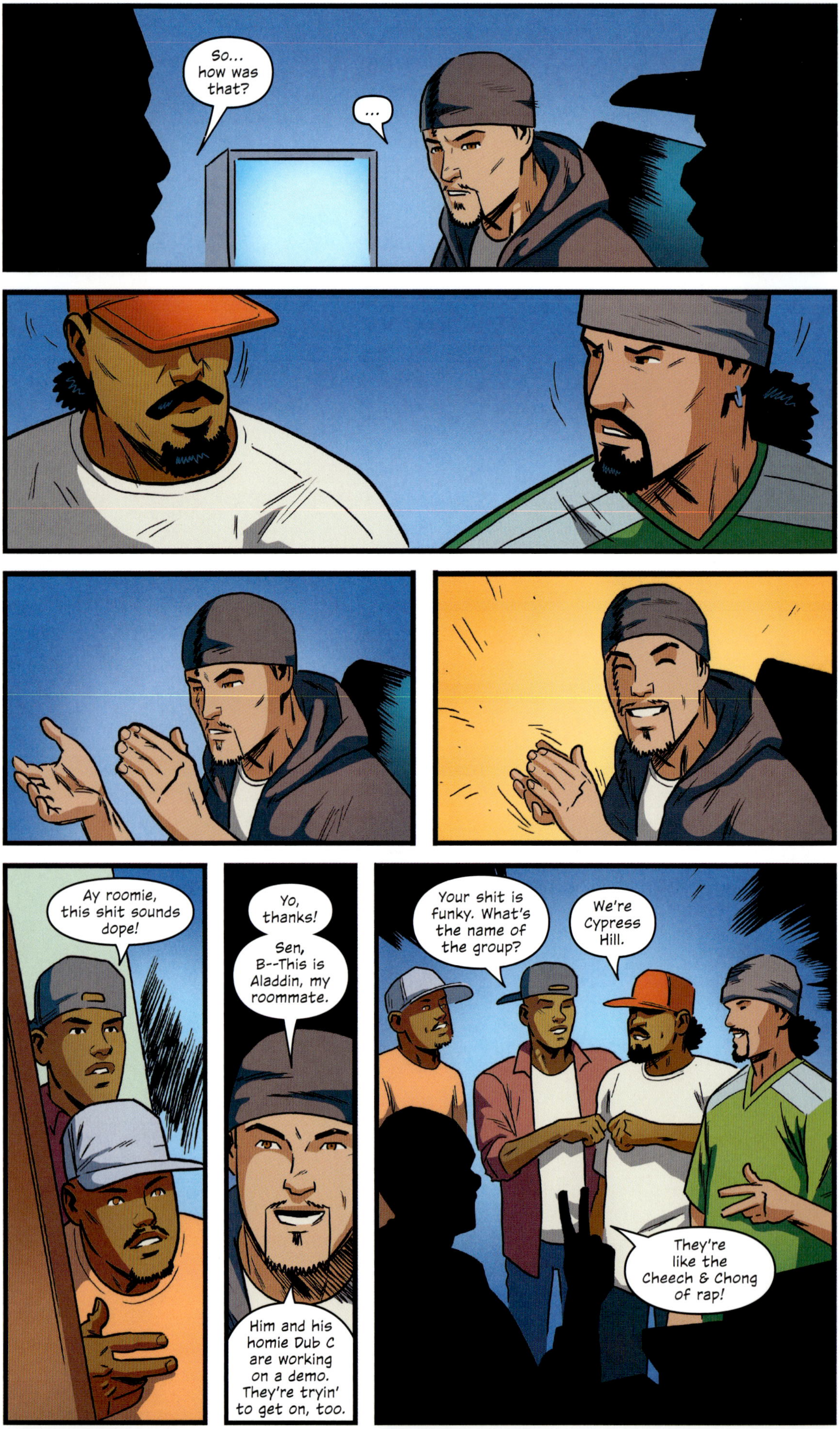
So... how was that?
...
Ay roomie, this shit sounds dope!
Yo, thanks!
Sen, B--This is Aladdin, my roommate.
Him and his homie Dub C are working on a demo. They're tryin' to get on, too.
Your shit is funky. What's the name of the group?
We're Cypress Hill.
They're like the Cheech & Chong of rap!

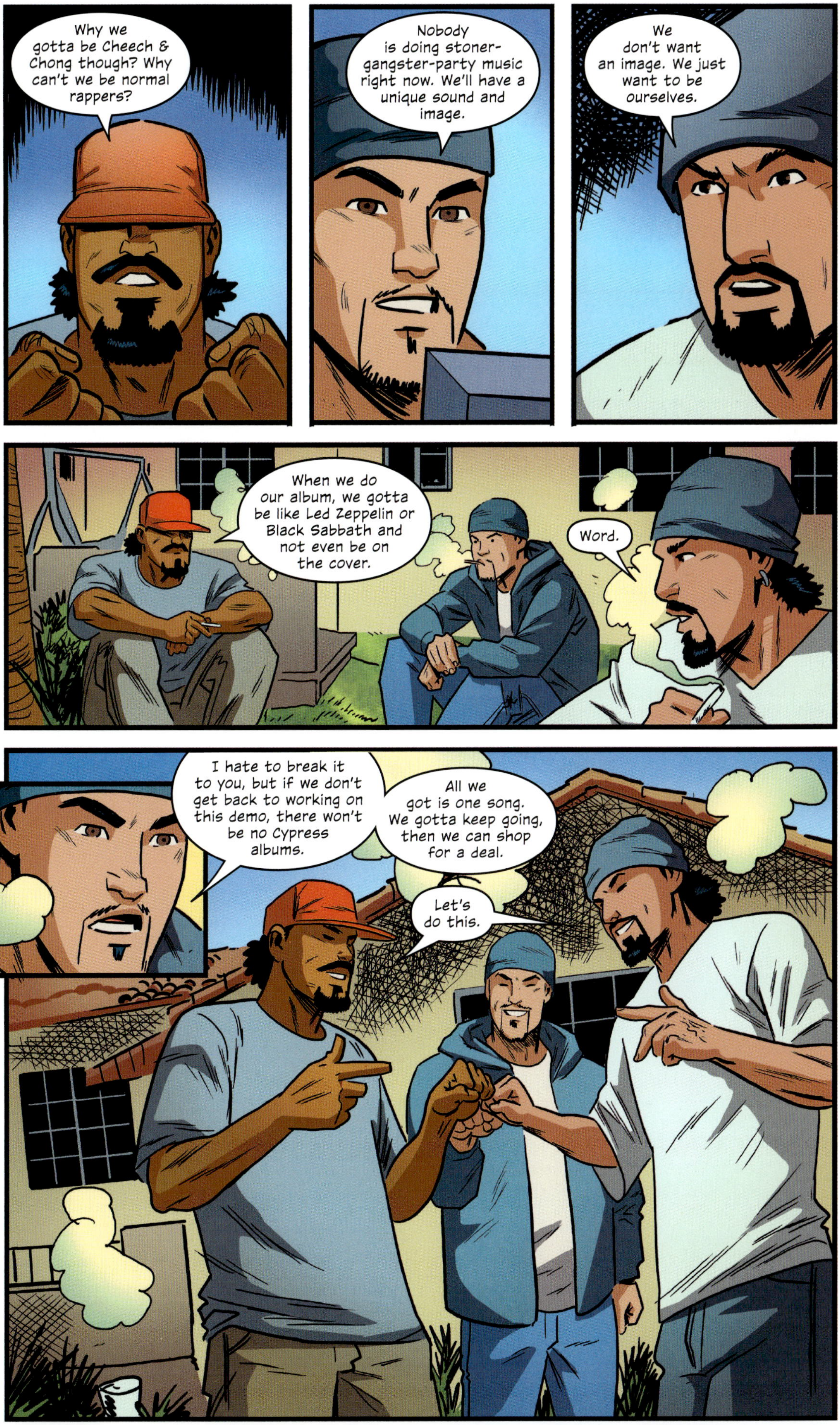
Why we gotta be Cheech & Chong though? Why can't we be normal rappers?
Nobody is doing stoner-gangster-party music right now. We'll have a unique sound and image.
We don't want an image. We just want to be ourselves.
When we do our album, we gotta be like Led Zeppelin or Black Sabbath and not even be on the cover.
Word.
I hate to break it to you, but if we don't get back to working on this demo, there won't be no Cypress albums.
All we got is one song. We gotta keep going, then we can shop for a deal.
Let's do this.

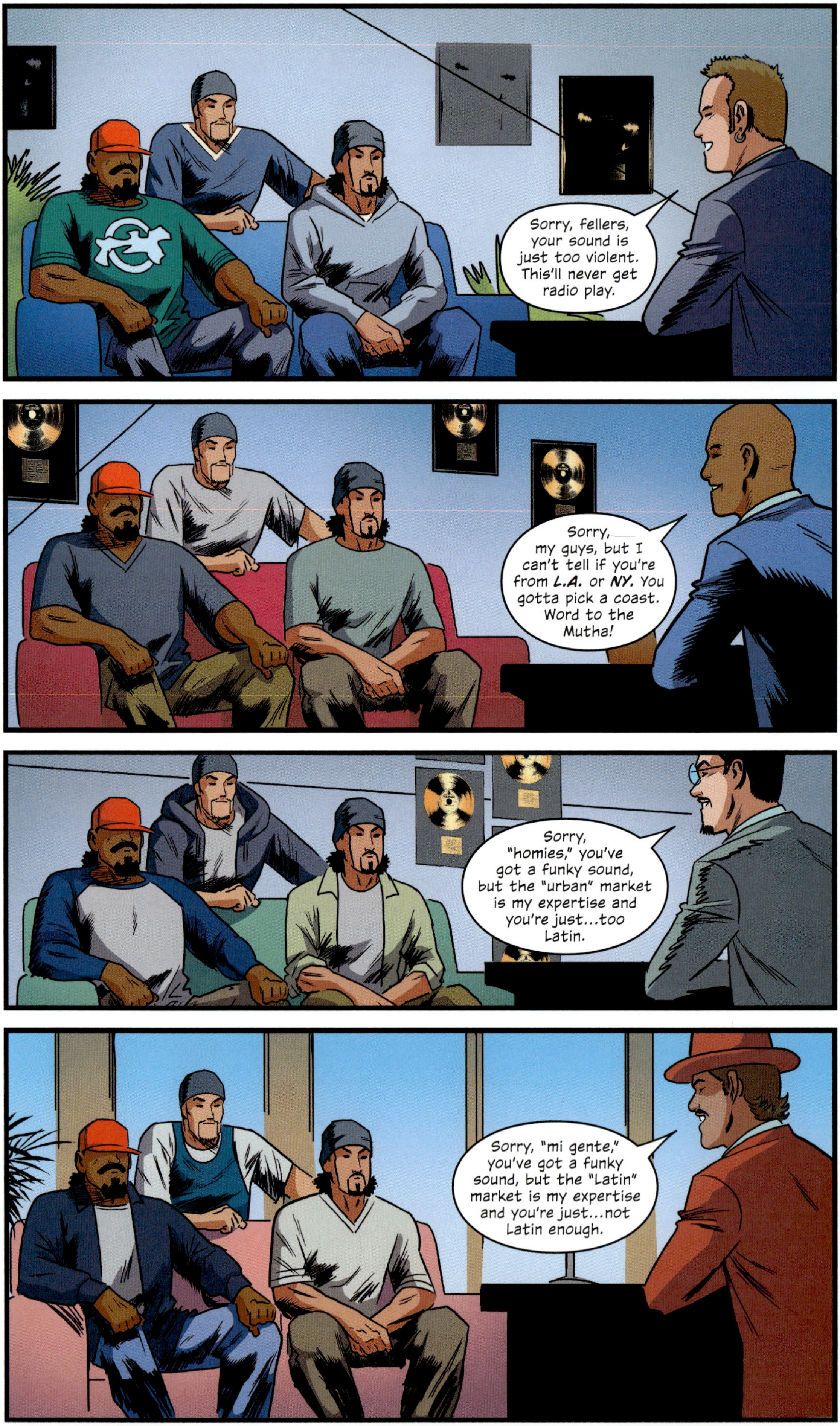
Sorry, fellers, your sound is just too violent. This'll never get radio play.
Sorry, my guys, but I can't tell if you're from **L.A.** or **NY.** You gotta pick a coast. Word to the Mutha!
Sorry, "homies," you've got a funky sound, but the "urban" market is my expertise and you're just...too Latin.
Sorry, "mi gente," you've got a funky sound, but the "Latin" market is my expertise and you're just...not Latin enough.

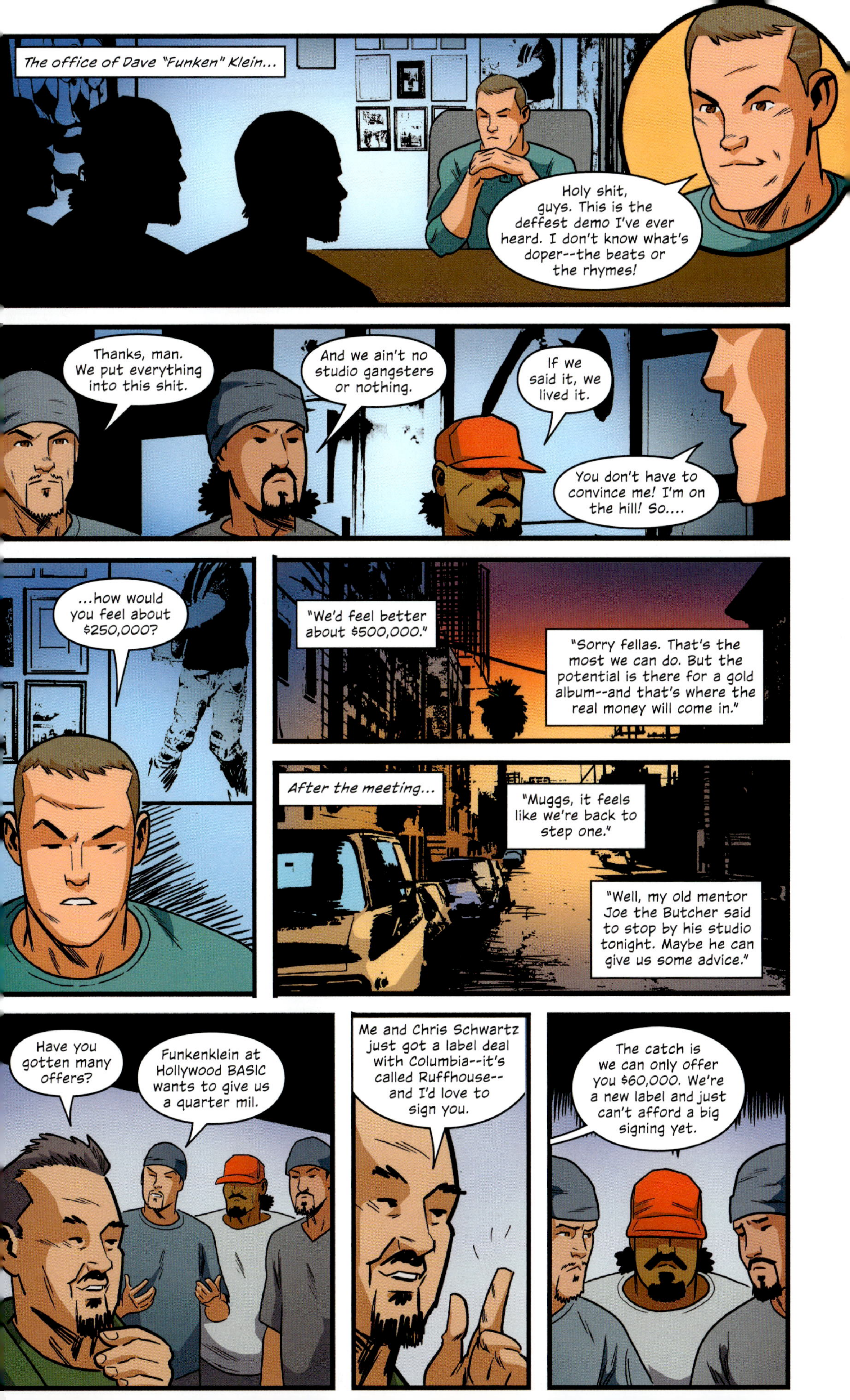
The office of Dave "Funken" Klein...
Holy shit, guys. This is the deffest demo I've ever heard. I don't know what's doper--the beats or the rhymes!
Thanks, man. We put everything into this shit.
And we ain't no studio gangsters or nothing.
If we said it, we lived it.
You don't have to convince me! I'm on the hill! So....
...how would you feel about $250,000?
"We'd feel better about $500,000."
"Sorry fellas. That's the most we can do. But the potential is there for a gold album--and that's where the real money will come in."
After the meeting...
"Muggs, it feels like we're back to step one."
"Well, my old mentor Joe the Butcher said to stop by his studio tonight. Maybe he can give us some advice."
Have you gotten many offers?
Funkenklein at Hollywood BASIC wants to give us a quarter mil.
Me and Chris Schwartz just got a label deal with Columbia--it's called Ruffhouse--and I'd love to sign you.
The catch is we can only offer you $60,000. We're a new label and just can't afford a big signing yet.

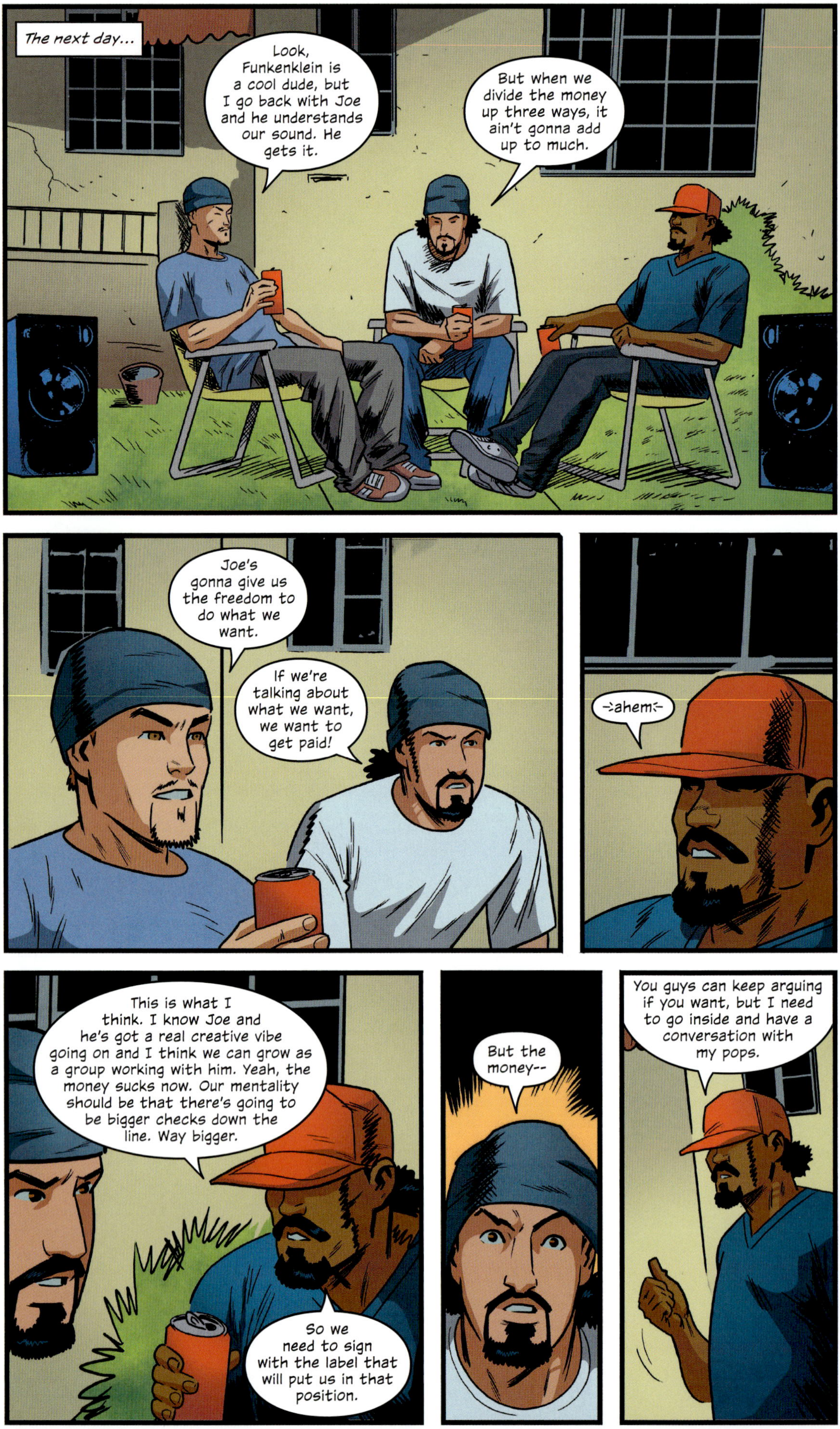

The next day...
Look, Funkenklein is a cool dude, but I go back with Joe and he understands our sound. He gets it.
But when we divide the money up three ways, it ain't gonna add up to much.
Joe's gonna give us the freedom to do what we want.
If we're talking about what we want, we want to get paid!
-ahem-
This is what I think. I know Joe and he's got a real creative vibe going on and I think we can grow as a group working with him. Yeah, the money sucks now. Our mentality should be that there's going to be bigger checks down the line. Way bigger.
So we need to sign with the label that will put us in that position.
But the money--
You guys can keep arguing if you want, but I need to go inside and have a conversation with my pops.

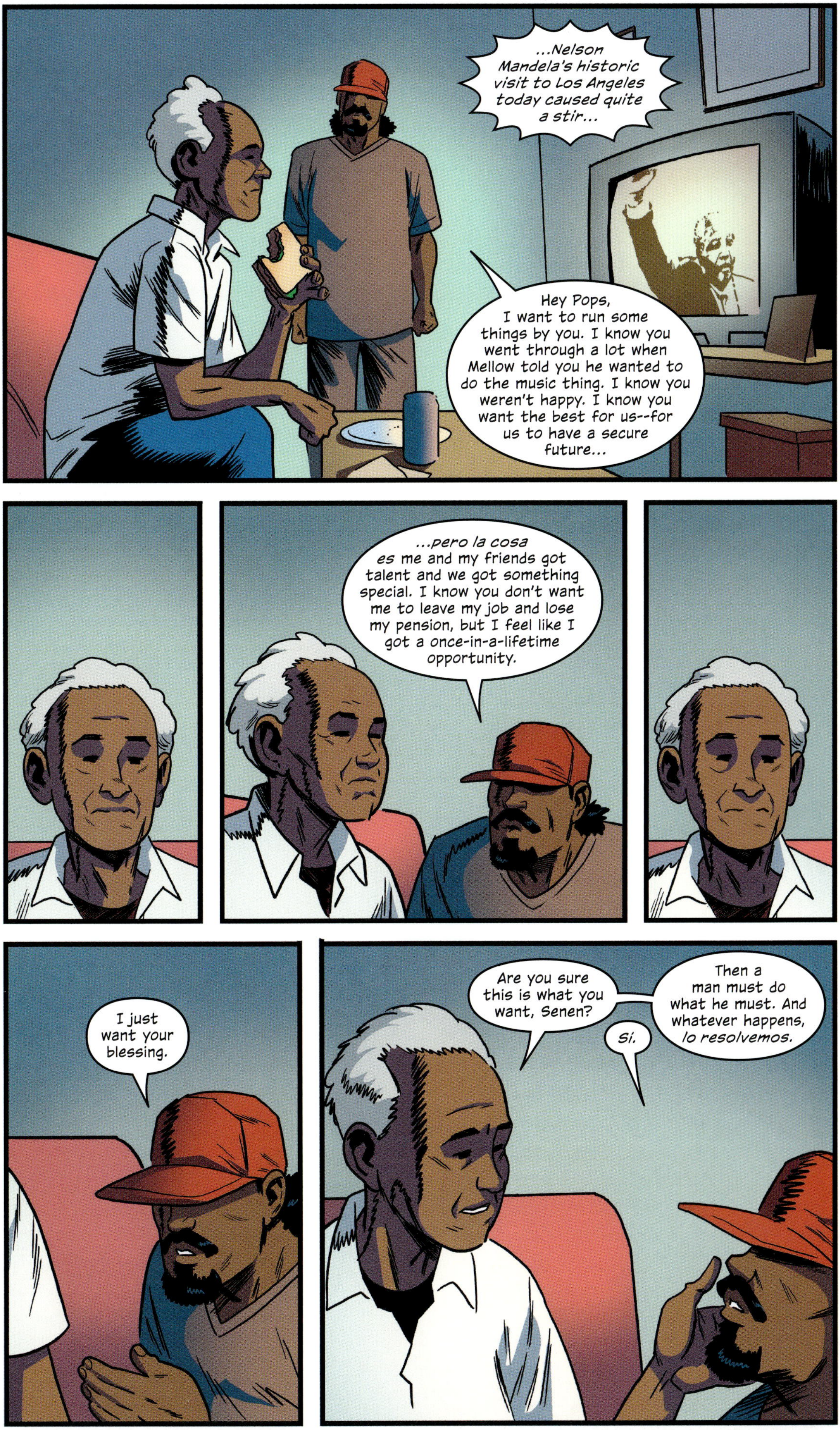
...Nelson Mandela's historic visit to Los Angeles today caused quite a stir...
Hey Pops, I want to run some things by you. I know you went through a lot when Mellow told you he wanted to do the music thing. I know you weren't happy. I know you want the best for us--for us to have a secure future...
...pero la cosa es me and my friends got talent and we got something special. I know you don't want me to leave my job and lose my pension, but I feel like I got a once-in-a-lifetime opportunity.
I just want your blessing.
Are you sure this is what you want, Senen?
Si.
Then a man must do what he must. And whatever happens, lo resolvemos.

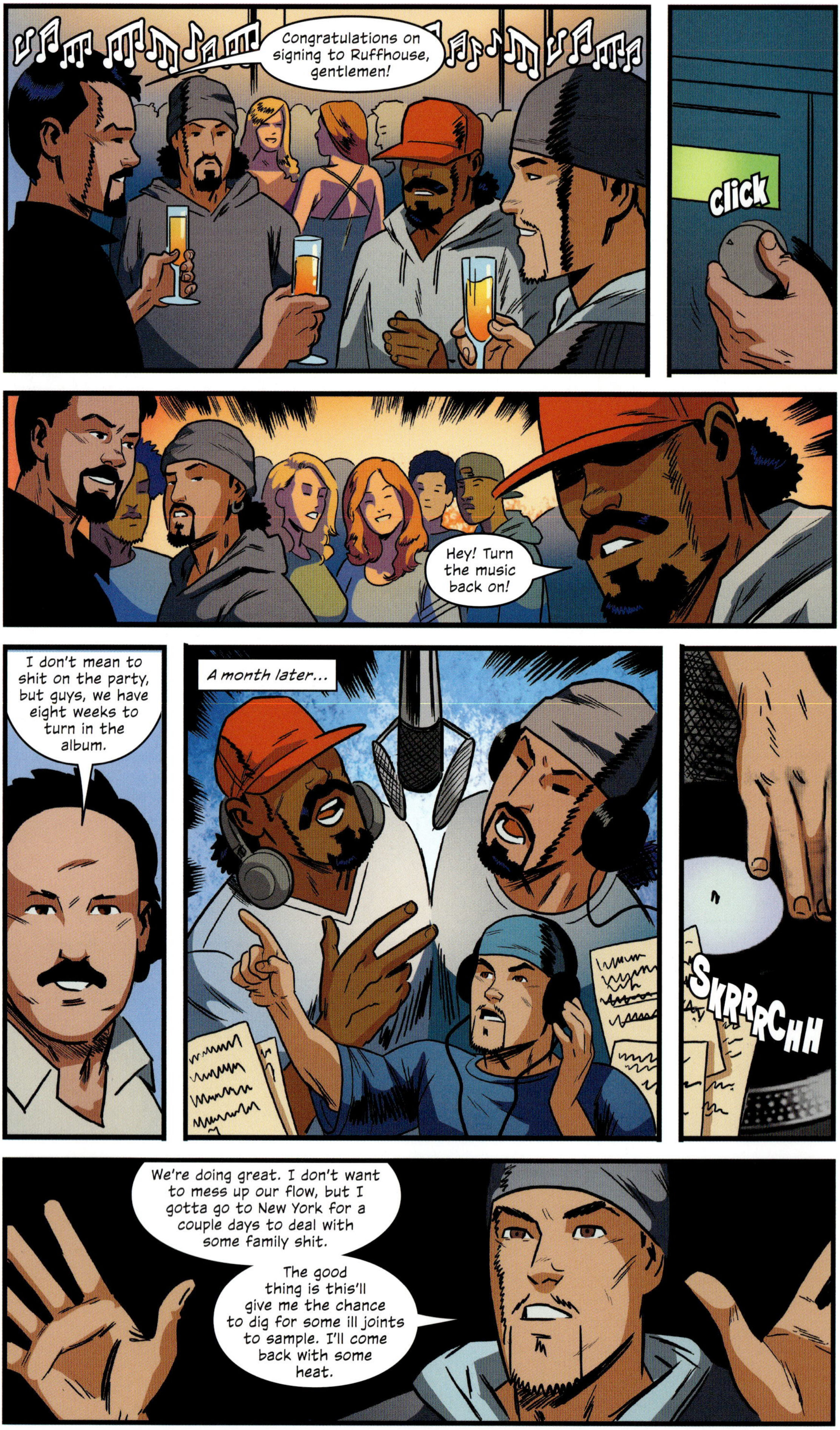
Congratulations on signing to Ruffhouse, gentlemen!
CLICK
Hey! Turn the music back on!
I don't mean to shit on the party, but guys, we have eight weeks to turn in the album.
A month later...
SKRRRCHH
We're doing great. I don't want to mess up our flow, but I gotta go to New York for a couple days to deal with some family shit.
The good thing is this'll give me the chance to dig for some ill joints to sample. I'll come back with some heat.

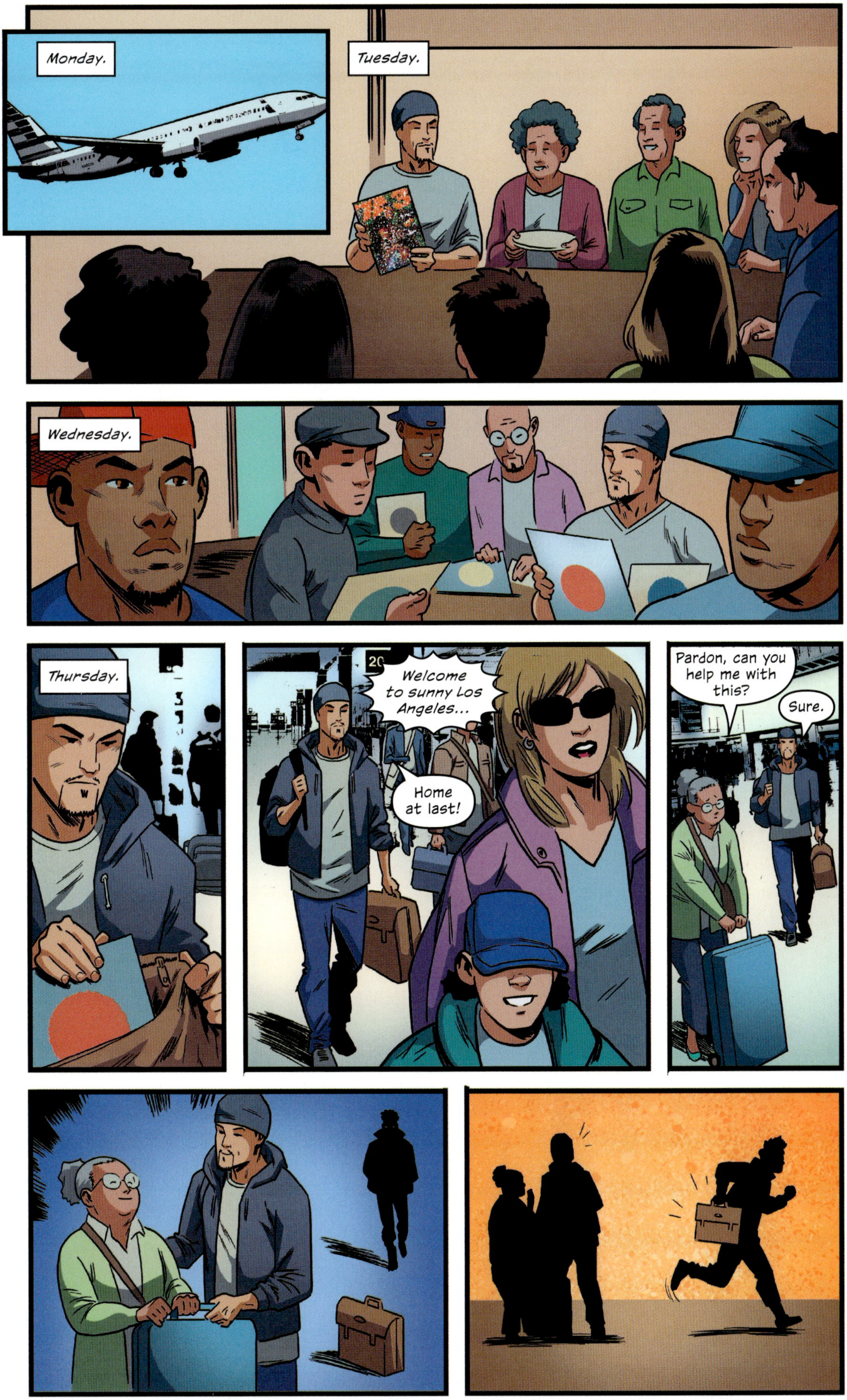

Monday.
Tuesday.
Wednesday.
Thursday.
Welcome to sunny Los Angeles...
Home at last!
Pardon, can you help me with this?
Sure.

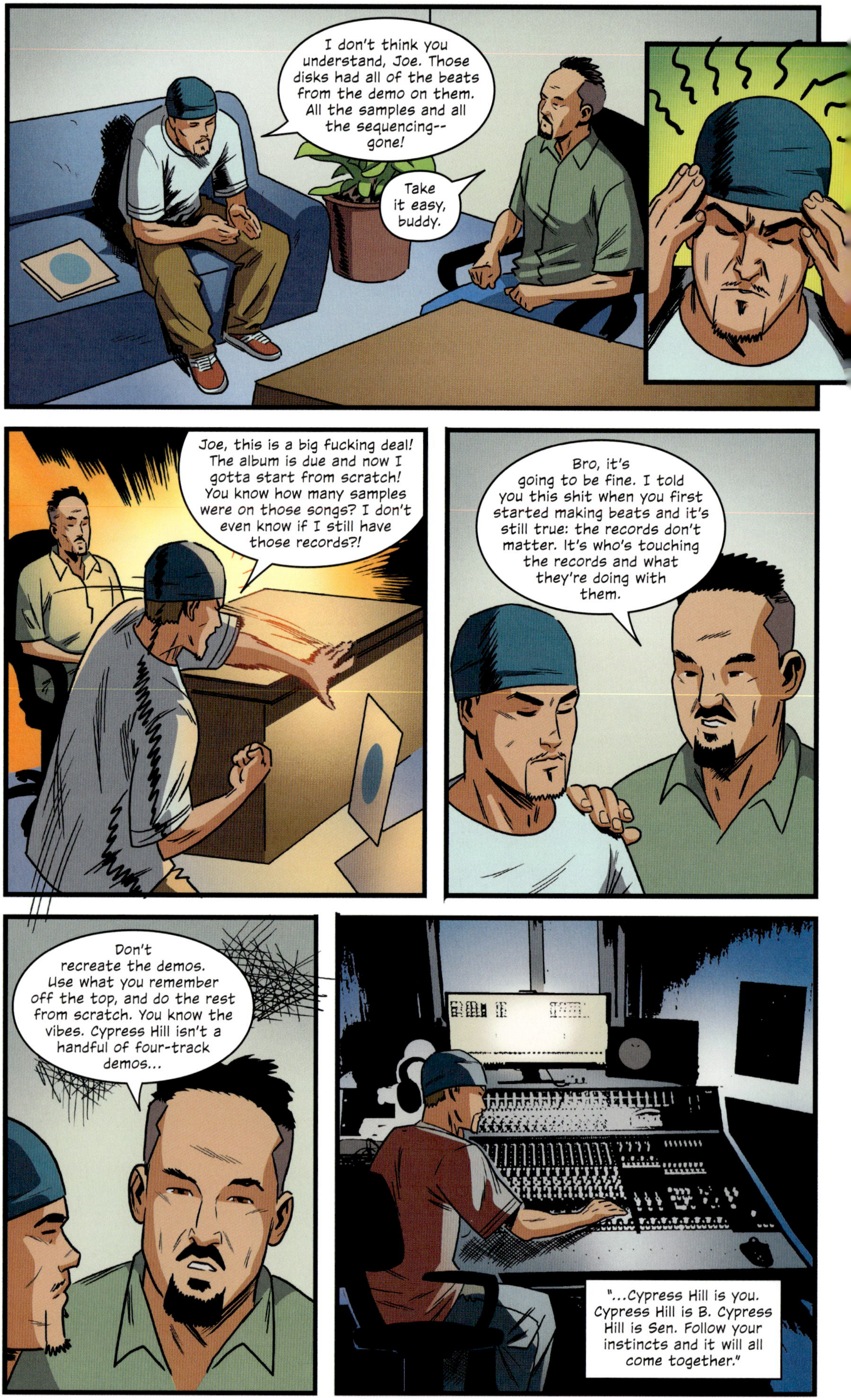
I don't think you understand, Joe. Those disks had all of the beats from the demo on them. All the samples and all the sequencing--gone!
Take it easy, buddy.
Joe, this is a big fucking deal! The album is due and now I gotta start from scratch! You know how many samples were on those songs? I don't even know if I still have those records?!
Bro, it's going to be fine. I told you this shit when you first started making beats and it's still true: the records don't matter. It's who's touching the records and what they're doing with them.
Don't recreate the demos. Use what you remember off the top, and do the rest from scratch. You know the vibes. Cypress Hill isn't a handful of four-track demos...
"...Cypress Hill is you. Cypress Hill is B. Cypress Hill is Sen. Follow your instincts and it will all come together."

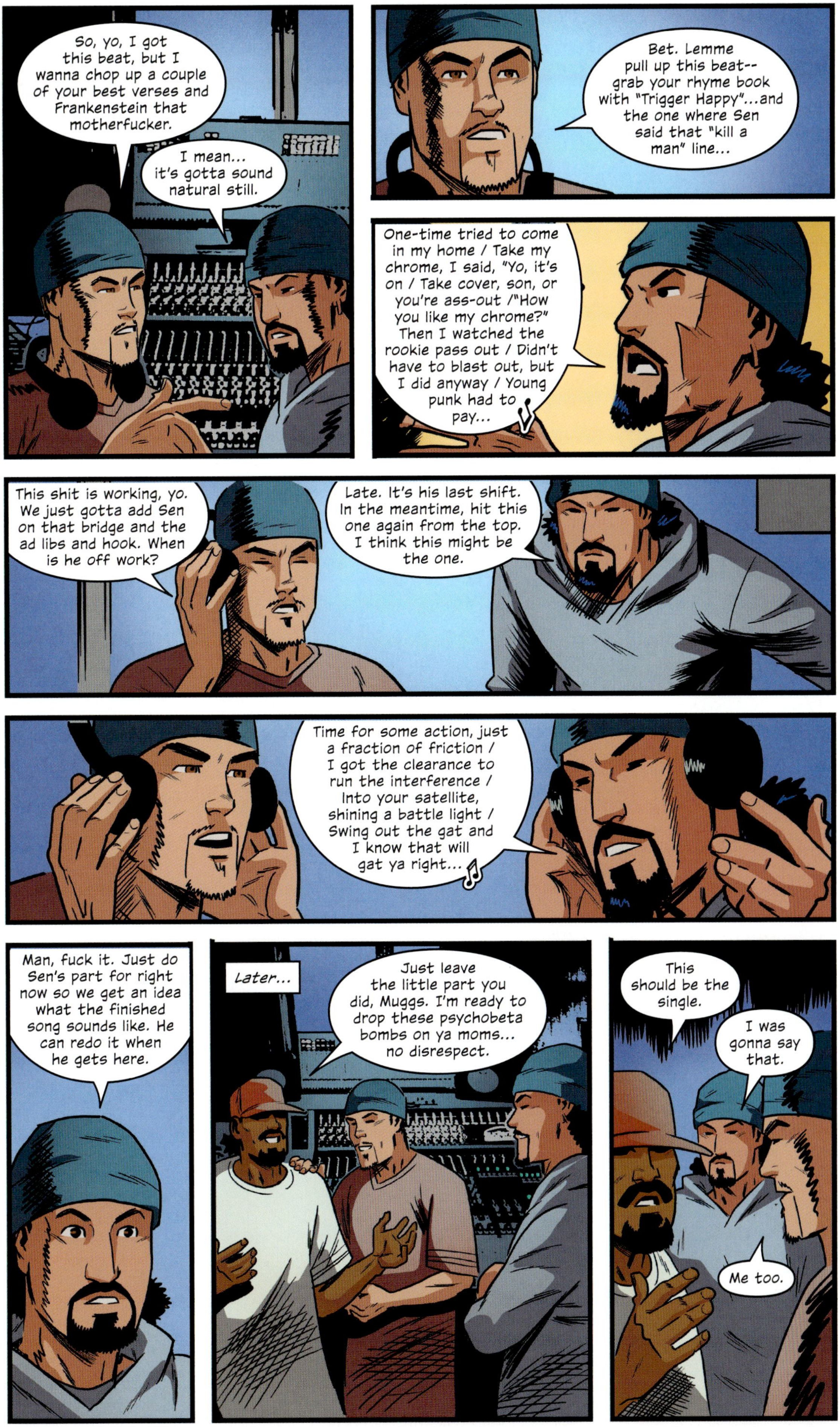
So, yo, I got this beat, but I wanna chop up a couple of your best verses and Frankenstein that motherfucker.
I mean... it's gotta sound natural still.
Bet. Lemme pull up this beat--grab your rhyme book with "Trigger Happy"...and the one where Sen said that "kill a man" line...
One-time tried to come in my home / Take my chrome, I said, "Yo, it's on / Take cover, son, or you're ass-out /"How you like my chrome?" Then I watched the rookie pass out / Didn't have to blast out, but I did anyway / Young punk had to pay...
This shit is working, yo. We just gotta add Sen on that bridge and the ad libs and hook. When is he off work?
Late. It's his last shift. In the meantime, hit this one again from the top. I think this might be the one.
Time for some action, just a fraction of friction / I got the clearance to run the interference / Into your satellite, shining a battle light / Swing out the gat and I know that will gat ya right...
Man, fuck it. Just do Sen's part for right now so we get an idea what the finished song sounds like. He can redo it when he gets here.
Later...
Just leave the little part you did, Muggs. I'm ready to drop these psychobeta bombs on ya moms... no disrespect.
This should be the single.
I was gonna say that.
Me too.

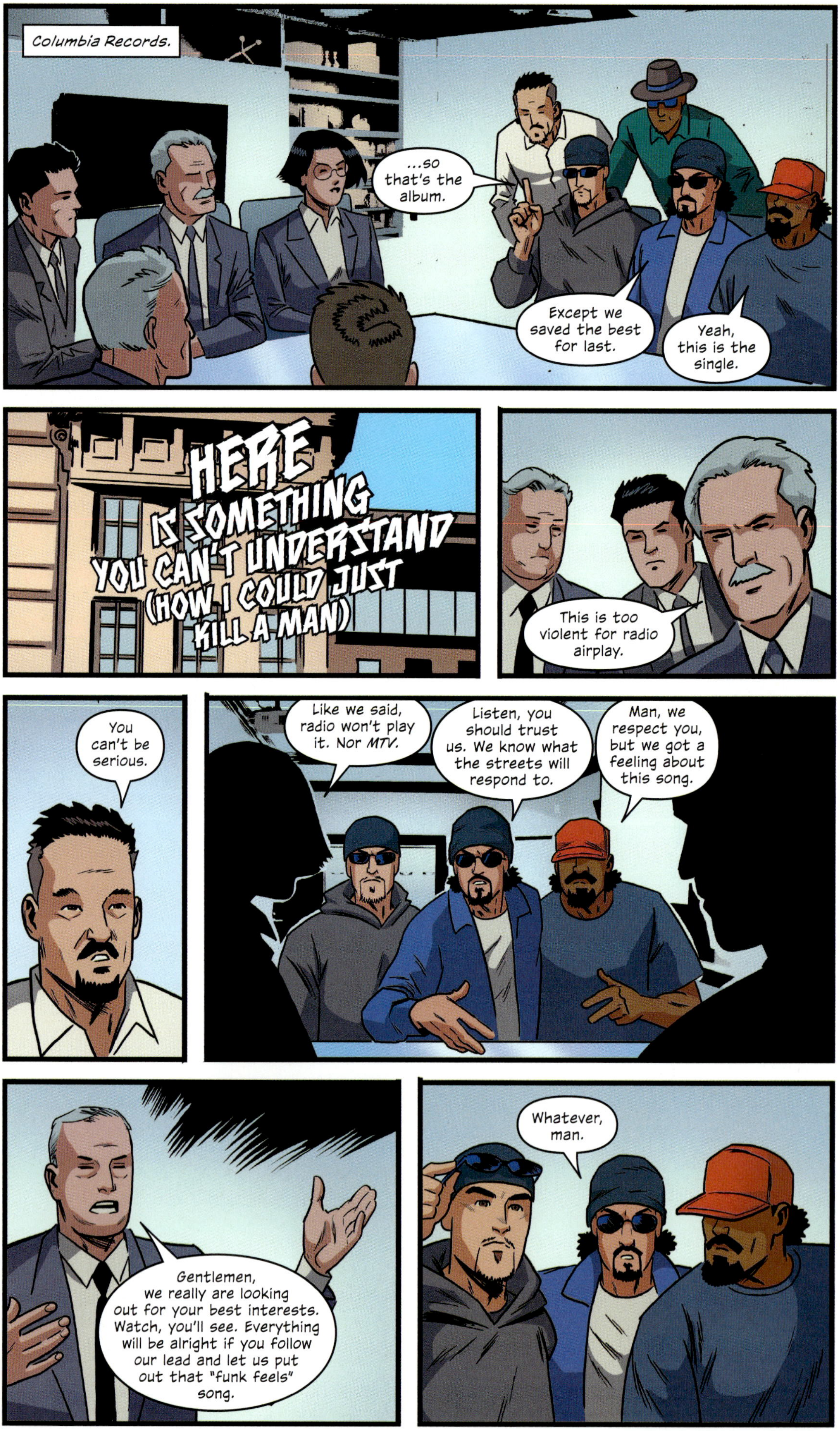
Columbia Records.
...so that's the album.
Except we saved the best for last.
Yeah, this is the single.
HERE IS SOMETHING YOU CAN'T UNDERSTAND (HOW I COULD JUST KILL A MAN)
This is too violent for radio airplay.
You can't be serious.
Like we said, radio won't play it. Nor MTV.
Listen, you should trust us. We know what the streets will respond to.
Man, we respect you, but we got a feeling about this song.
Gentlemen, we really are looking out for your best interests. Watch, you'll see. Everything will be alright if you follow our lead and let us put out that "funk feels" song.
Whatever, man.

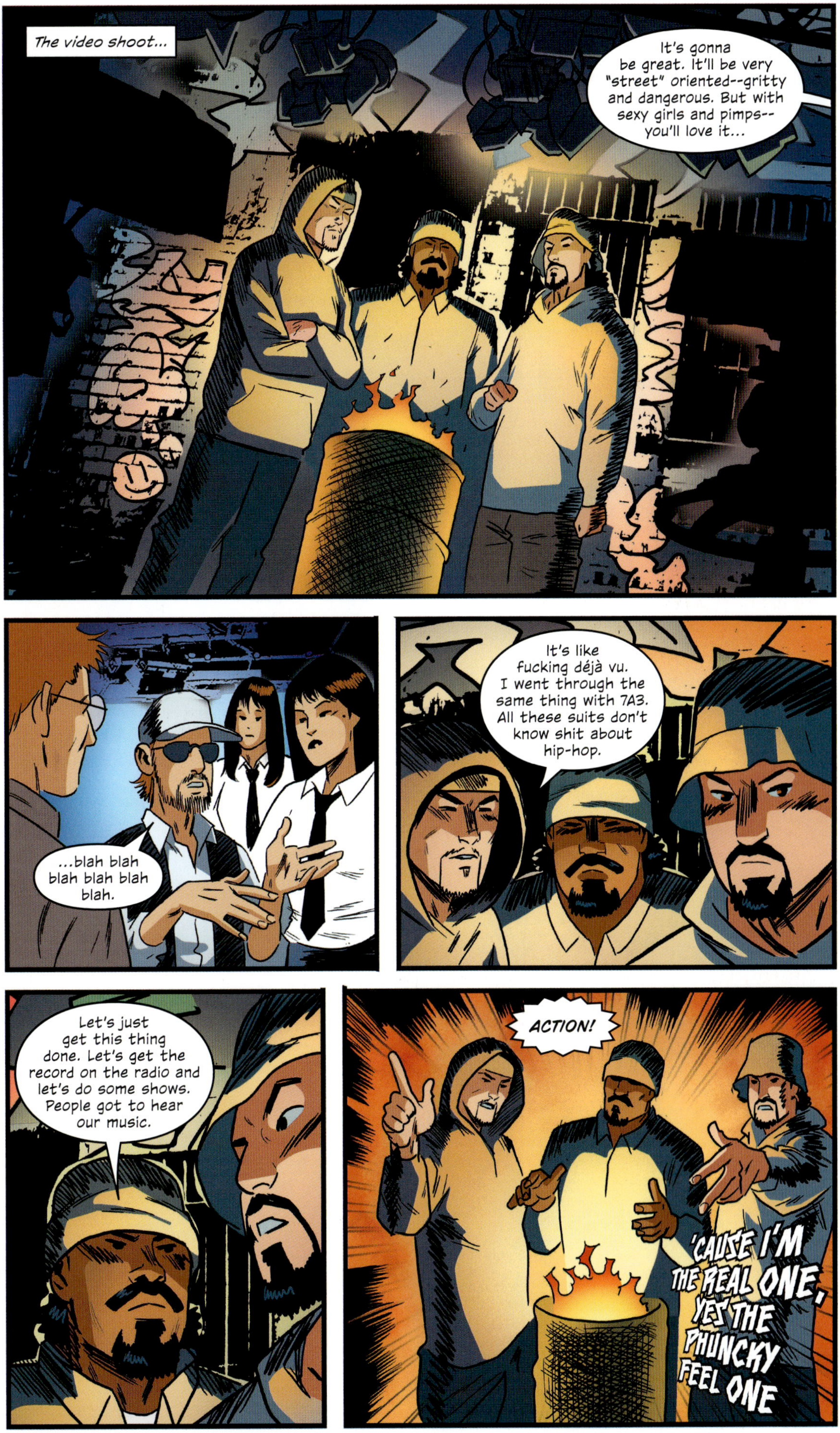
The video shoot...
It's gonna be great. It'll be very "street" oriented--gritty and dangerous. But with sexy girls and pimps--you'll love it...
...blah blah blah blah blah blah.
It's like fucking déjà vu. I went through the same thing with 7A3. All these suits don't know shit about hip-hop.
Let's just get this thing done. Let's get the record on the radio and let's do some shows. People got to hear our music.
ACTION!
'CAUSE I'M THE REAL ONE, YES THE PHUNCKY FEEL ONE

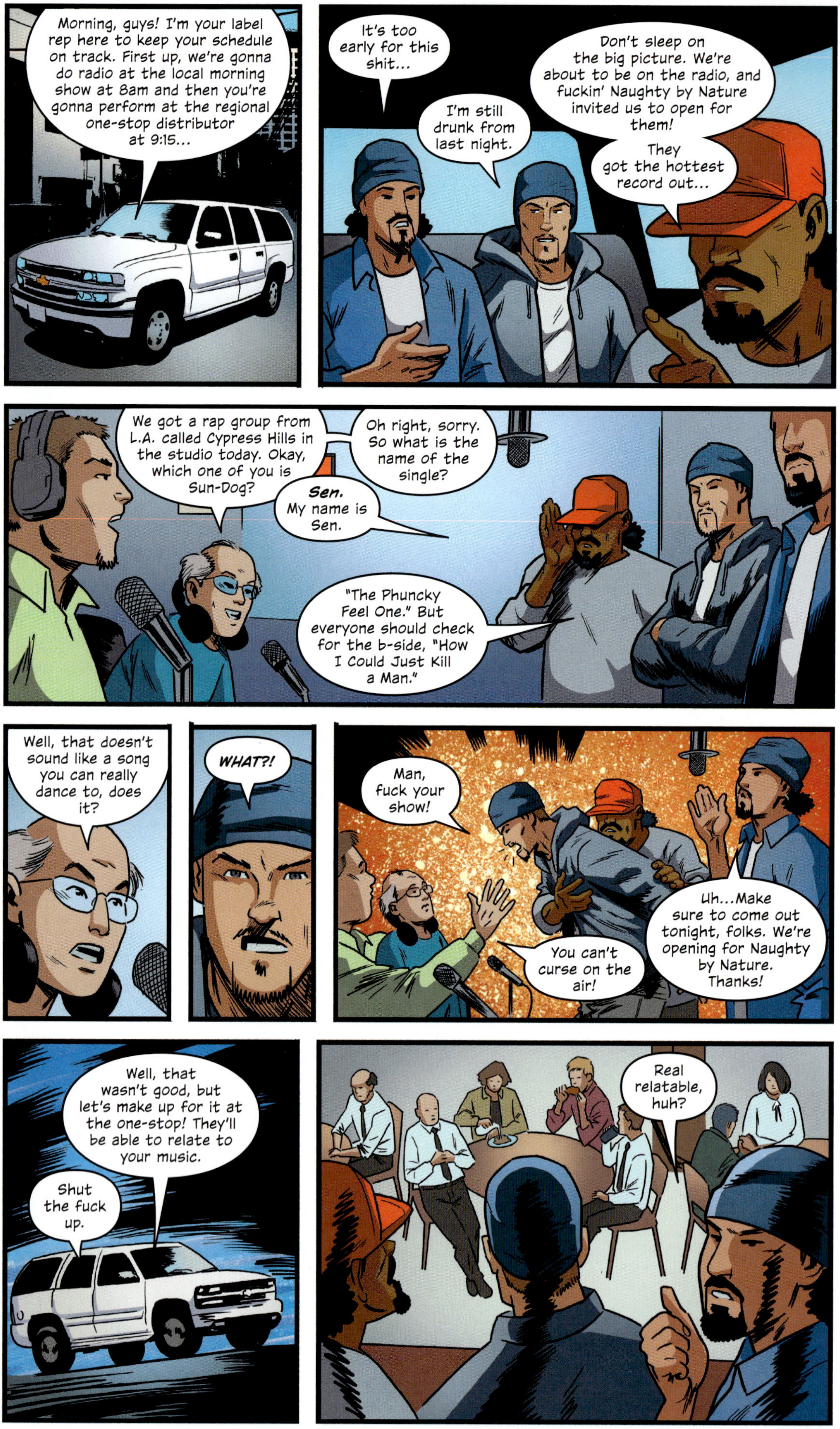
Morning, guys! I'm your label rep here to keep your schedule on track. First up, we're gonna do radio at the local morning show at 8am and then you're gonna perform at the regional one-stop distributor at 9:15...
It's too early for this shit...
I'm still drunk from last night.
Don't sleep on the big picture. We're about to be on the radio, and fuckin' Naughty by Nature invited us to open for them!
They got the hottest record out...
We got a rap group from L.A. called Cypress Hills in the studio today. Okay, which one of you is Sun-Dog?
Sen. My name is Sen.
Oh right, sorry. So what is the name of the single?
"The Phuncky Feel One." But everyone should check for the b-side, "How I Could Just Kill a Man."
Well, that doesn't sound like a song you can really dance to, does it?
WHAT?!
Man, fuck your show!
You can't curse on the air!
Uh...Make sure to come out tonight, folks. We're opening for Naughty by Nature. Thanks!
Well, that wasn't good, but let's make up for it at the one-stop! They'll be able to relate to your music.
Shut the fuck up.
Real relatable, huh?

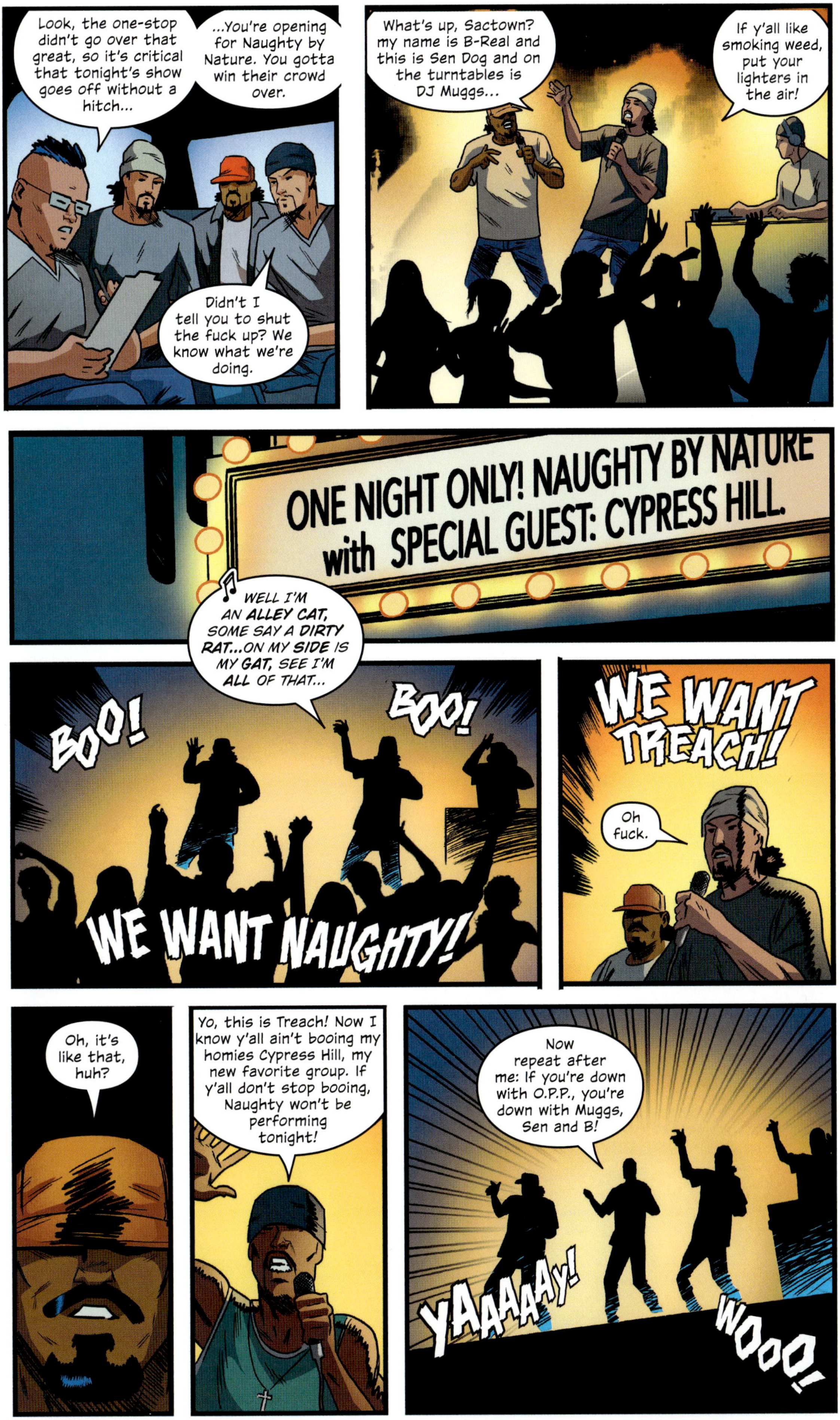
Look, the one-stop didn't go over that great, so it's critical that tonight's show goes off without a hitch...
...You're opening for Naughty by Nature. You gotta win their crowd over.
Didn't I tell you to shut the fuck up? We know what we're doing.
What's up, Sactown? my name is B-Real and this is Sen Dog and on the turntables is DJ Muggs...
If y'all like smoking weed, put your lighters in the air!
ONE NIGHT ONLY! NAUGHTY BY NATURE
with SPECIAL GUEST: CYPRESS HILL.
WELL I'M AN ALLEY CAT, SOME SAY A DIRTY RAT...ON MY SIDE IS MY GAT, SEE I'M ALL OF THAT...
BOO!
BOO!
WE WANT NAUGHTY!
WE WANT TREACH!
Oh fuck.
Oh, it's like that, huh?
Yo, this is Treach! Now I know y'all ain't booing my homies Cypress Hill, my new favorite group. If y'all don't stop booing, Naughty won't be performing tonight!
Now repeat after me: If you're down with O.P.P., you're down with Muggs, Sen and B!
YAAAAAY!
WOOO!

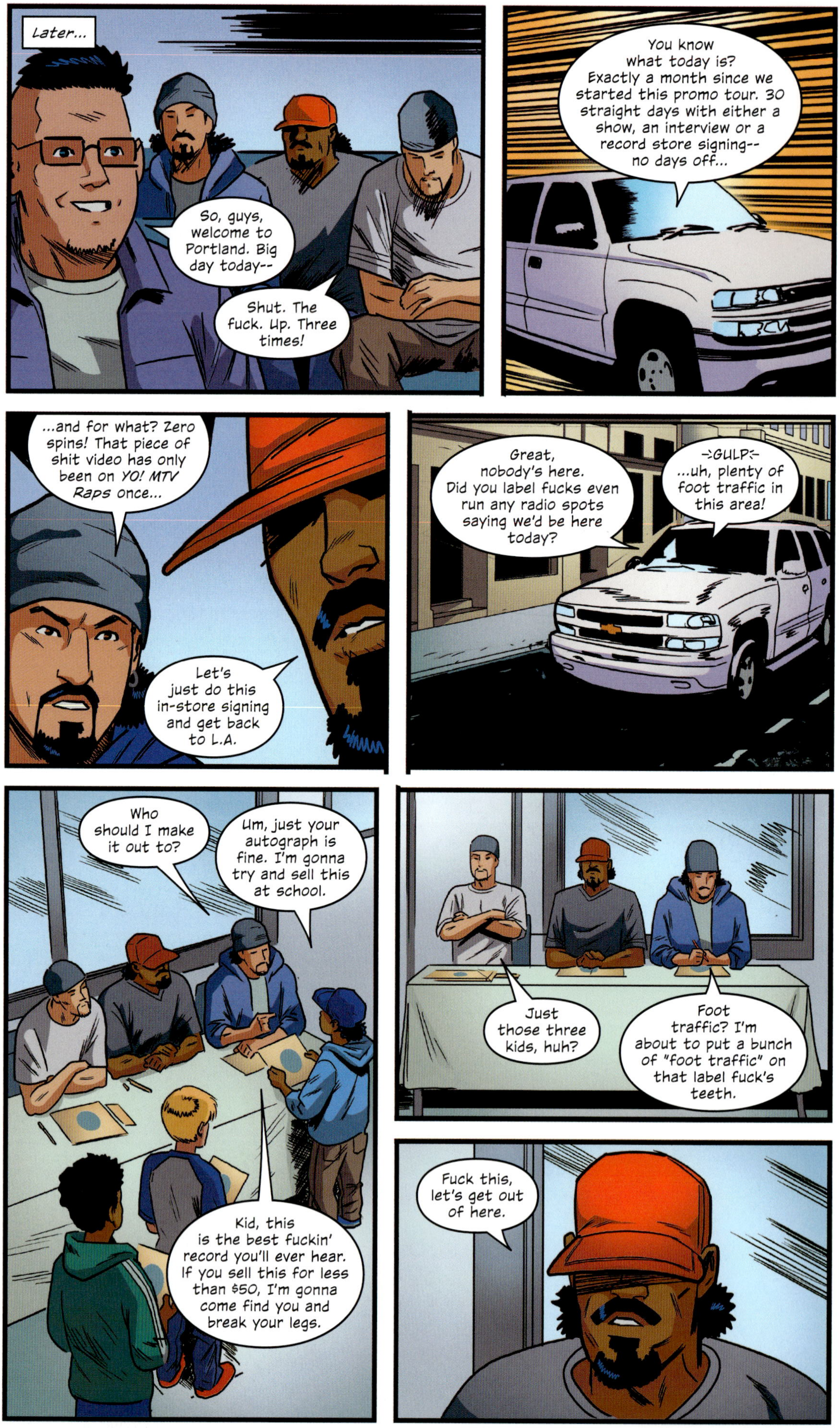
Later...
So, guys, welcome to Portland. Big day today--
Shut. The fuck. Up. Three times!
You know what today is? Exactly a month since we started this promo tour. 30 straight days with either a show, an interview or a record store signing-- no days off...
...and for what? Zero spins! That piece of shit video has only been on *YO! MTV Raps* once...
Let's just do this in-store signing and get back to L.A.
Great, nobody's here. Did you label fucks even run any radio spots saying we'd be here today?
-GULP-
...uh, plenty of foot traffic in this area!
Who should I make it out to?
Um, just your autograph is fine. I'm gonna try and sell this at school.
Kid, this is the best fuckin' record you'll ever hear. If you sell this for less than $50, I'm gonna come find you and break your legs.
Just those three kids, huh?
Foot traffic? I'm about to put a bunch of "foot traffic" on that label fuck's teeth.
Fuck this, let's get out of here.

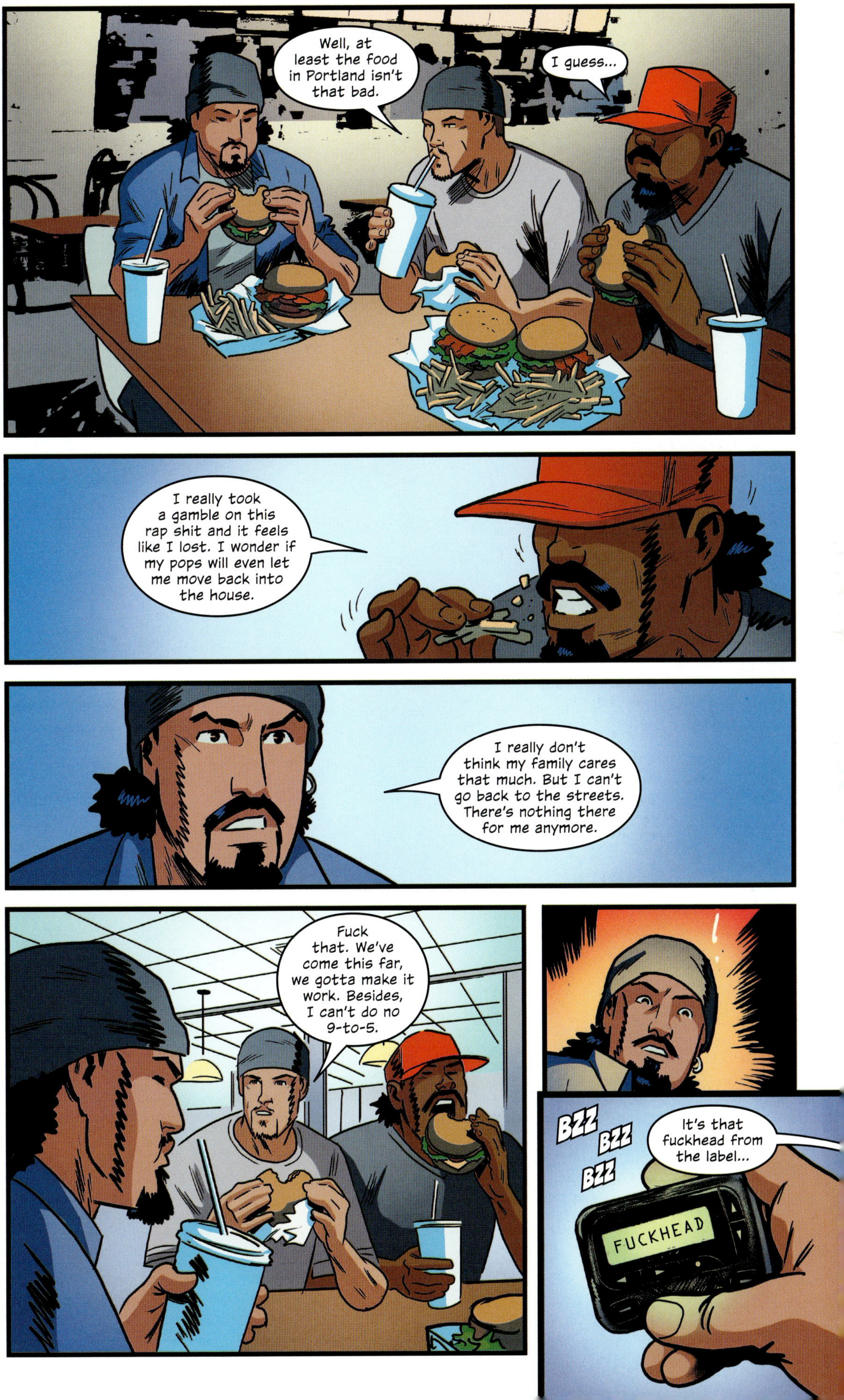
Well, at least the food in Portland isn't that bad.
I guess...
I really took a gamble on this rap shit and it feels like I lost. I wonder if my pops will even let me move back into the house.
I really don't think my family cares that much. But I can't go back to the streets. There's nothing there for me anymore.
Fuck that. We've come this far, we gotta make it work. Besides, I can't do no 9-to-5.
!
BZZ
BZZ
BZZ
It's that fuckhead from the label...
FUCKHEAD

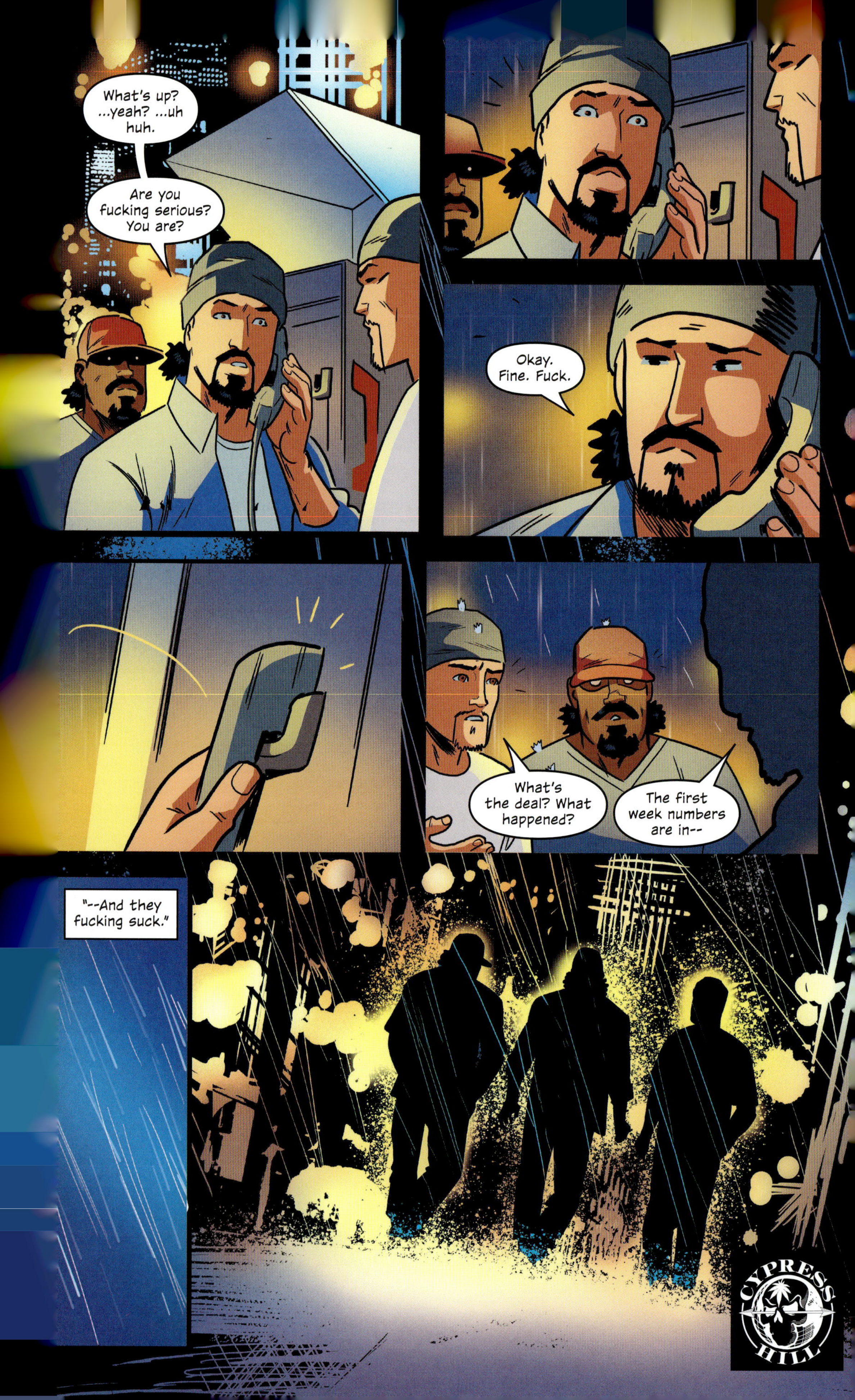
What's up? ...yeah? ...uh huh.
Are you fucking serious? You are?
Okay. Fine. Fuck.
What's the deal? What happened?
The first week numbers are in--
"--And they fucking suck."
CYPRESS HILL

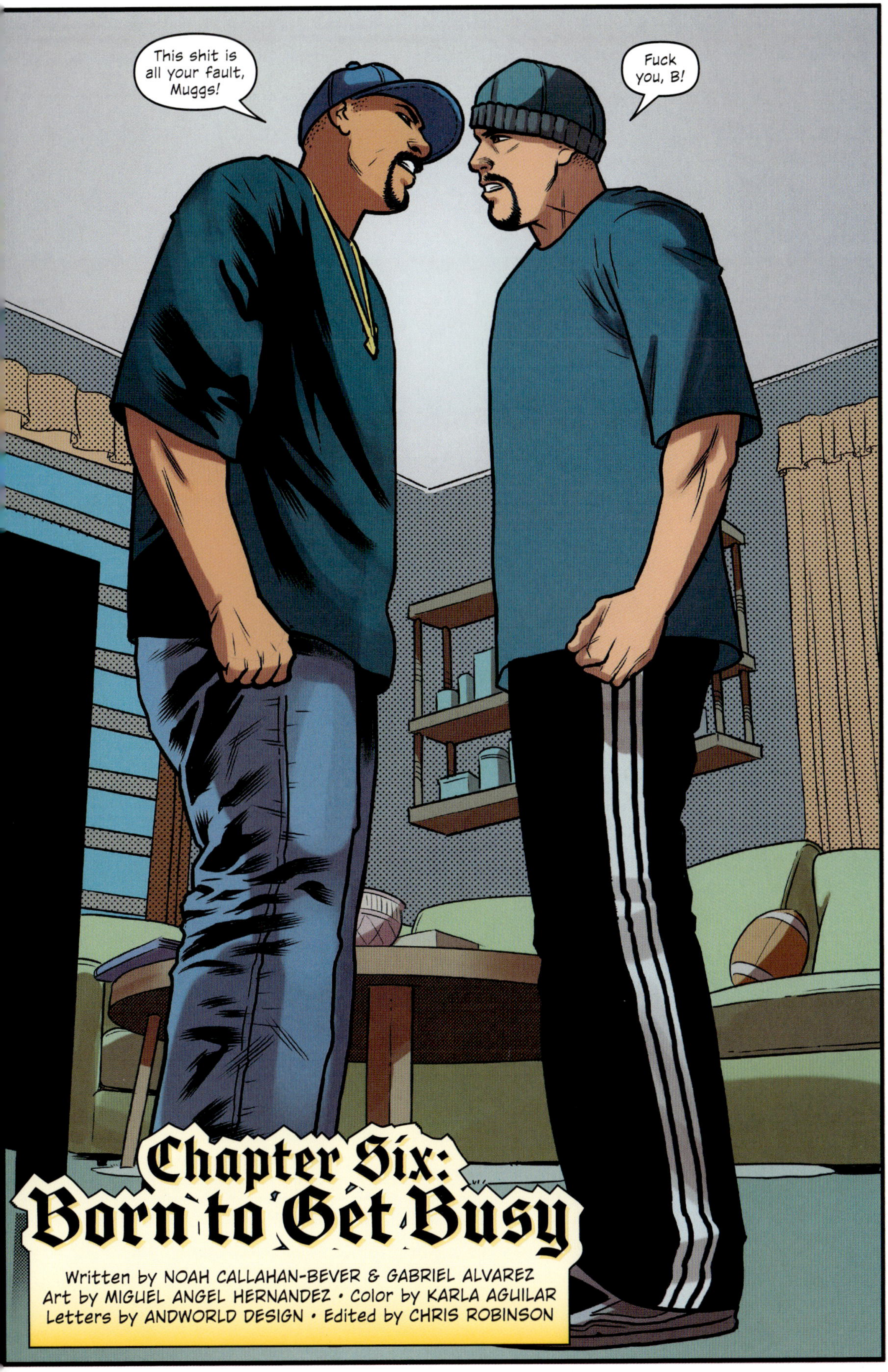
This shit is all your fault, Muggs!
Fuck you, B!
Chapter Six: Born to Get Busy
Written by NOAH CALLAHAN-BEVER & GABRIEL ALVAREZ
Art by MIGUEL ANGEL HERNANDEZ • Color by KARLA AGUILAR
Letters by ANDWORLD DESIGN • Edited by CHRIS ROBINSON

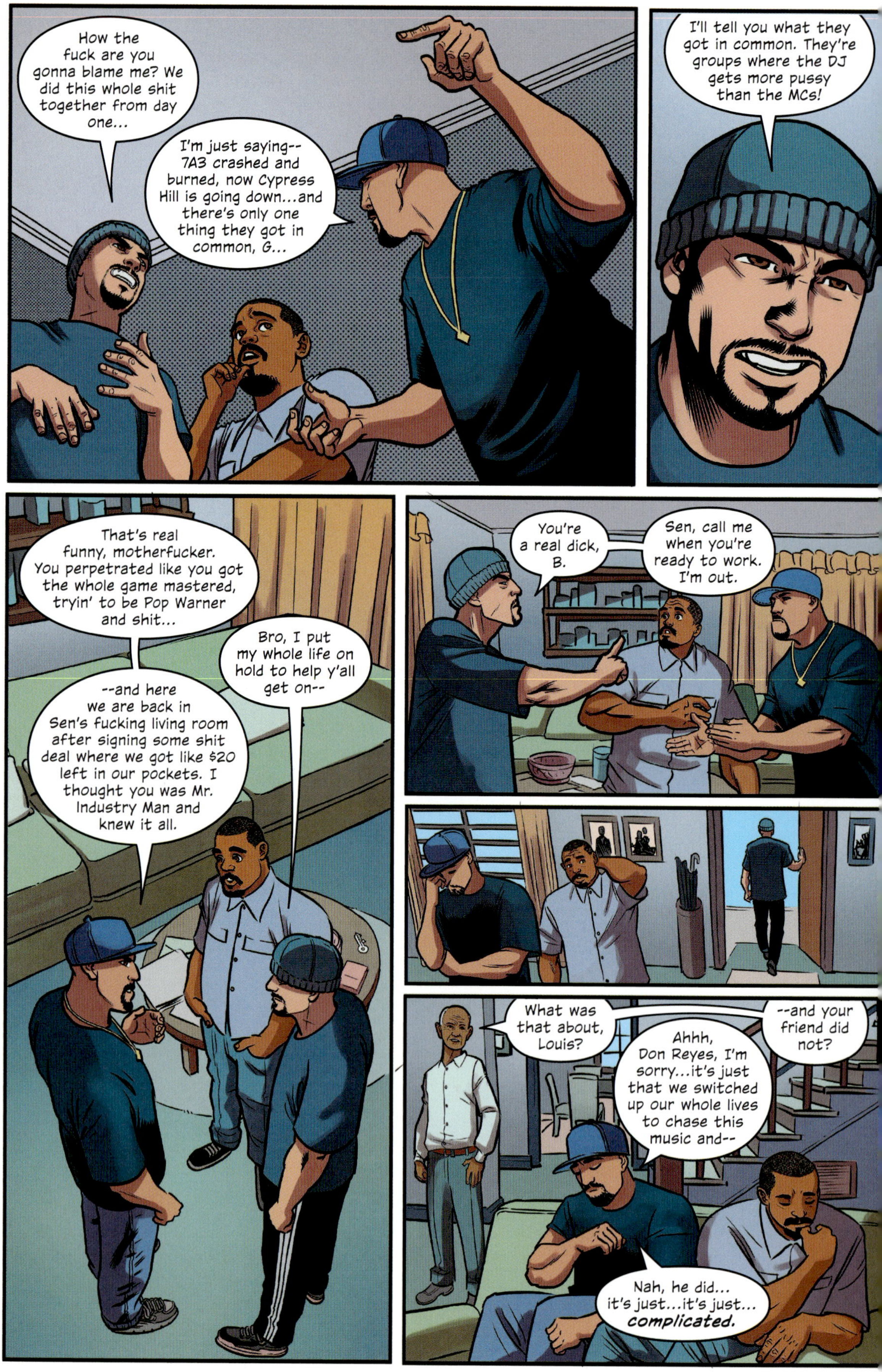
How the fuck are you gonna blame me? We did this whole shit together from day one...
I'm just saying-- 7A3 crashed and burned, now Cypress Hill is going down...and there's only one thing they got in common, G...
I'll tell you what they got in common. They're groups where the DJ gets more pussy than the MCs!
That's real funny, motherfucker. You perpetrated like you got the whole game mastered, tryin' to be Pop Warner and shit...
Bro, I put my whole life on hold to help y'all get on--
--and here we are back in Sen's fucking living room after signing some shit deal where we got like $20 left in our pockets. I thought you was Mr. Industry Man and knew it all.
You're a real dick, B.
Sen, call me when you're ready to work. I'm out.
What was that about, Louis?
--and your friend did not?
Ahhh, Don Reyes, I'm sorry...it's just that we switched up our whole lives to chase this music and--
Nah, he did... it's just...it's just... ***complicated.***

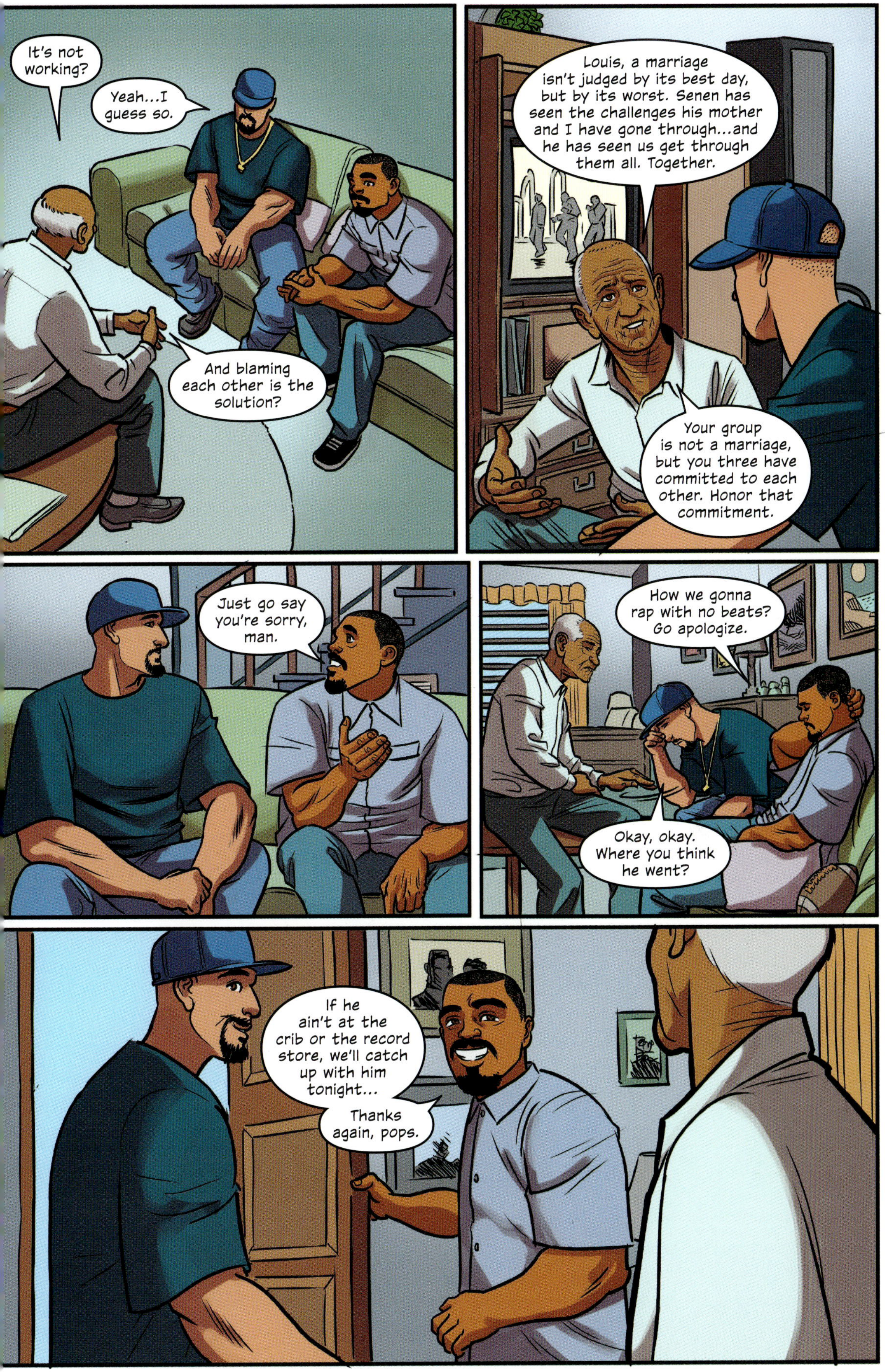
It's not working?
Yeah...I guess so.
And blaming each other is the solution?
Louis, a marriage isn't judged by its best day, but by its worst. Senen has seen the challenges his mother and I have gone through...and he has seen us get through them all. Together.
Your group is not a marriage, but you three have committed to each other. Honor that commitment.
Just go say you're sorry, man.
How we gonna rap with no beats? Go apologize.
Okay, okay. Where you think he went?
If he ain't at the crib or the record store, we'll catch up with him tonight...
Thanks again, pops.

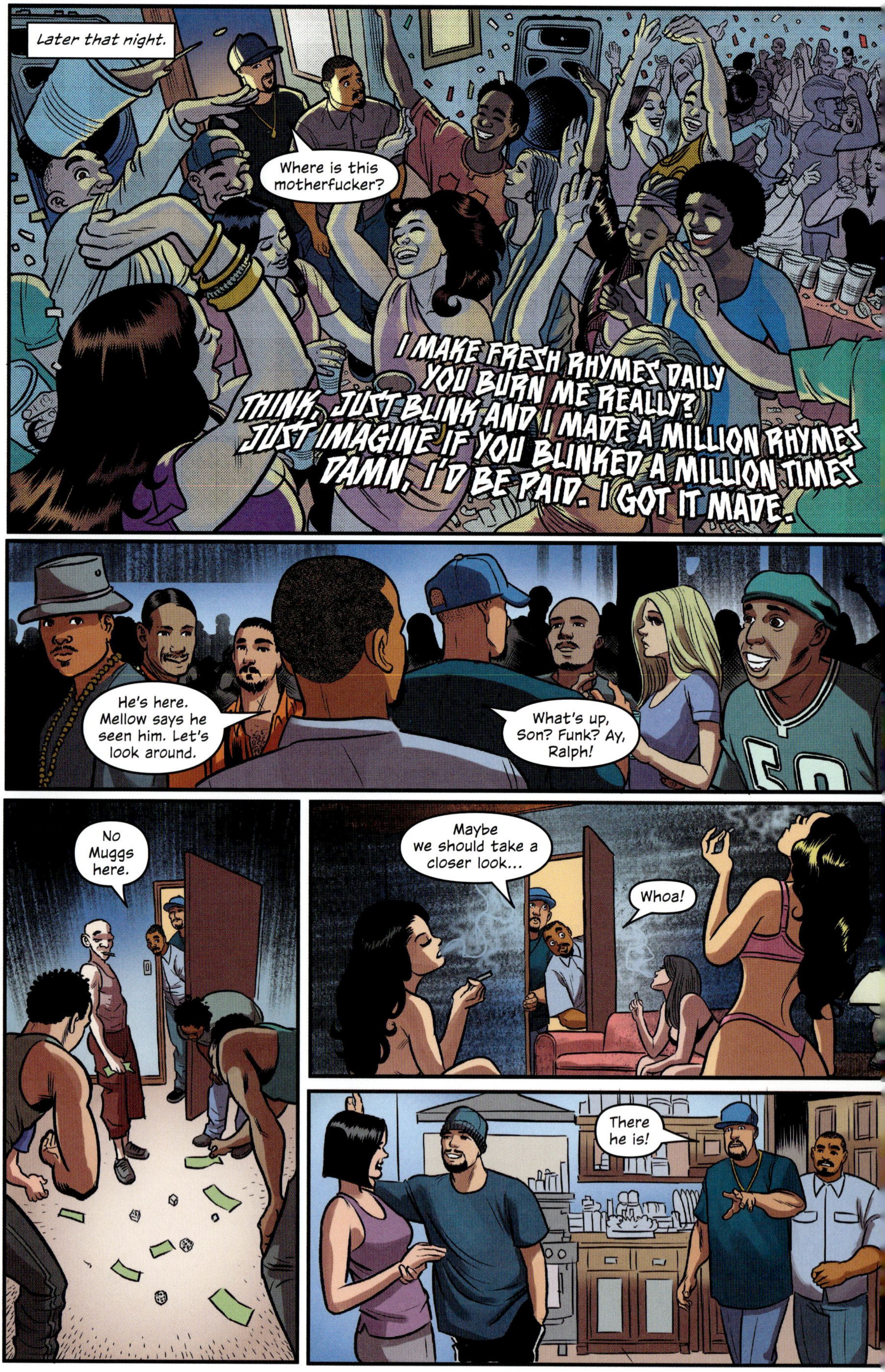
Later that night.
Where is this motherfucker?
I MAKE FRESH RHYMES DAILY
YOU BURN ME REALLY?
THINK, JUST BLINK AND I MADE A MILLION RHYMES
JUST IMAGINE IF YOU BLINKED A MILLION TIMES
DAMN, I'D BE PAID. I GOT IT MADE.
He's here. Mellow says he seen him. Let's look around.
What's up, Son? Funk? Ay, Ralph!
No Muggs here.
Maybe we should take a closer look...
Whoa!
There he is!

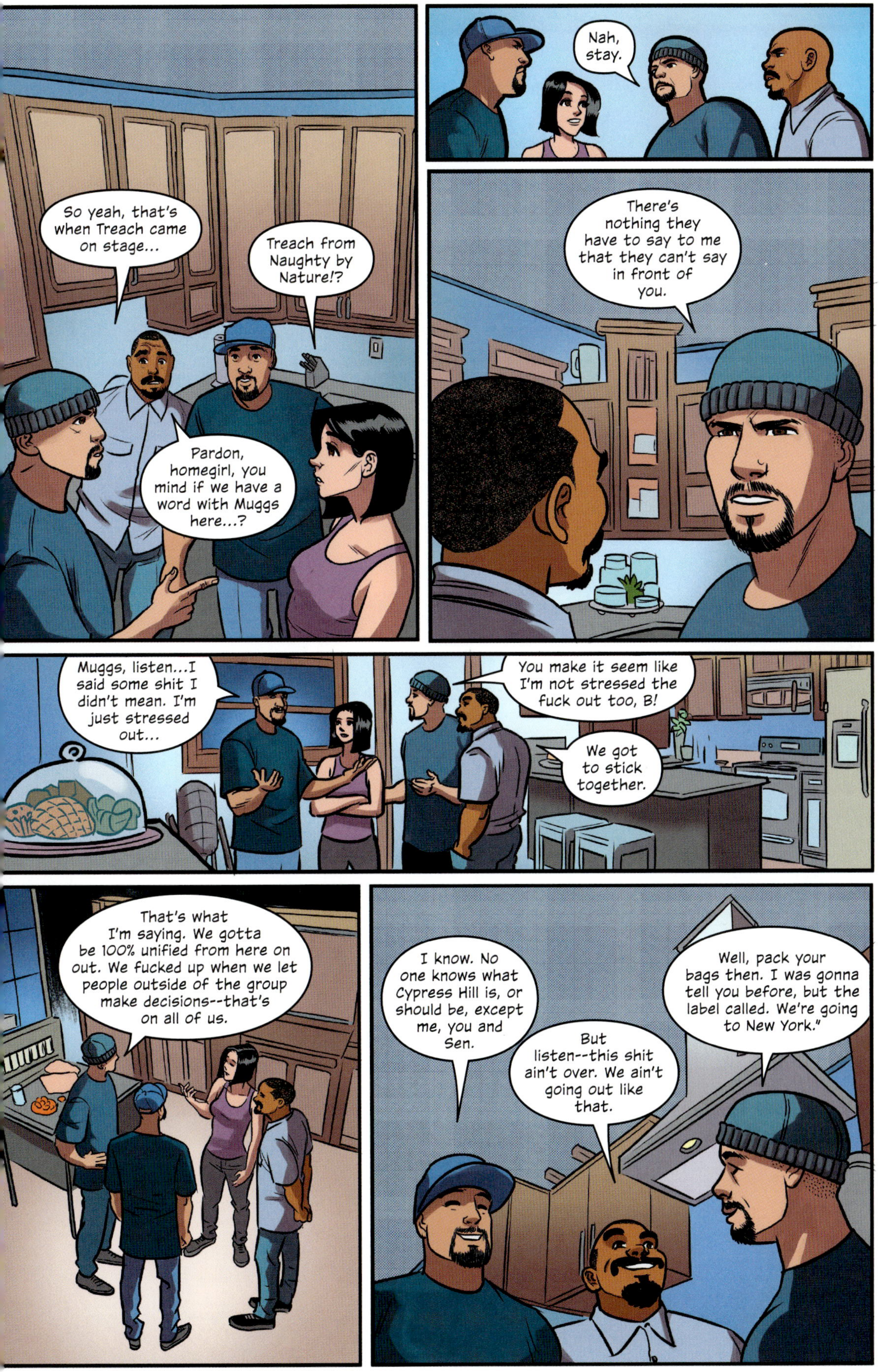
So yeah, that's when Treach came on stage...
Treach from Naughty by Nature!?
Pardon, homegirl, you mind if we have a word with Muggs here...?
Nah, stay.
There's nothing they have to say to me that they can't say in front of you.
Muggs, listen...I said some shit I didn't mean. I'm just stressed out...
You make it seem like I'm not stressed the fuck out too, B!
We got to stick together.
That's what I'm saying. We gotta be 100% unified from here on out. We fucked up when we let people outside of the group make decisions--that's on all of us.
I know. No one knows what Cypress Hill is, or should be, except me, you and Sen.
But listen--this shit ain't over. We ain't going out like that.
Well, pack your bags then. I was gonna tell you before, but the label called. We're going to New York."

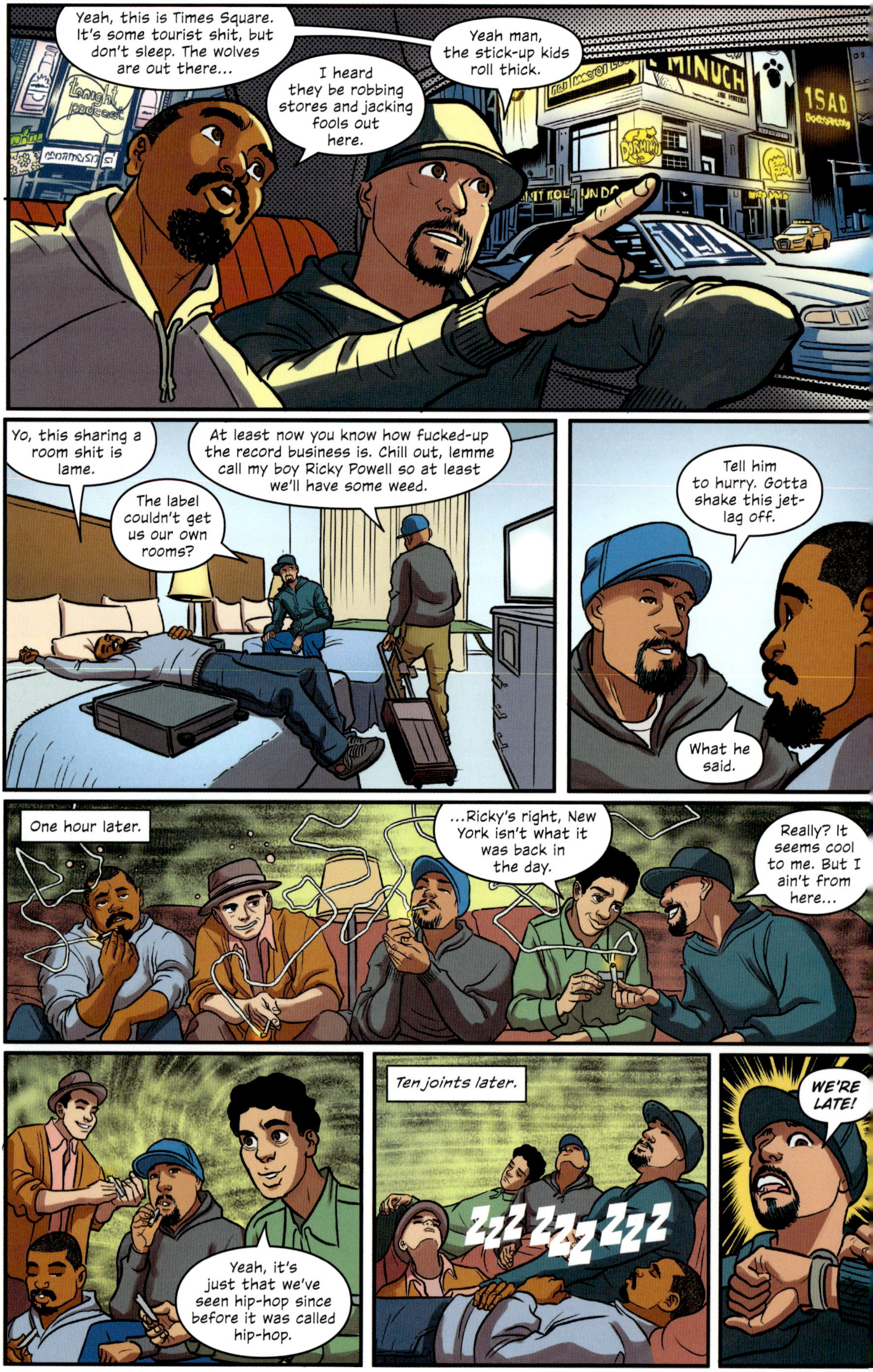

Yeah, this is Times Square. It's some tourist shit, but don't sleep. The wolves are out there...
I heard they be robbing stores and jacking fools out here.
Yeah man, the stick-up kids roll thick.
Yo, this sharing a room shit is lame.
The label couldn't get us our own rooms?
At least now you know how fucked-up the record business is. Chill out, lemme call my boy Ricky Powell so at least we'll have some weed.
Tell him to hurry. Gotta shake this jet-lag off.
What he said.
One hour later.
...Ricky's right, New York isn't what it was back in the day.
Really? It seems cool to me. But I ain't from here...
Yeah, it's just that we've seen hip-hop since before it was called hip-hop.
Ten joints later.
ZZZ ZZZ ZZZ
WE'RE LATE!

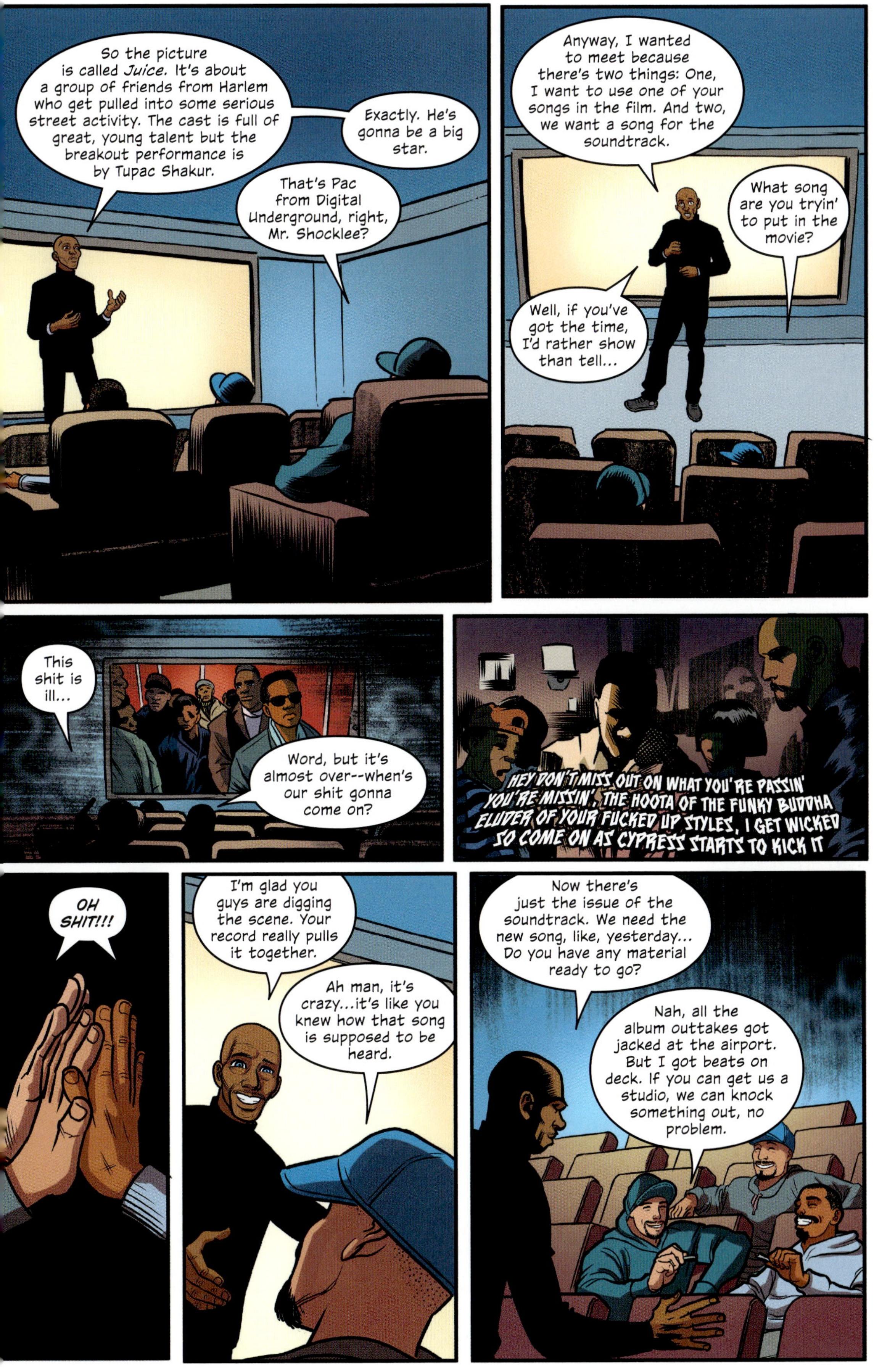
So the picture is called *Juice.* It's about a group of friends from Harlem who get pulled into some serious street activity. The cast is full of great, young talent but the breakout performance is by Tupac Shakur.
That's Pac from Digital Underground, right, Mr. Shocklee?
Exactly. He's gonna be a big star.
Anyway, I wanted to meet because there's two things: One, I want to use one of your songs in the film. And two, we want a song for the soundtrack.
What song are you tryin' to put in the movie?
Well, if you've got the time, I'd rather show than tell...
This shit is ill...
Word, but it's almost over--when's our shit gonna come on?
HEY DON'T MISS OUT ON WHAT YOU'RE PASSIN' YOU'RE MISSIN', THE HOOTA OF THE FUNKY BUDDHA ELUDER OF YOUR FUCKED UP STYLES, I GET WICKED SO COME ON AS CYPRESS STARTS TO KICK IT
OH SHIT!!!
I'm glad you guys are digging the scene. Your record really pulls it together.
Ah man, it's crazy...it's like you knew how that song is supposed to be heard.
Now there's just the issue of the soundtrack. We need the new song, like, yesterday... Do you have any material ready to go?
Nah, all the album outtakes got jacked at the airport. But I got beats on deck. If you can get us a studio, we can knock something out, no problem.

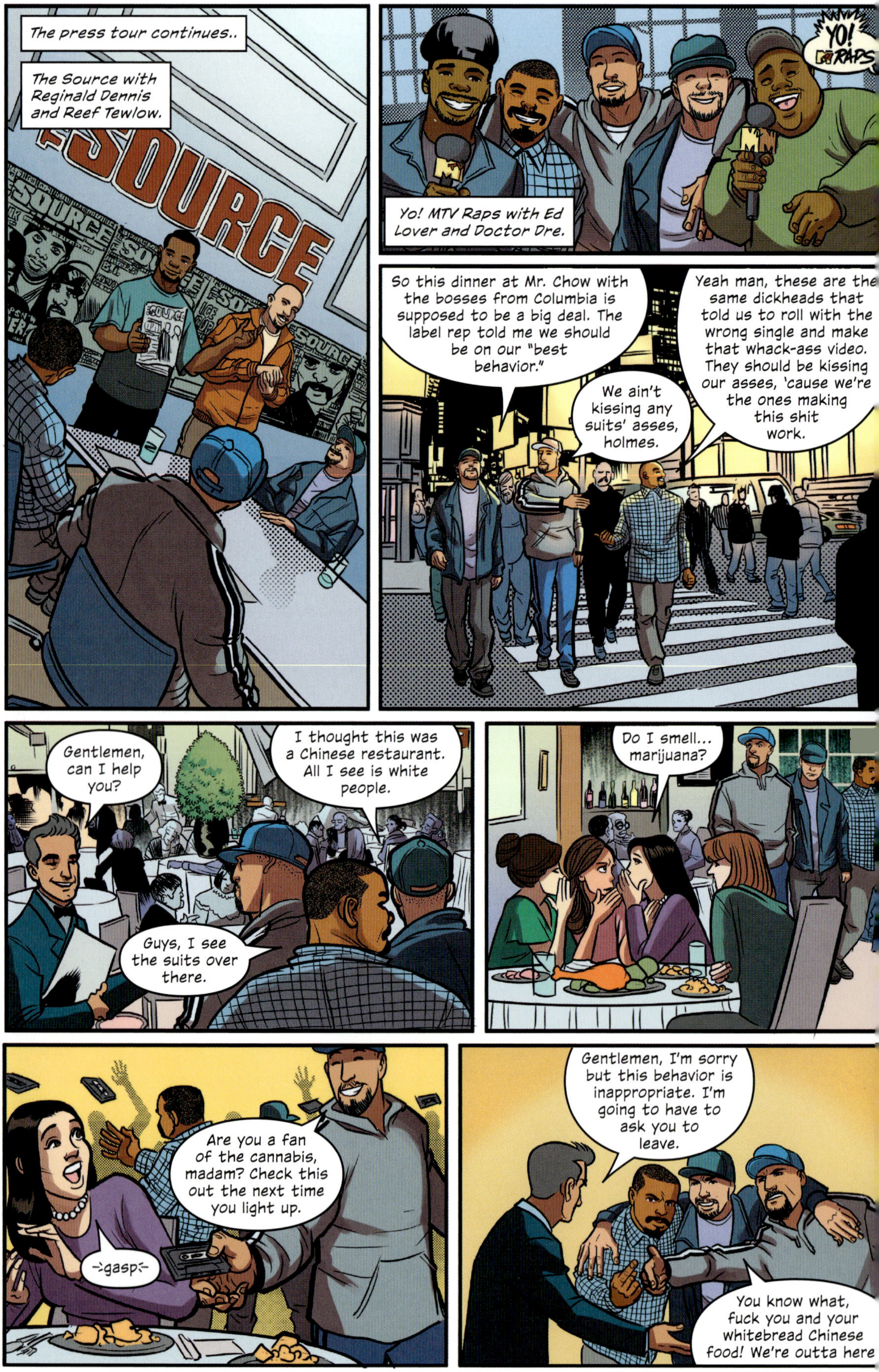

The press tour continues..
The Source with Reginald Dennis and Reef Tewlow.
SOURCE
YO! RAPS
Yo! MTV Raps with Ed Lover and Doctor Dre.
So this dinner at Mr. Chow with the bosses from Columbia is supposed to be a big deal. The label rep told me we should be on our "best behavior."
We ain't kissing any suits' asses, holmes.
Yeah man, these are the same dickheads that told us to roll with the wrong single and make that whack-ass video. They should be kissing our asses, 'cause we're the ones making this shit work.
Gentlemen, can I help you?
I thought this was a Chinese restaurant. All I see is white people.
Guys, I see the suits over there.
Do I smell... marijuana?
Are you a fan of the cannabis, madam? Check this out the next time you light up.
gasp
Gentlemen, I'm sorry but this behavior is inappropriate. I'm going to have to ask you to leave.
You know what, fuck you and your whitebread Chinese food! We're outta here

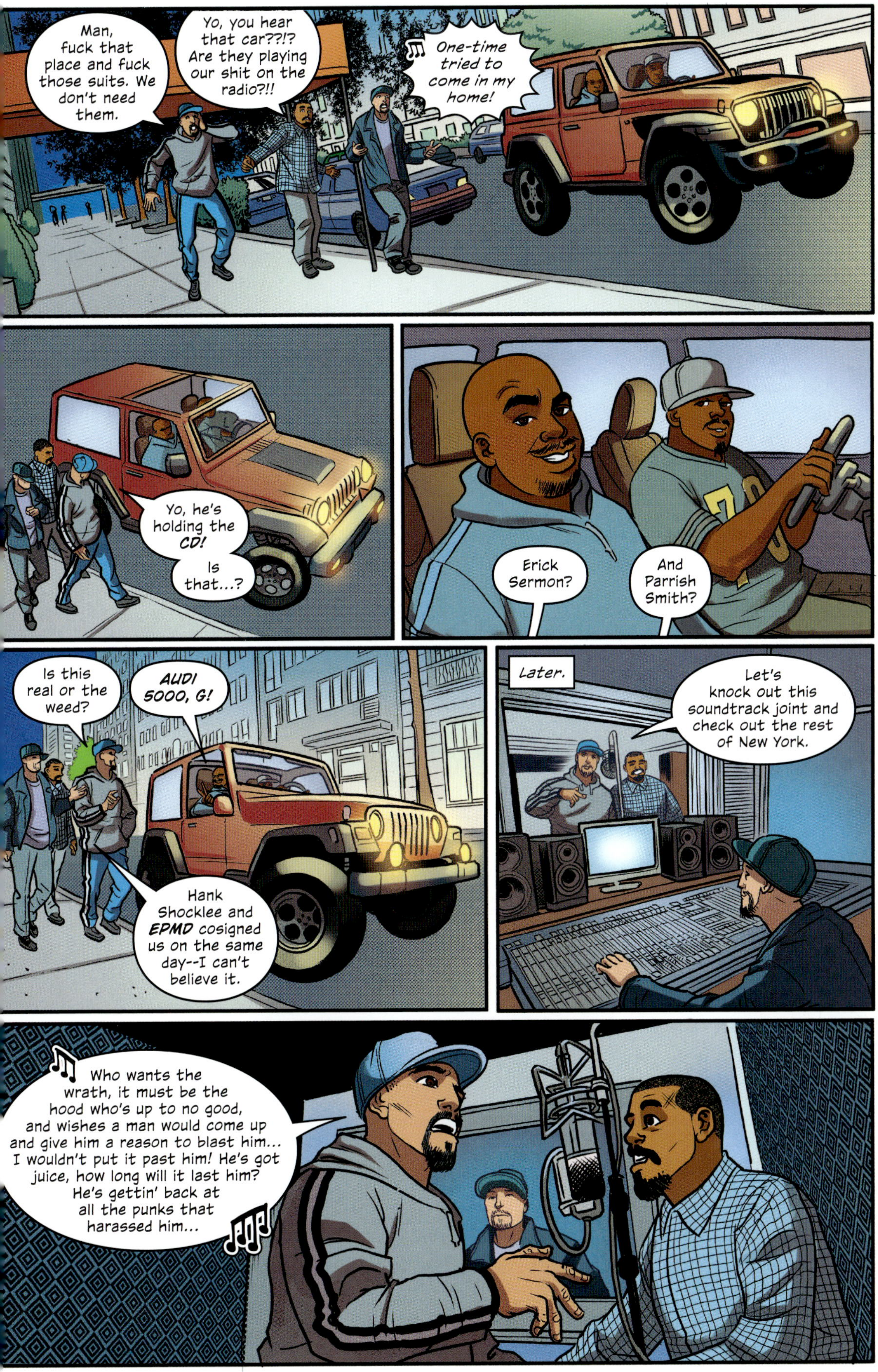

Man, fuck that place and fuck those suits. We don't need them.
Yo, you hear that car??!? Are they playing our shit on the radio?!!
One-time tried to come in my home!
Yo, he's holding the CD!
Is that...?
Erick Sermon?
And Parrish Smith?
Is this real or the weed?
AUDI 5000, G!
Hank Shocklee and EPMD cosigned us on the same day--I can't believe it.
Later.
Let's knock out this soundtrack joint and check out the rest of New York.
Who wants the wrath, it must be the hood who's up to no good, and wishes a man would come up and give him a reason to blast him... I wouldn't put it past him! He's got juice, how long will it last him? He's gettin' back at all the punks that harassed him...

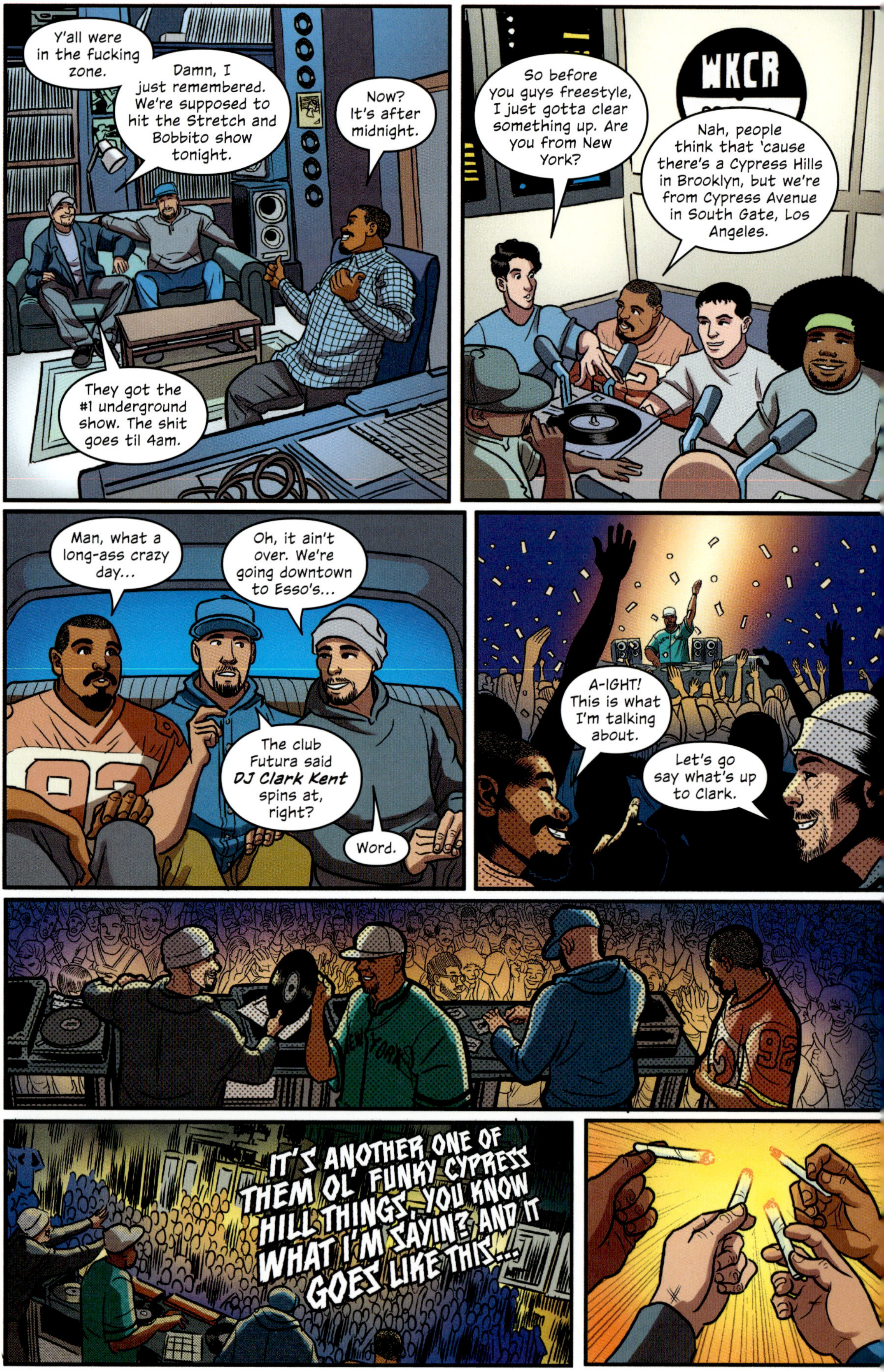
Y'all were in the fucking zone.
Damn, I just remembered. We're supposed to hit the Stretch and Bobbito show tonight.
Now? It's after midnight.
They got the #1 underground show. The shit goes til 4am.
WKCR
So before you guys freestyle, I just gotta clear something up. Are you from New York?
Nah, people think that 'cause there's a Cypress Hills in Brooklyn, but we're from Cypress Avenue in South Gate, Los Angeles.
Man, what a long-ass crazy day...
Oh, it ain't over. We're going downtown to Esso's...
The club Futura said DJ Clark Kent spins at, right?
Word.
A-IGHT! This is what I'm talking about.
Let's go say what's up to Clark.
IT'S ANOTHER ONE OF THEM OL' FUNKY CYPRESS HILL THINGS, YOU KNOW WHAT I'M SAYIN? AND IT GOES LIKE THIS...

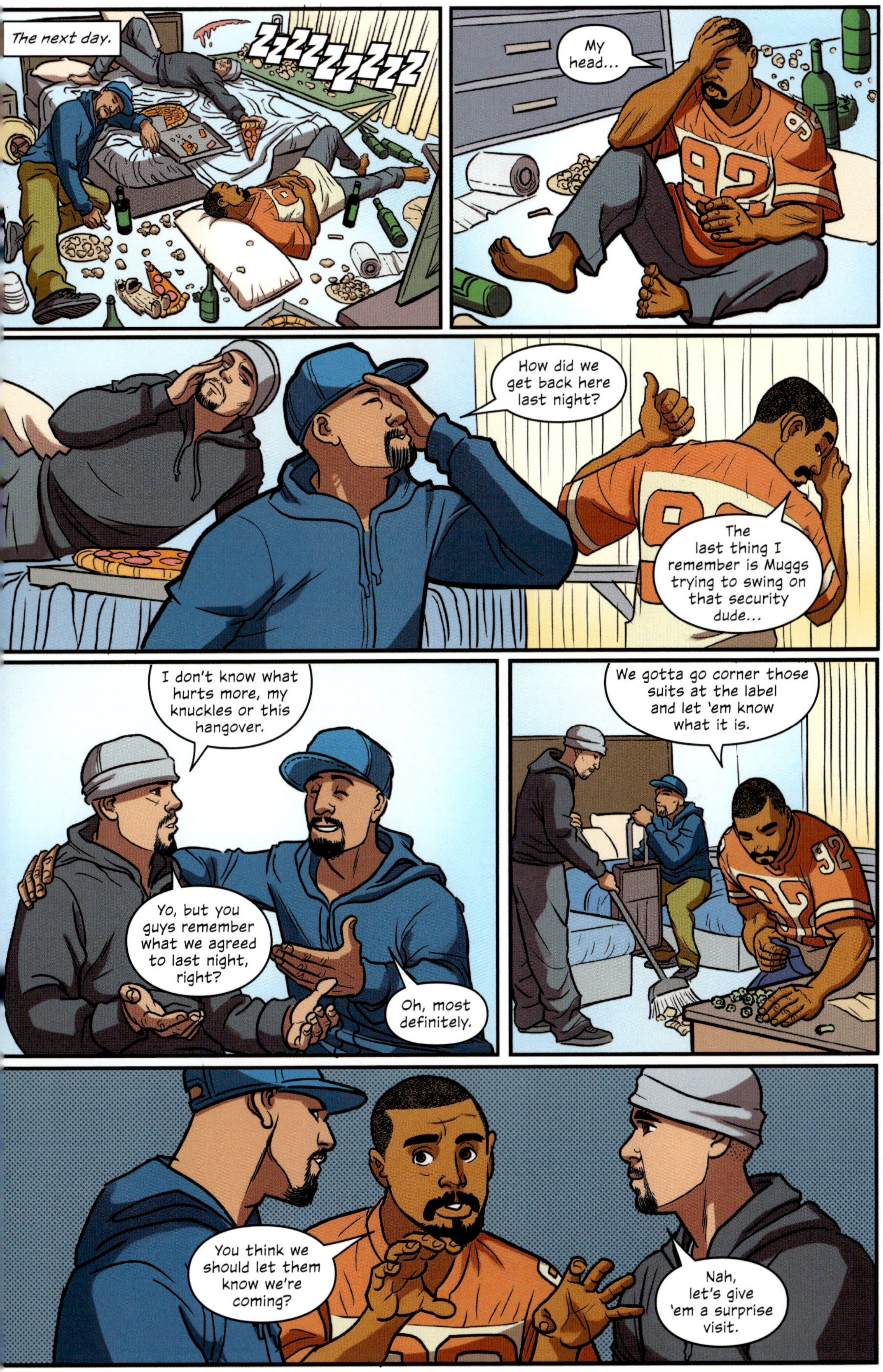
The next day.
ZZZZZZZZ
My head...
How did we get back here last night?
The last thing I remember is Muggs trying to swing on that security dude...
I don't know what hurts more, my knuckles or this hangover.
Yo, but you guys remember what we agreed to last night, right?
Oh, most definitely.
We gotta go corner those suits at the label and let 'em know what it is.
You think we should let them know we're coming?
Nah, let's give 'em a surprise visit.

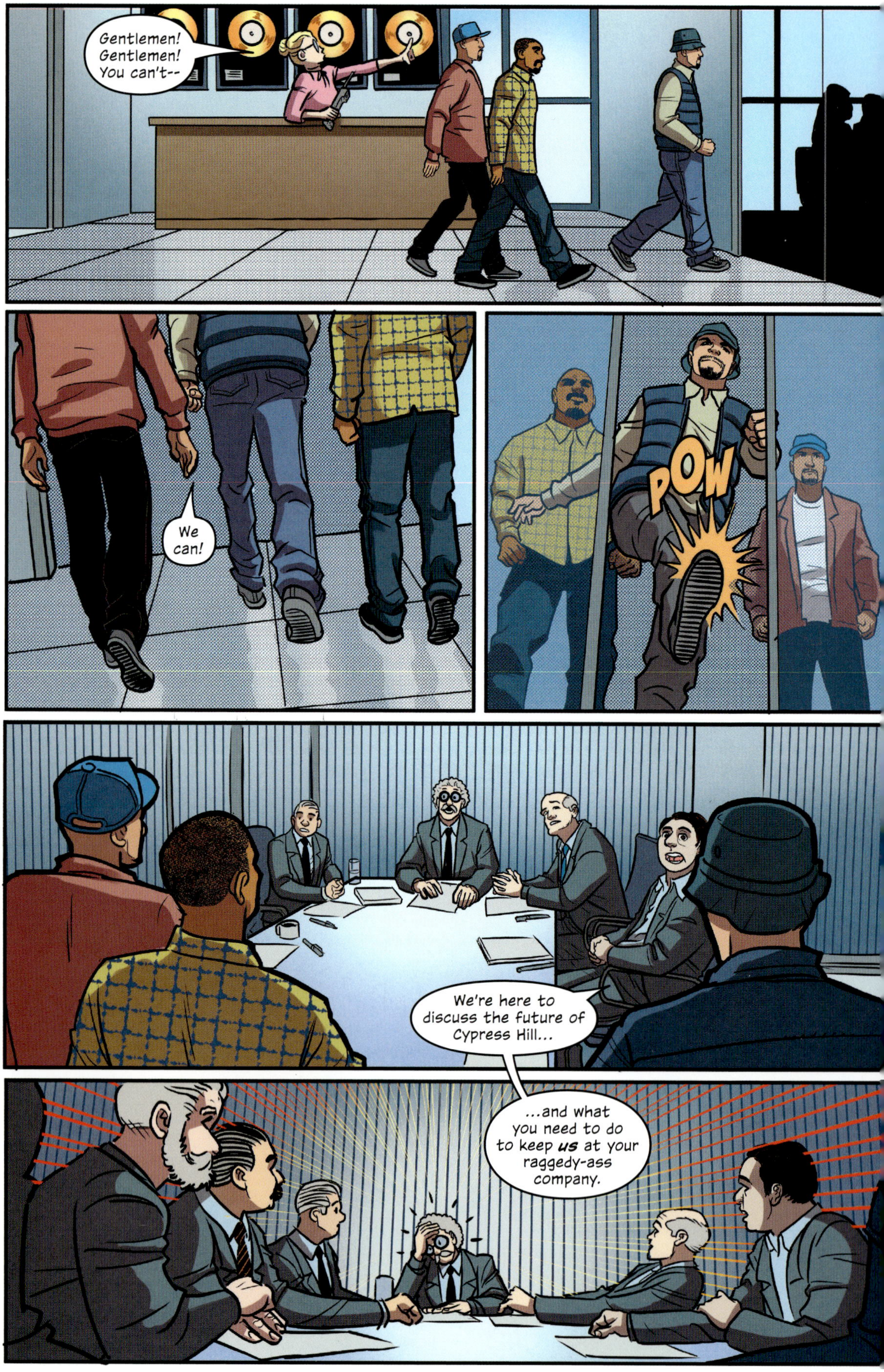
Gentlemen! Gentlemen! You can't--
We can!
POW
We're here to discuss the future of Cypress Hill...
...and what you need to do to keep *us* at your raggedy-ass company.

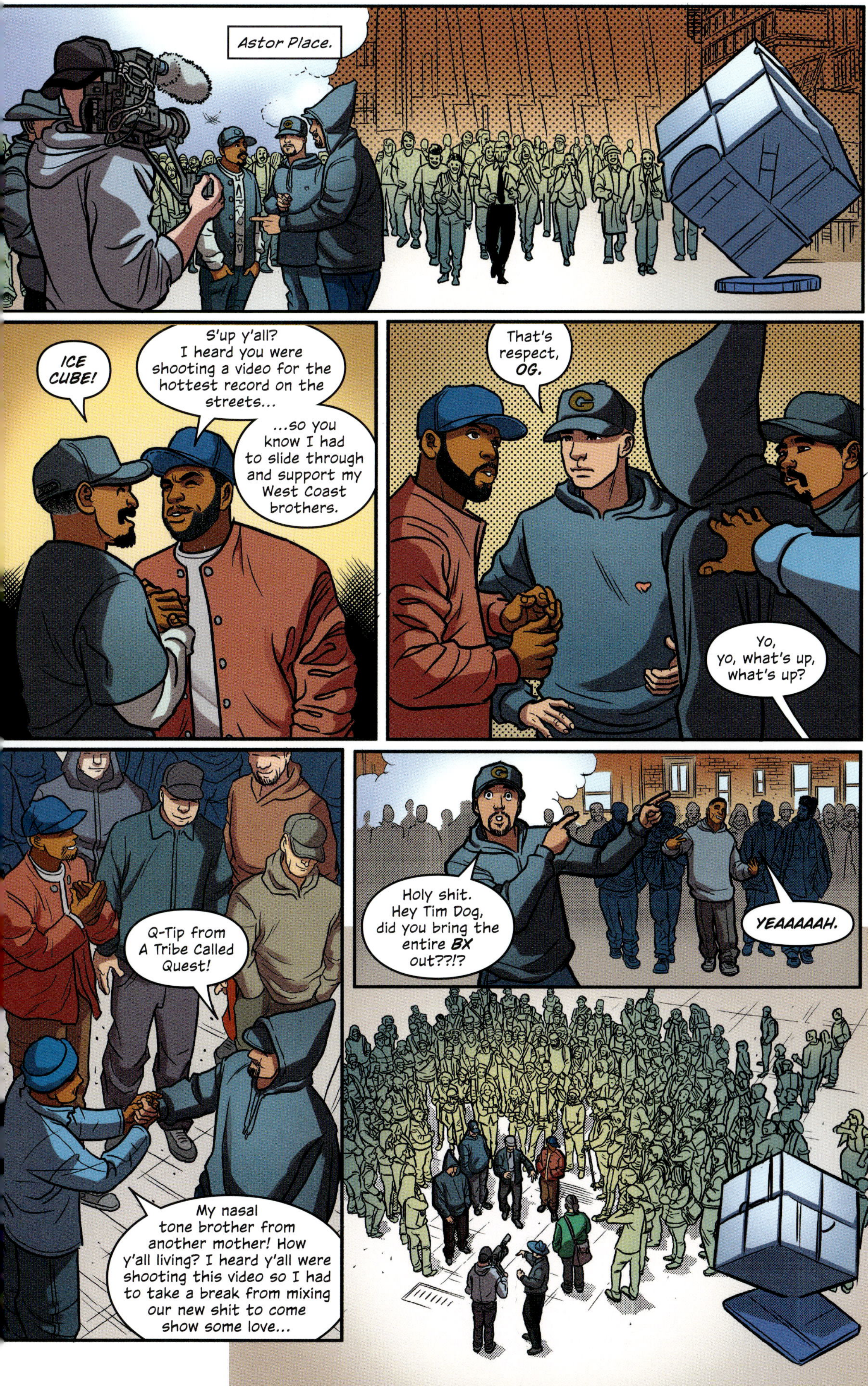
Astor Place.
ICE CUBE!
S'up y'all? I heard you were shooting a video for the hottest record on the streets...
...so you know I had to slide through and support my West Coast brothers.
That's respect, OG.
Yo, yo, what's up, what's up?
Q-Tip from A Tribe Called Quest!
My nasal tone brother from another mother! How y'all living? I heard y'all were shooting this video so I had to take a break from mixing our new shit to come show some love...
Holy shit. Hey Tim Dog, did you bring the entire BX out??!?
YEAAAAAH.

On tour a week later...

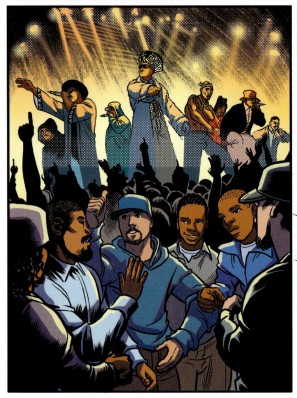

NO BACKSTAGE PASS, NO ENTRY

THE FREAKS OF THE INDUSTRY

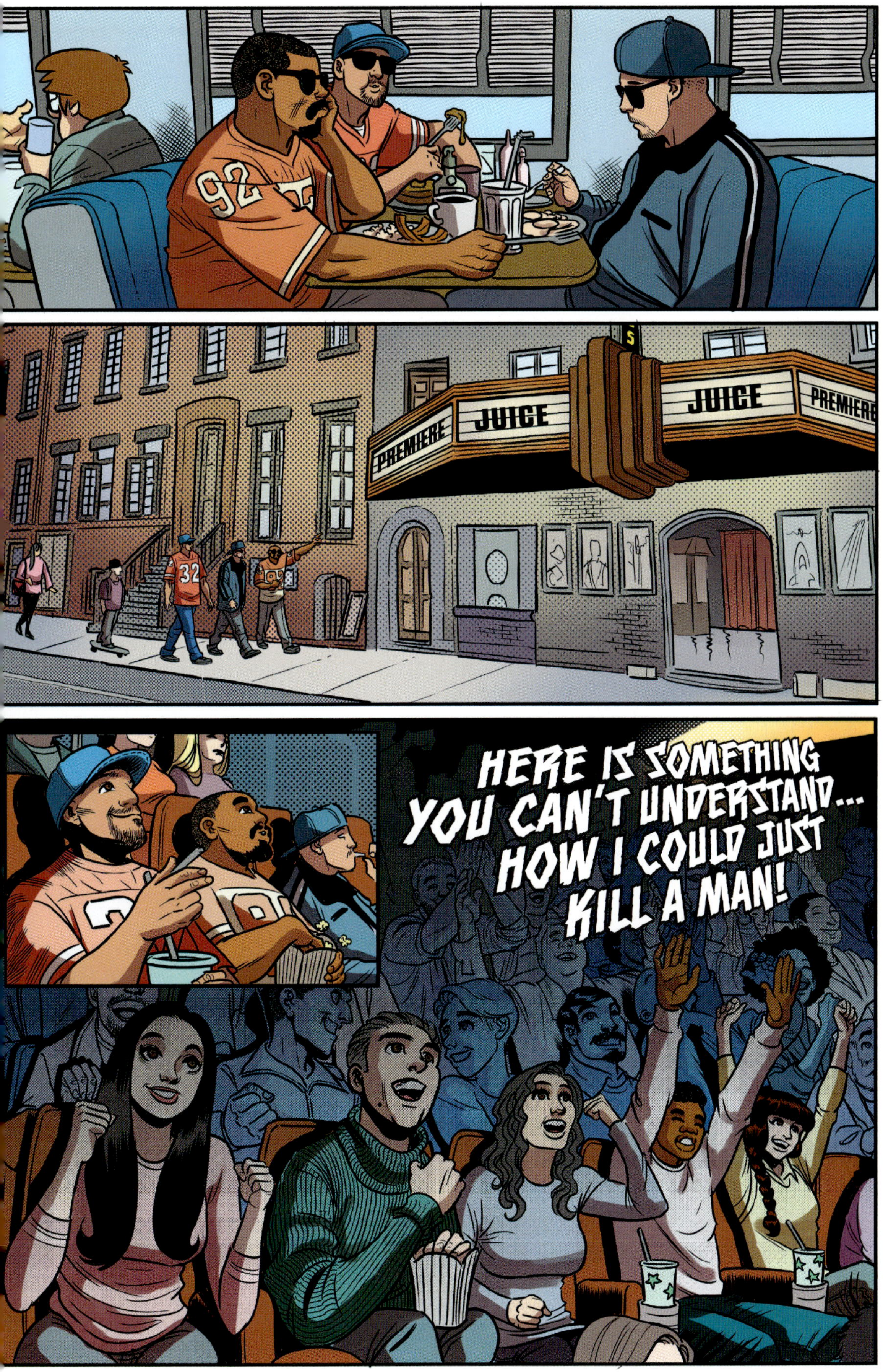

PREMIERE
JUICE
JUICE
PREMIERE
HERE IS SOMETHING YOU CAN'T UNDERSTAND... HOW I COULD JUST KILL A MAN!

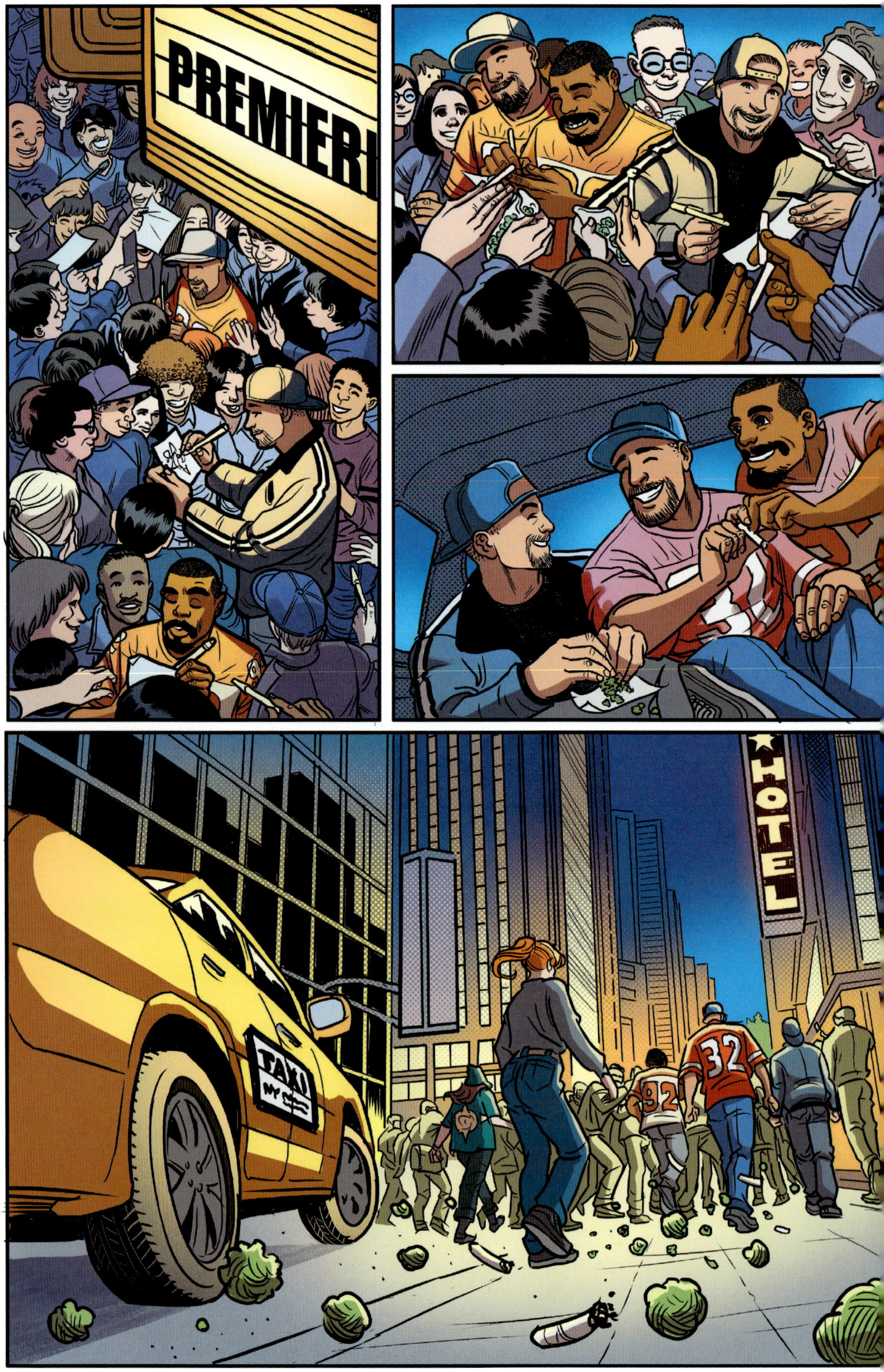

PREMIER
HOTEL
TAXI
92
32

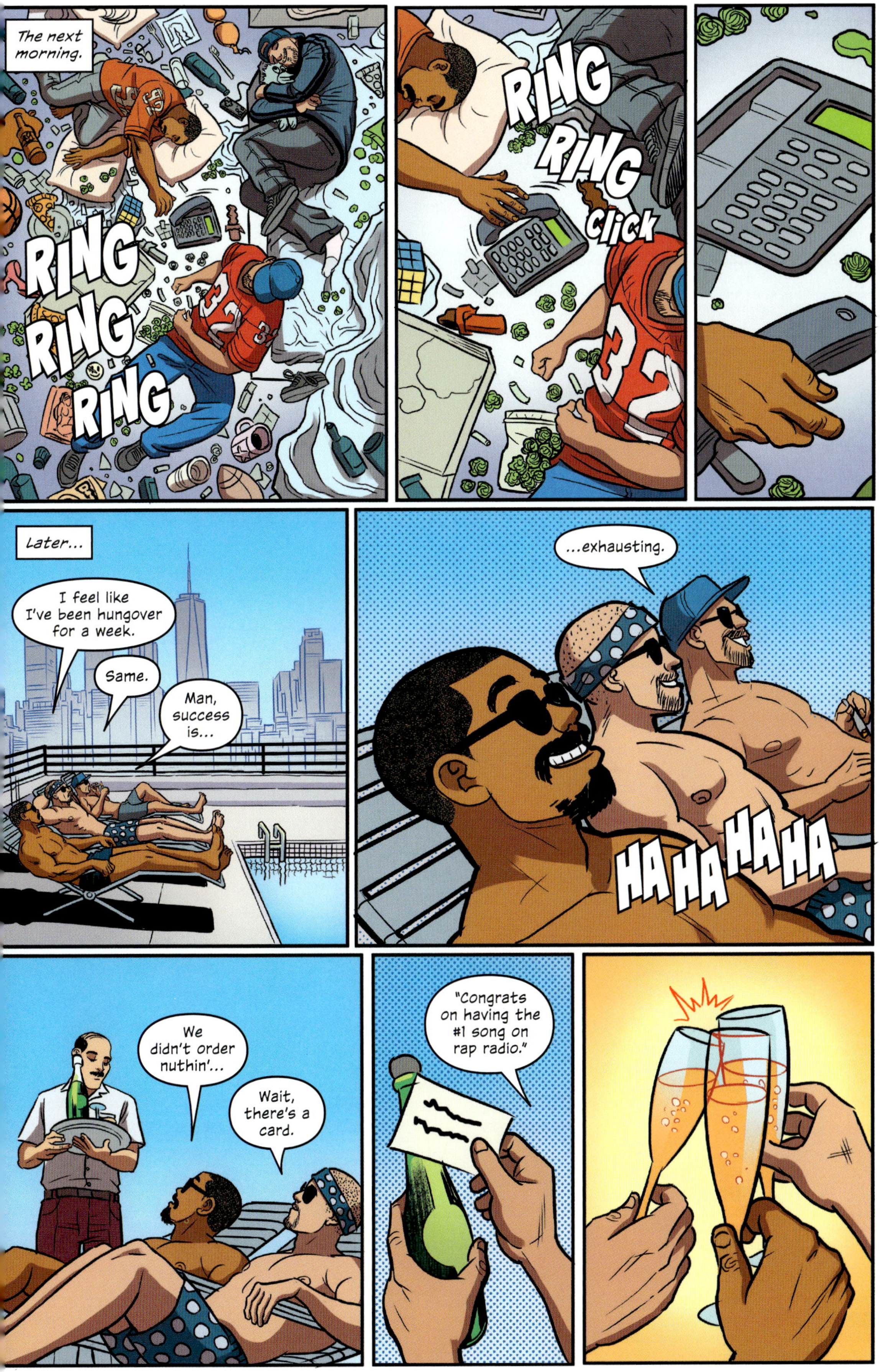
The next morning.
RING RING RING
RING RING
CLICK
Later...
I feel like I've been hungover for a week.
Same.
Man, success is...
...exhausting.
HAHAHAHAHA
We didn't order nuthin'...
Wait, there's a card.
"Congrats on having the #1 song on rap radio."

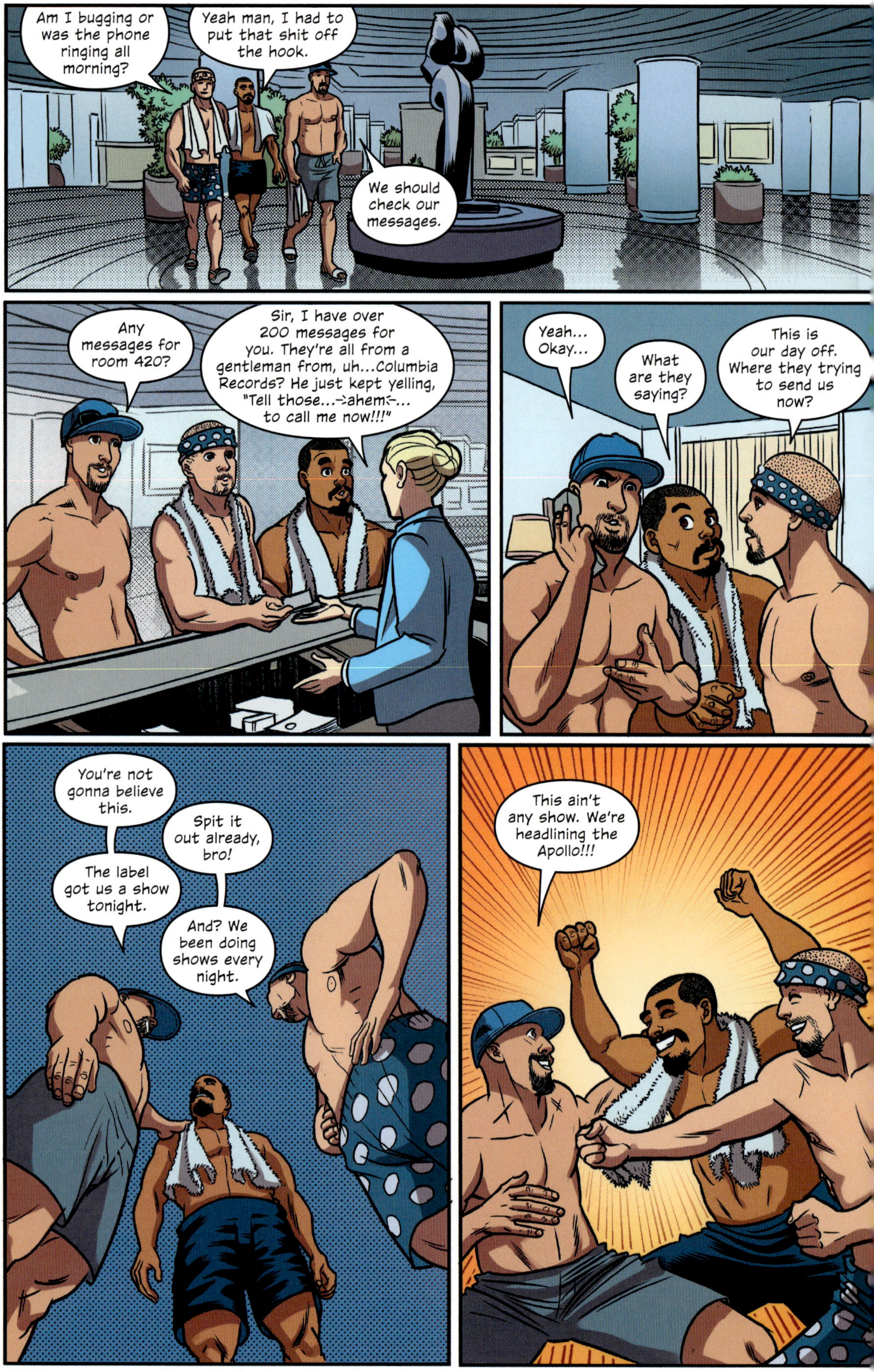
Am I bugging or was the phone ringing all morning?
Yeah man, I had to put that shit off the hook.
We should check our messages.
Any messages for room 420?
Sir, I have over 200 messages for you. They're all from a gentleman from, uh...Columbia Records? He just kept yelling, "Tell those...-ahem-... to call me now!!!"
Yeah... Okay...
What are they saying?
This is our day off. Where they trying to send us now?
You're not gonna believe this.
Spit it out already, bro!
The label got us a show tonight.
And? We been doing shows every night.
This ain't any show. We're headlining the Apollo!!!

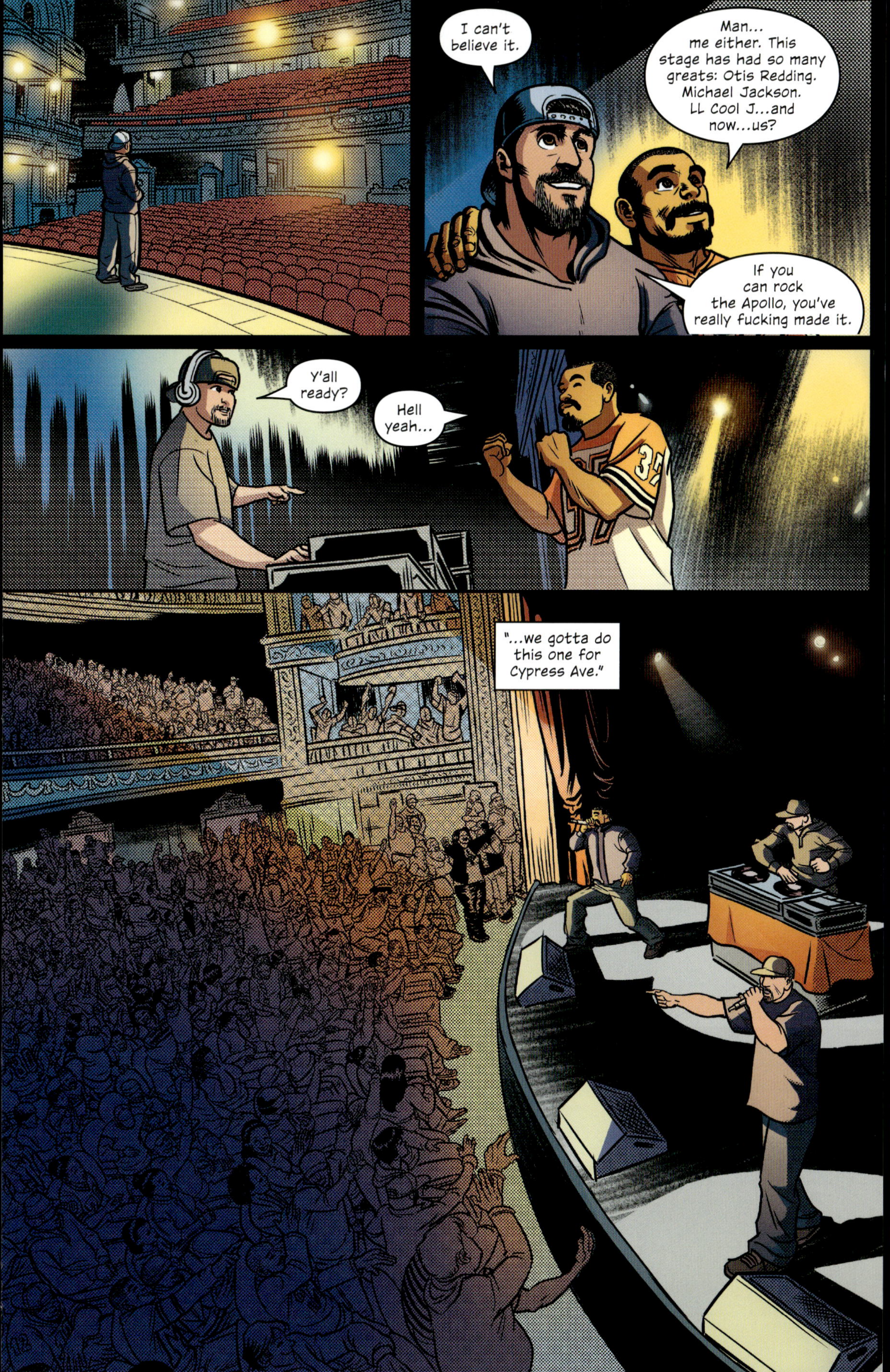
I can't believe it.
Man... me either. This stage has had so many greats: Otis Redding. Michael Jackson. LL Cool J...and now...us?
If you can rock the Apollo, you've really fucking made it.
Y'all ready?
Hell yeah...
"...we gotta do this one for Cypress Ave."

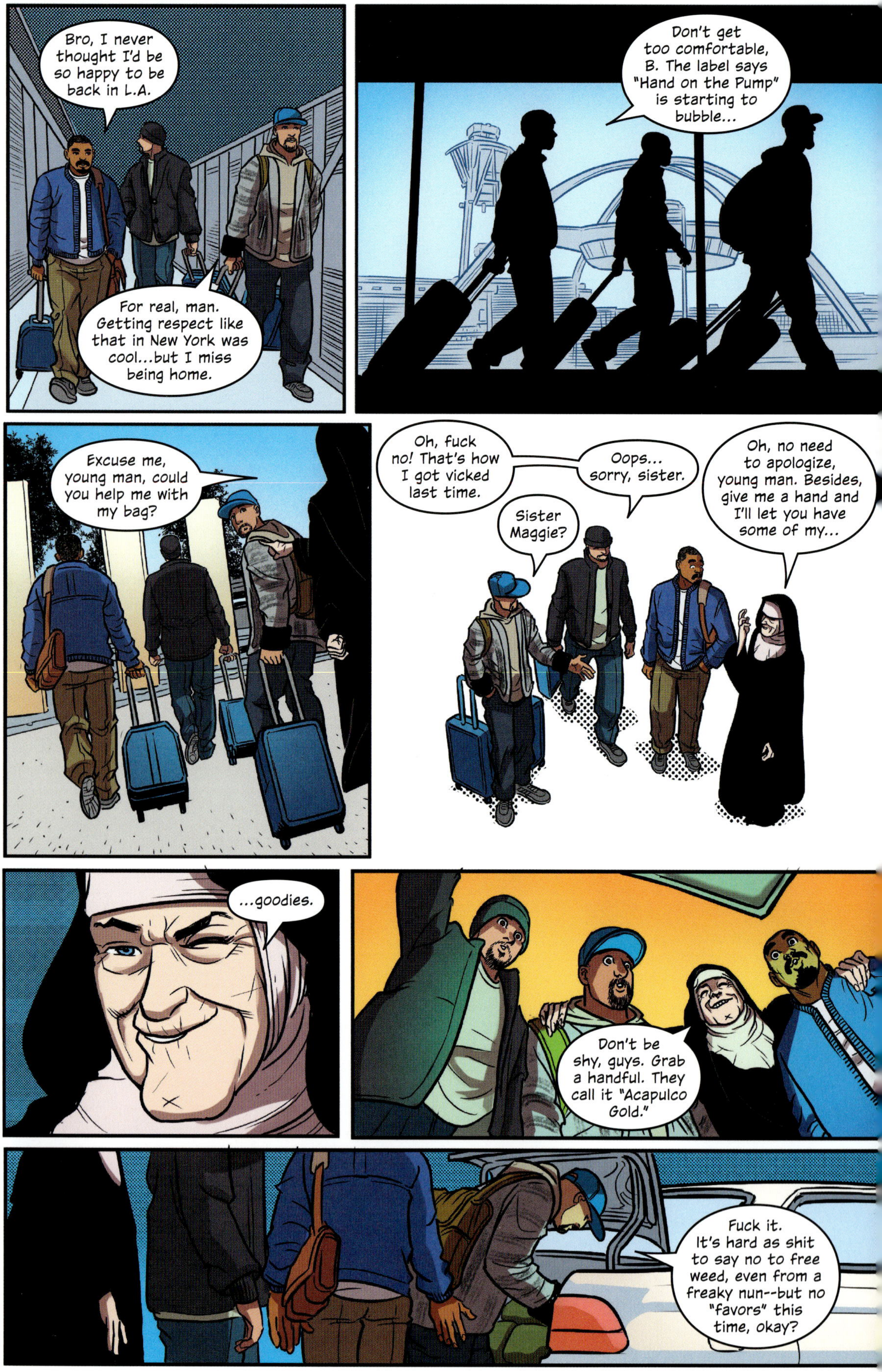
Bro, I never thought I'd be so happy to be back in L.A.
For real, man. Getting respect like that in New York was cool...but I miss being home.
Don't get too comfortable, B. The label says "Hand on the Pump" is starting to bubble...
Excuse me, young man, could you help me with my bag?
Oh, fuck no! That's how I got vicked last time.
Oops... sorry, sister.
Sister Maggie?
Oh, no need to apologize, young man. Besides, give me a hand and I'll let you have some of my...
...goodies.
Don't be shy, guys. Grab a handful. They call it "Acapulco Gold."
Fuck it. It's hard as shit to say no to free weed, even from a freaky nun--but no "favors" this time, okay?

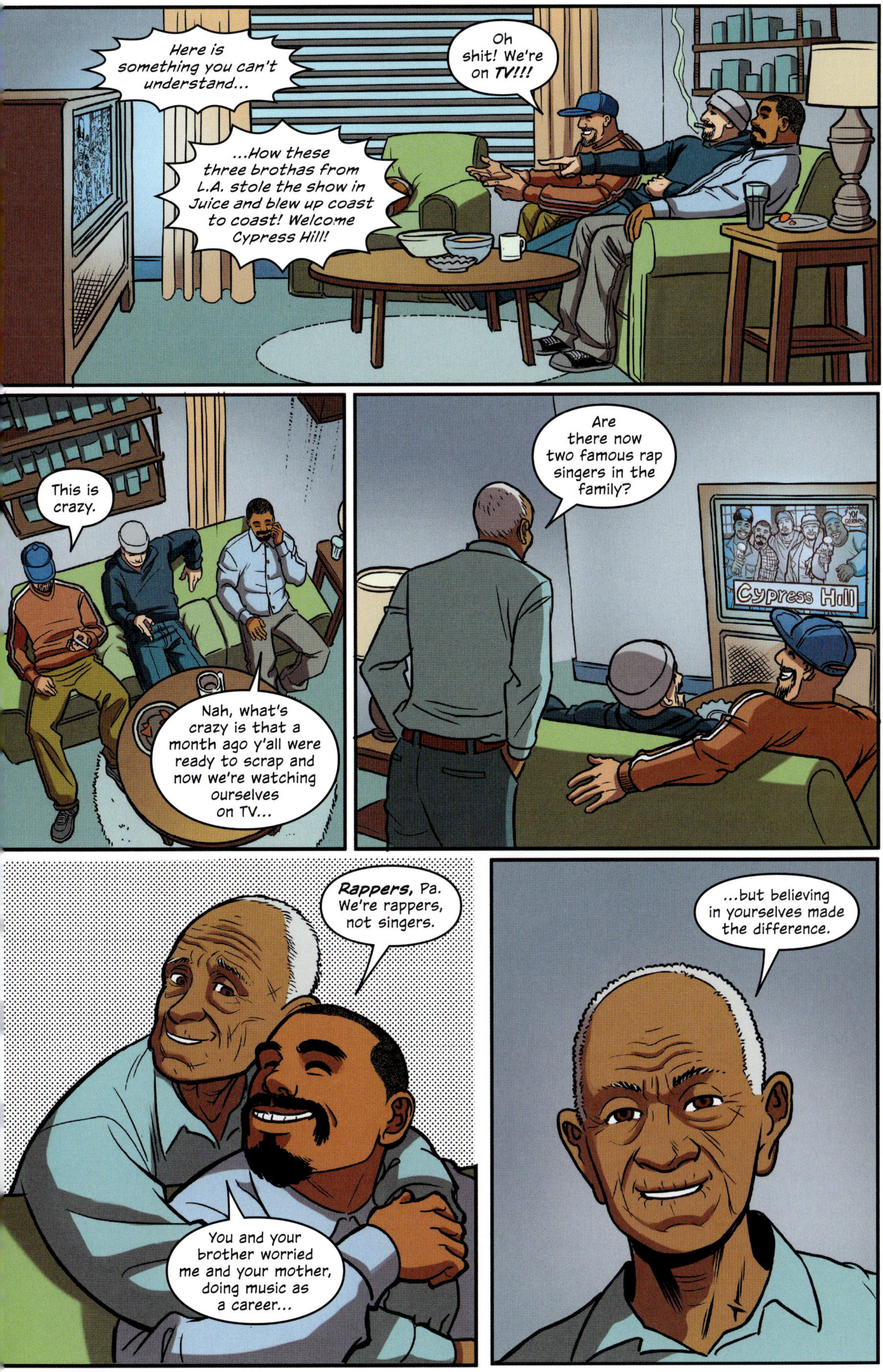
Here is something you can't understand...
Oh shit! We're on TV!!!
...How these three brothas from L.A. stole the show in Juice and blew up coast to coast! Welcome Cypress Hill!
This is crazy.
Nah, what's crazy is that a month ago y'all were ready to scrap and now we're watching ourselves on TV...
Are there now two famous rap singers in the family?
Cypress Hill
Rappers, Pa. We're rappers, not singers.
You and your brother worried me and your mother, doing music as a career...
...but believing in yourselves made the difference.

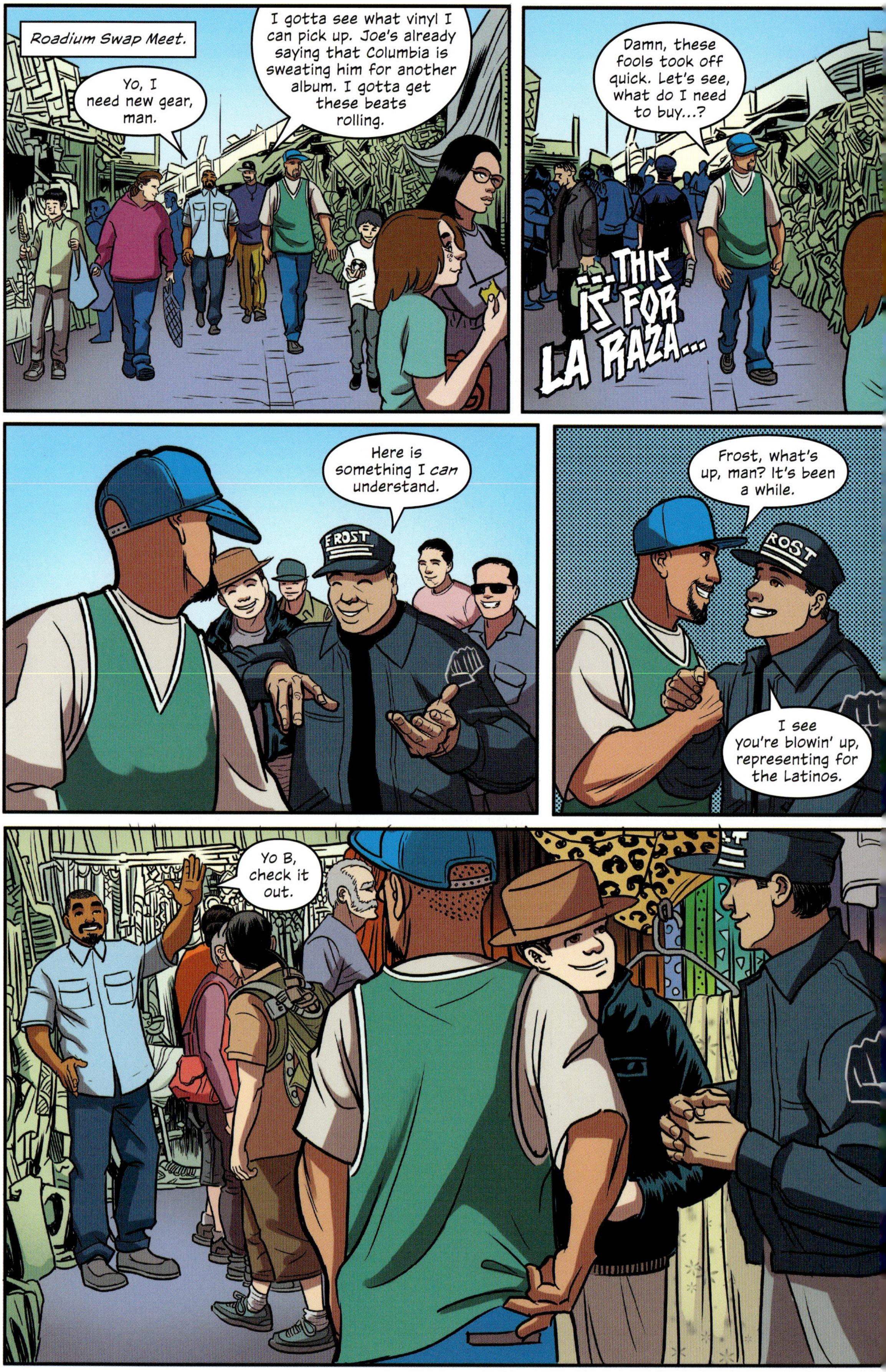
Roadium Swap Meet.
Yo, I need new gear, man.
I gotta see what vinyl I can pick up. Joe's already saying that Columbia is sweating him for another album. I gotta get these beats rolling.
Damn, these fools took off quick. Let's see, what do I need to buy...?
...THIS IS FOR LA RAZA...
Here is something I *can* understand.
Frost, what's up, man? It's been a while.
I see you're blowin' up, representing for the Latinos.
Yo B, check it out.

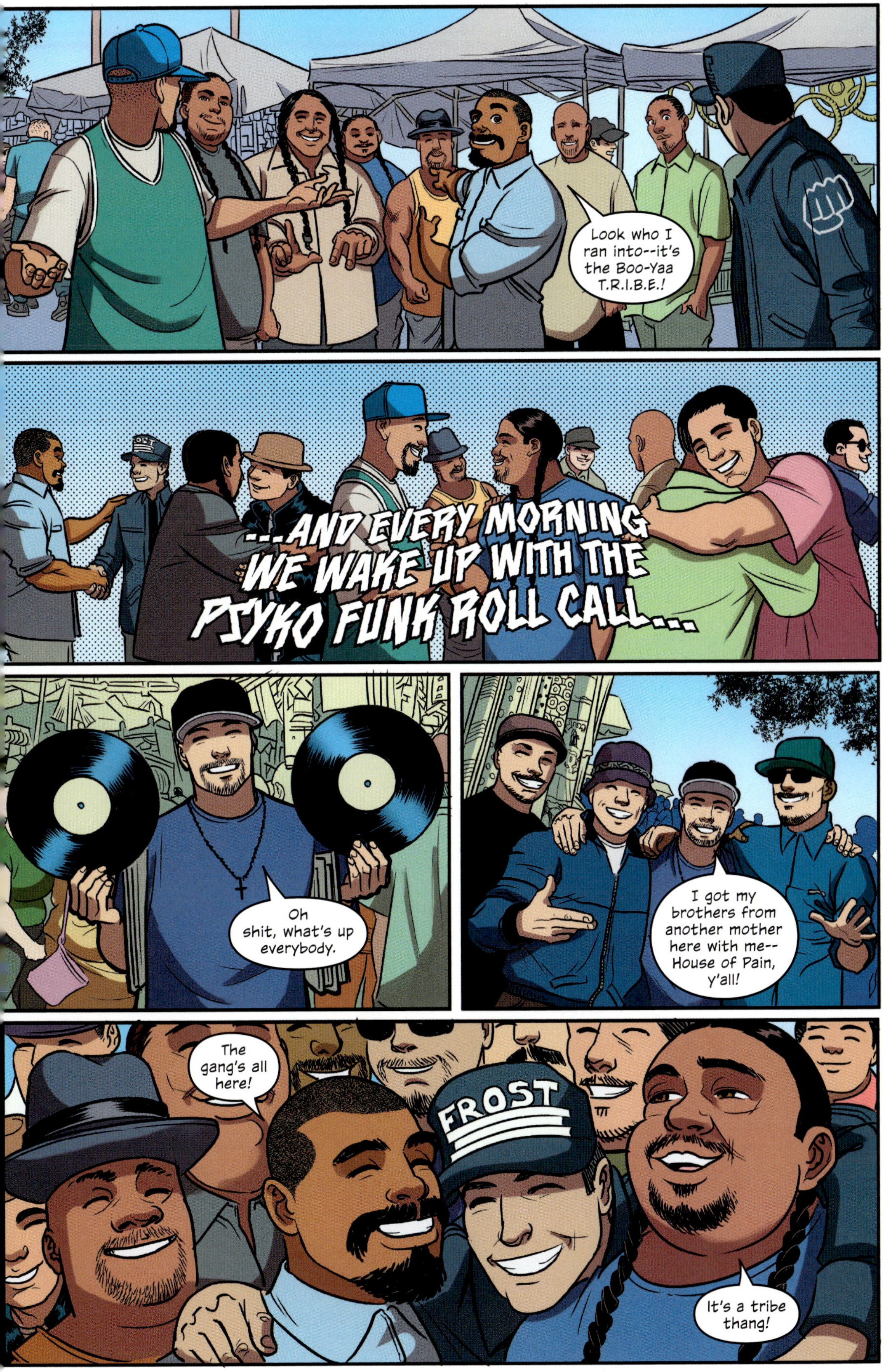
Look who I ran into--it's the Boo-Yaa T.R.I.B.E.!
...AND EVERY MORNING WE WAKE UP WITH THE PSYKO FUNK ROLL CALL...
Oh shit, what's up everybody.
I got my brothers from another mother here with me-- House of Pain, y'all!
The gang's all here!
FROST
It's a tribe thang!

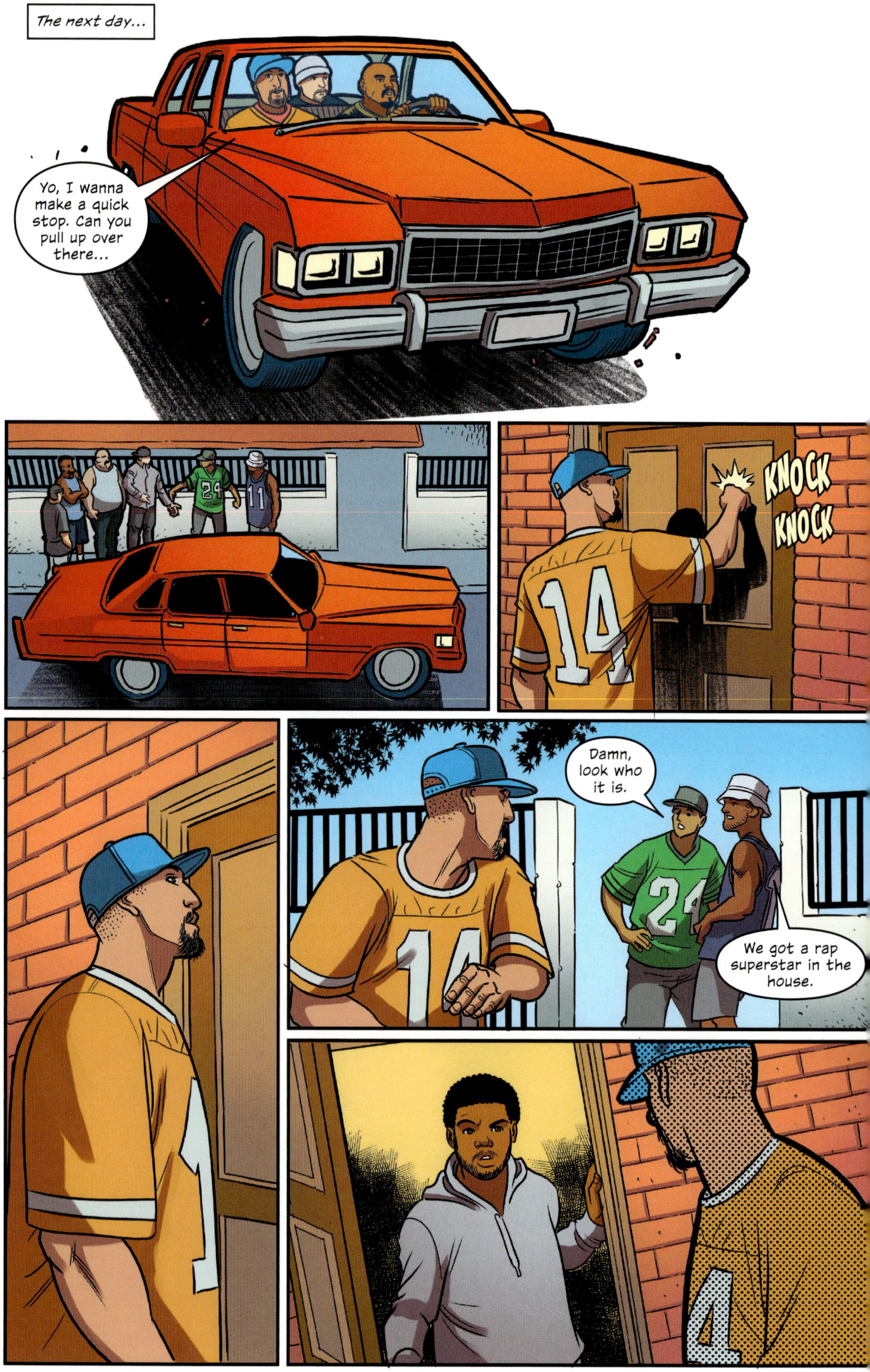
The next day...
Yo, I wanna make a quick stop. Can you pull up over there...
KNOCK KNOCK
Damn, look who it is.
We got a rap superstar in the house.

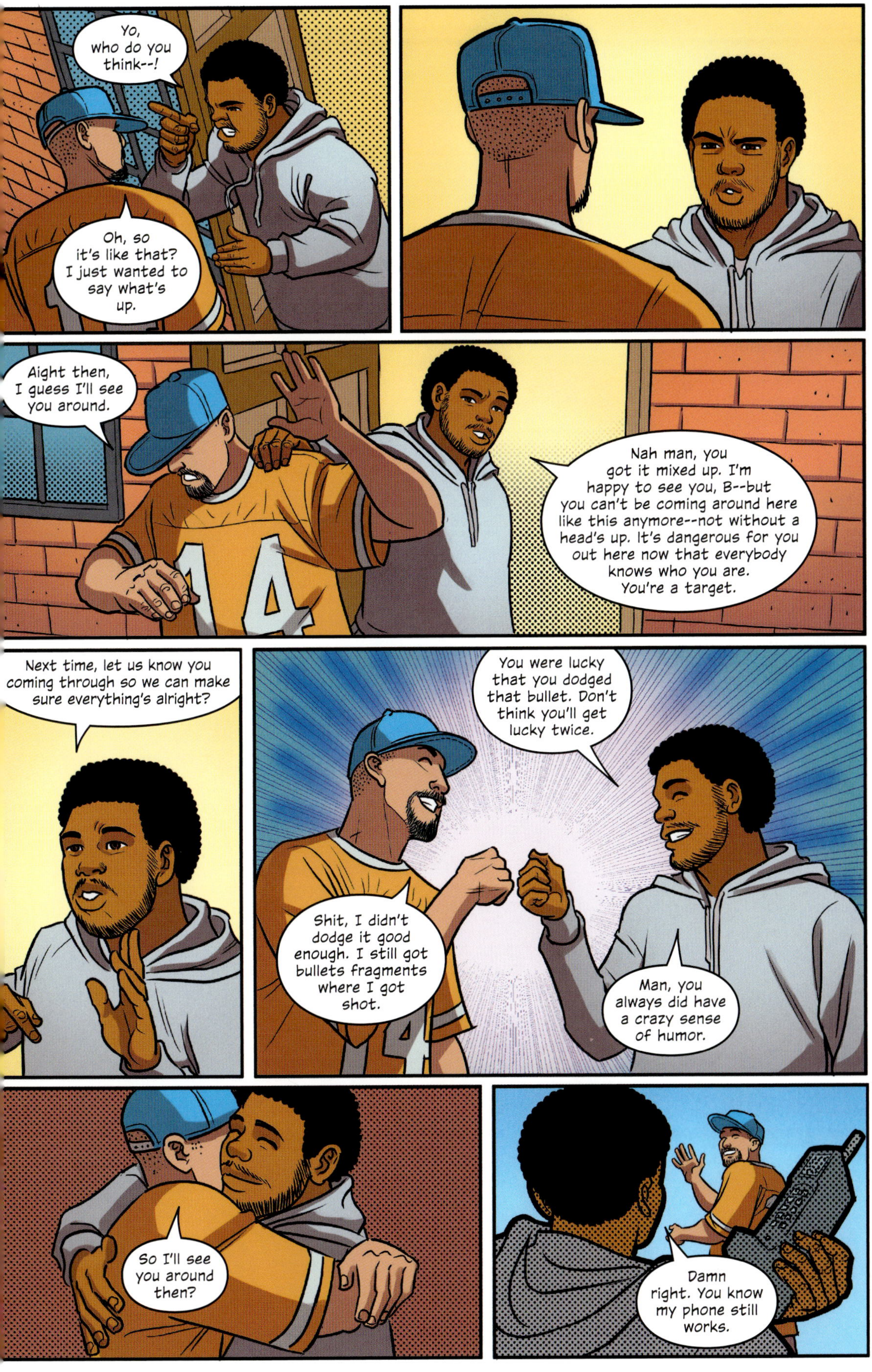
Yo, who do you think--!
Oh, so it's like that? I just wanted to say what's up.
Aight then, I guess I'll see you around.
Nah man, you got it mixed up. I'm happy to see you, B--but you can't be coming around here like this anymore--not without a head's up. It's dangerous for you out here now that everybody knows who you are. You're a target.
Next time, let us know you coming through so we can make sure everything's alright?
You were lucky that you dodged that bullet. Don't think you'll get lucky twice.
Shit, I didn't dodge it good enough. I still got bullets fragments where I got shot.
Man, you always did have a crazy sense of humor.
So I'll see you around then?
Damn right. You know my phone still works.

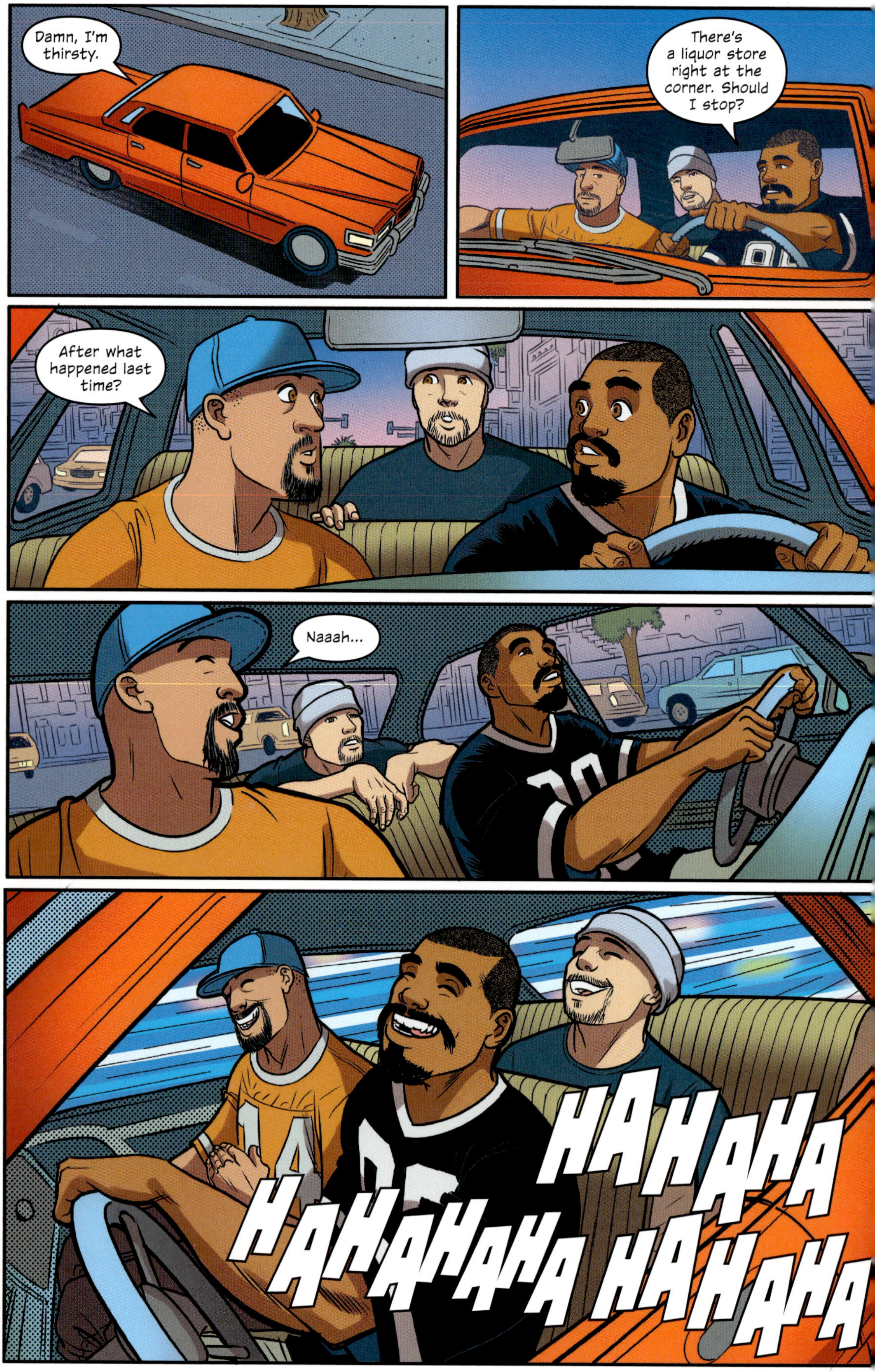
Damn, I'm thirsty.
There's a liquor store right at the corner. Should I stop?
After what happened last time?
Naaah...
HAHAHA
HAHAHAHA HAHAHA

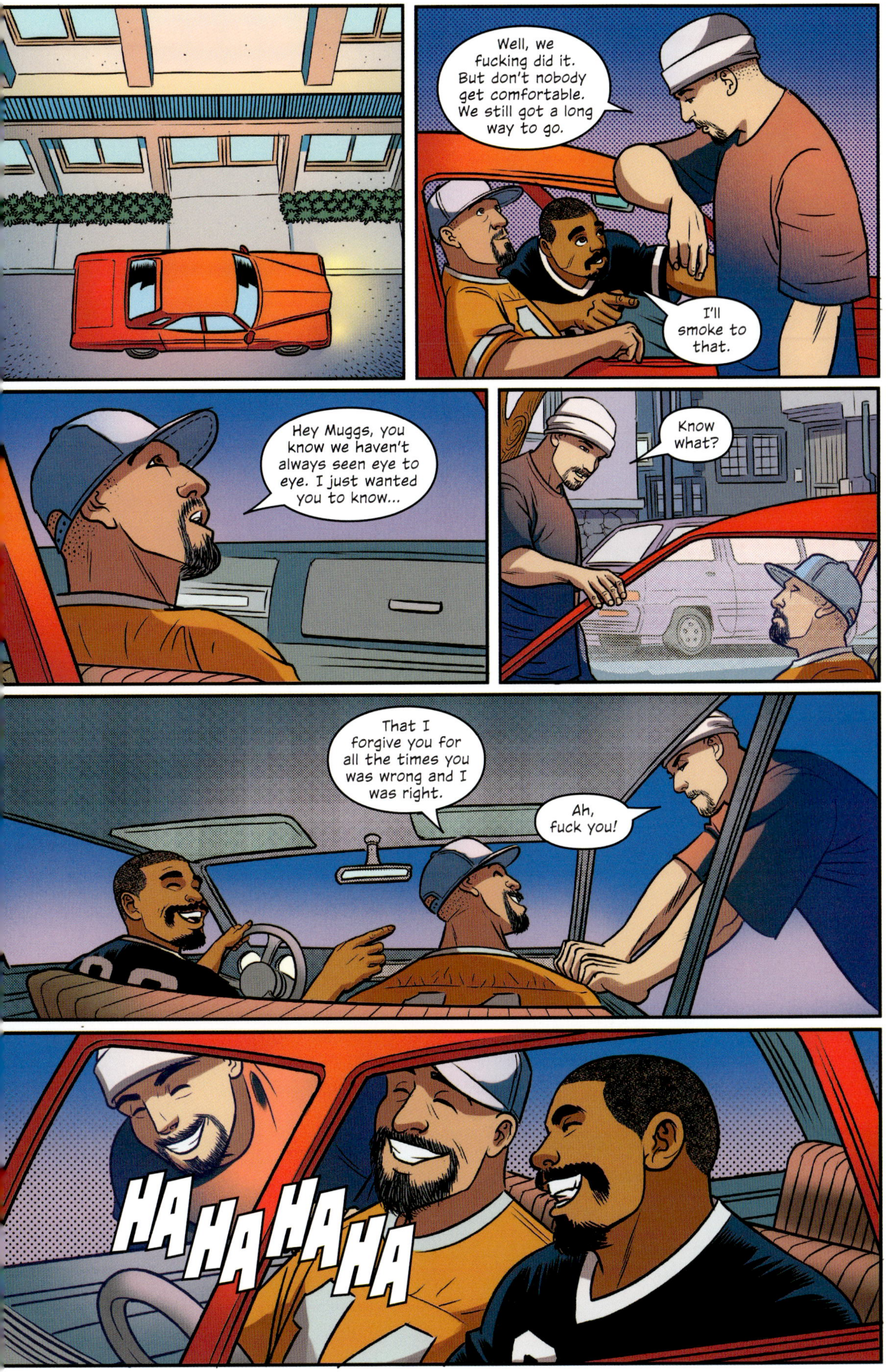
Well, we fucking did it. But don't nobody get comfortable. We still got a long way to go.
I'll smoke to that.
Hey Muggs, you know we haven't always seen eye to eye. I just wanted you to know...
Know what?
That I forgive you for all the times you was wrong and I was right.
Ah, fuck you!
HA HA HA HA HA HA

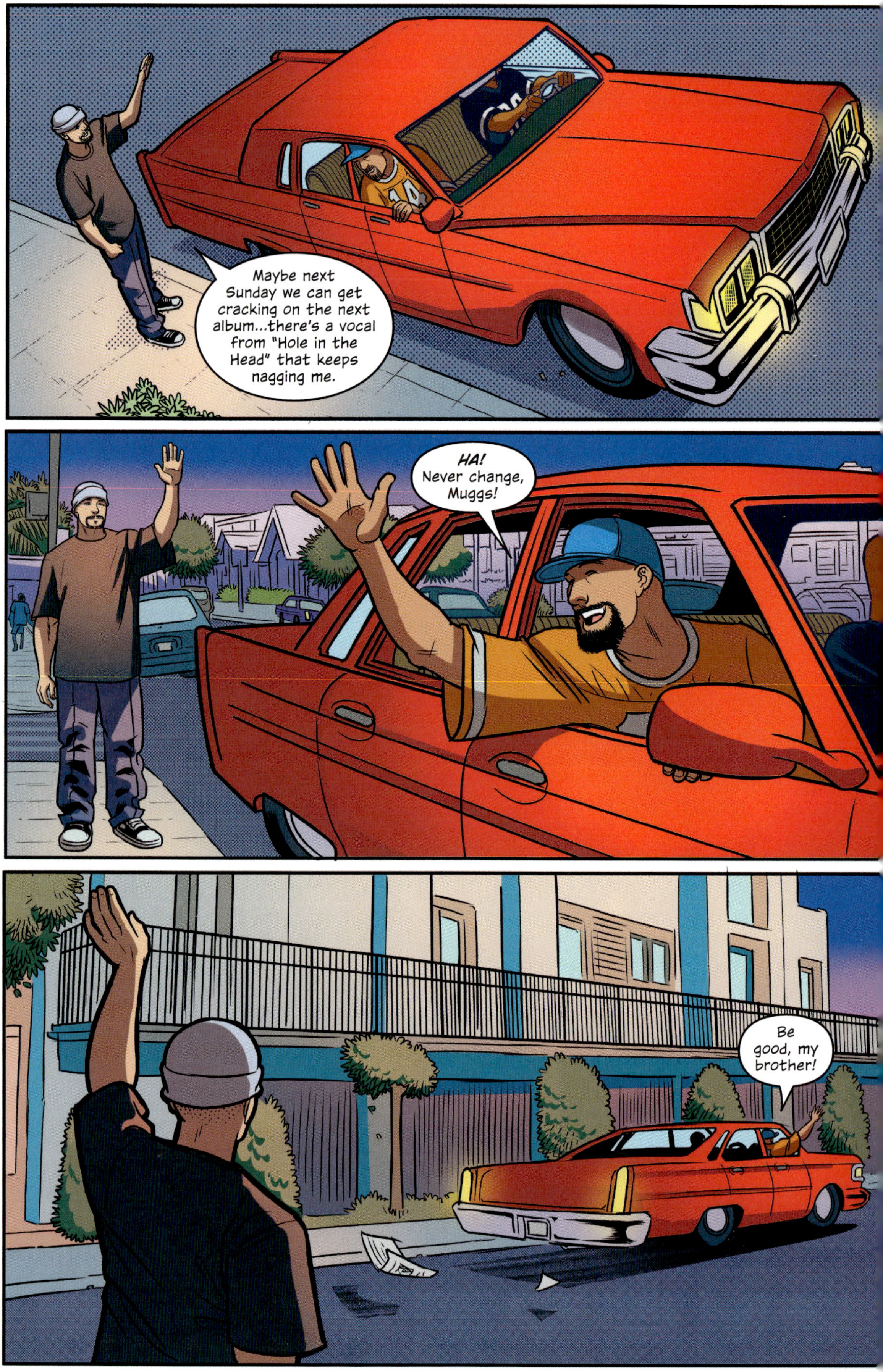
Maybe next Sunday we can get cracking on the next album...there's a vocal from "Hole in the Head" that keeps nagging me.
HA! Never change, Muggs!
Be good, my brother!

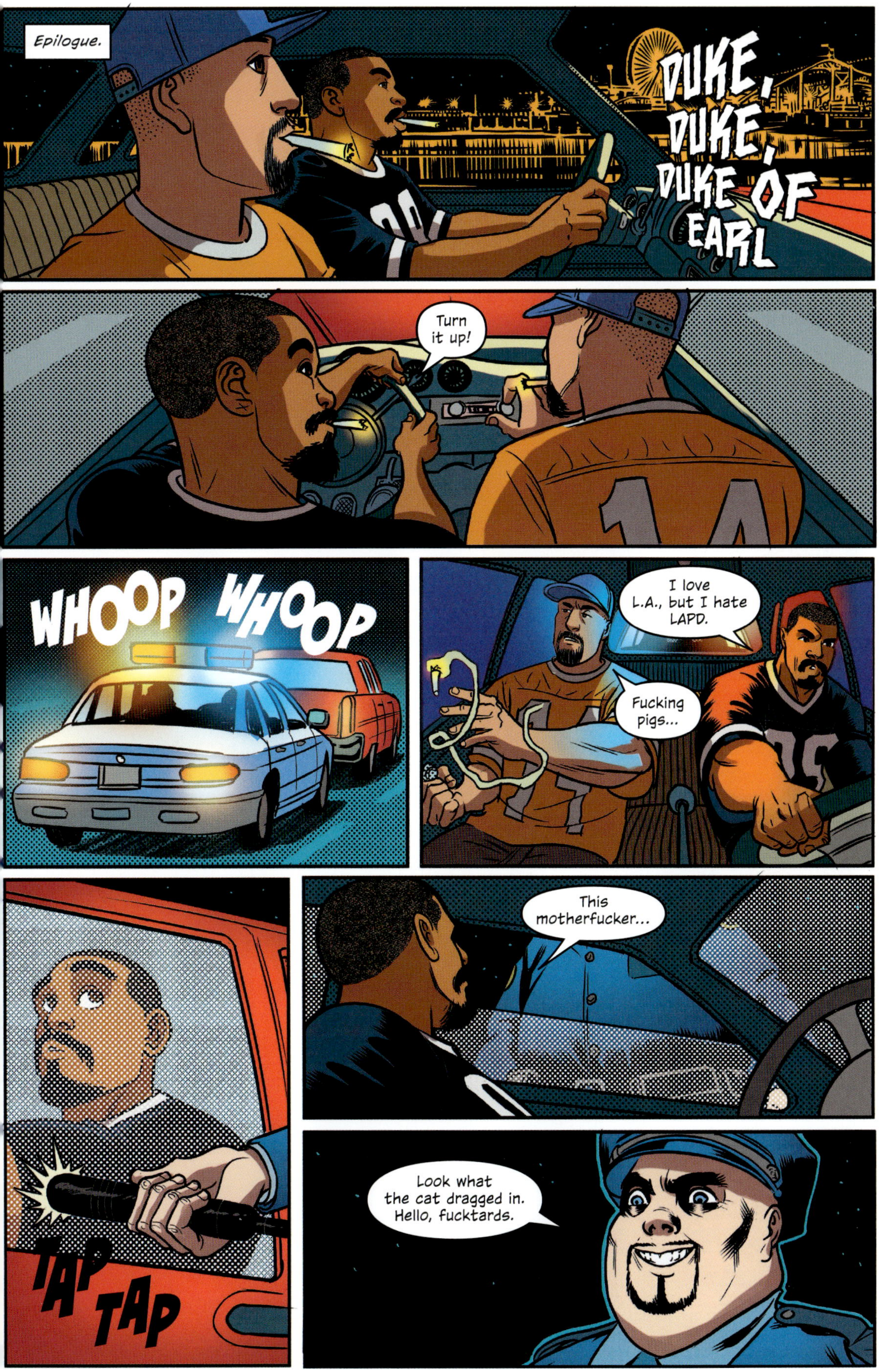
Epilogue.
DUKE, DUKE, DUKE OF EARL
Turn it up!
WHOOP WHOOP
I love L.A., but I hate LAPD.
Fucking pigs...
TAP TAP
This motherfucker...
Look what the cat dragged in. Hello, fucktards.

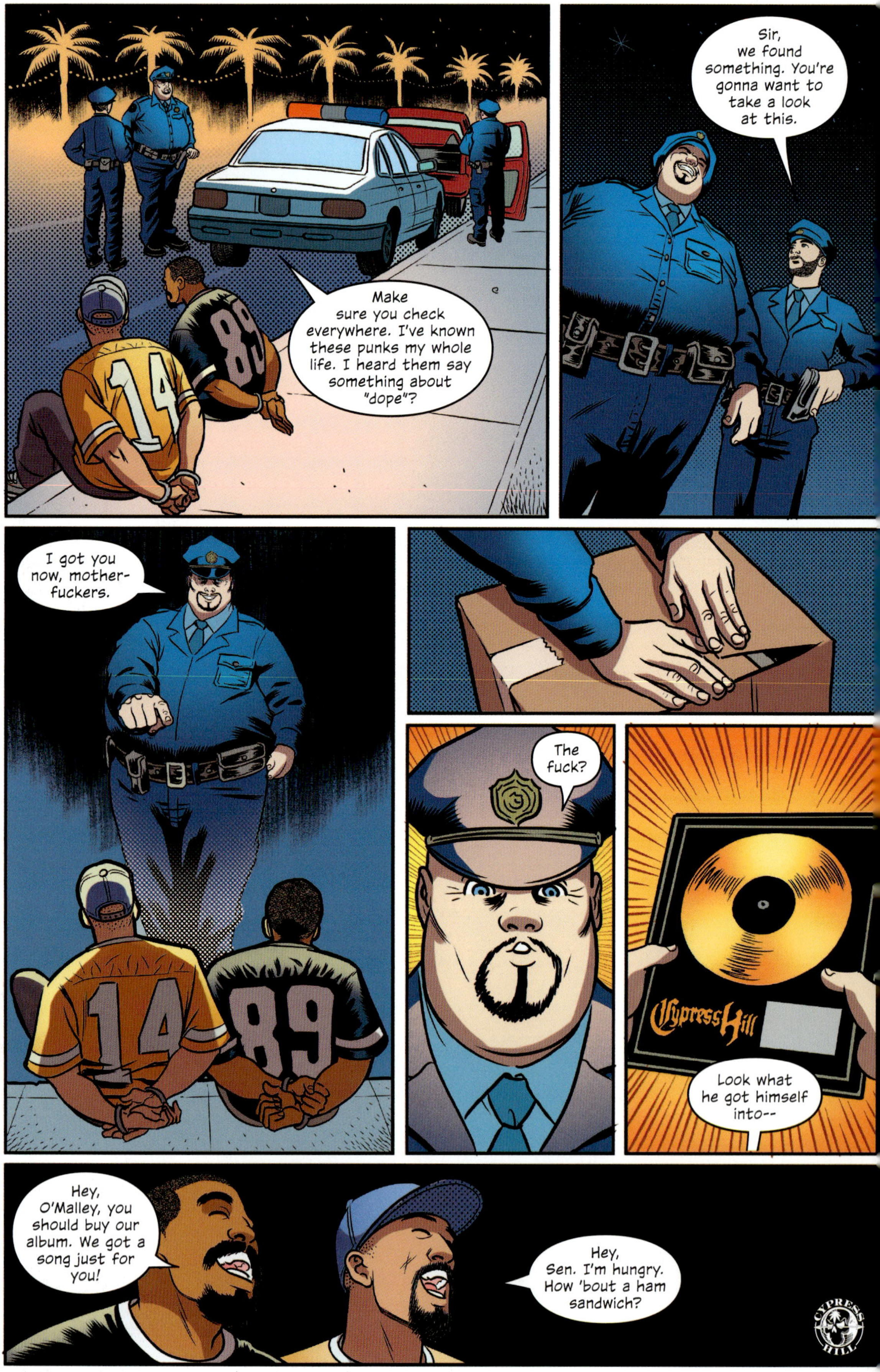
Make sure you check everywhere. I've known these punks my whole life. I heard them say something about "dope"?
Sir, we found something. You're gonna want to take a look at this.
I got you now, mother-fuckers.
The fuck?
Cypress Hill
Look what he got himself into--
Hey, O'Malley, you should buy our album. We got a song just for you!
Hey, Sen. I'm hungry. How 'bout a ham sandwich?

# PROCESS

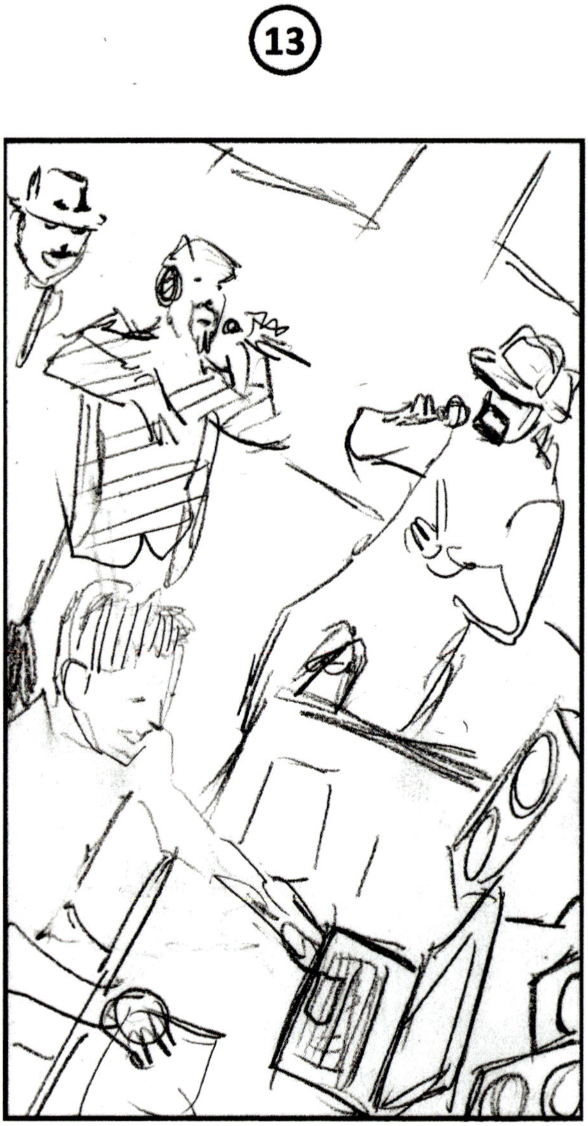
13

PAGE 13

**PANEL 1:** Back at the studio. B-REAL starts spitting and we get like a montage of him and SEN performing "Real Estate" and maybe some cool illustrative superpower shit to convey the nasal flow and SEN's booming PSYCHOBETA voice.

B: ...I'M NOT A LOCO BUT I'M LOCO JUST A POCO...

SEN: BOO-YAA! 'CAUSE I SAID, 'STEP OFF!'

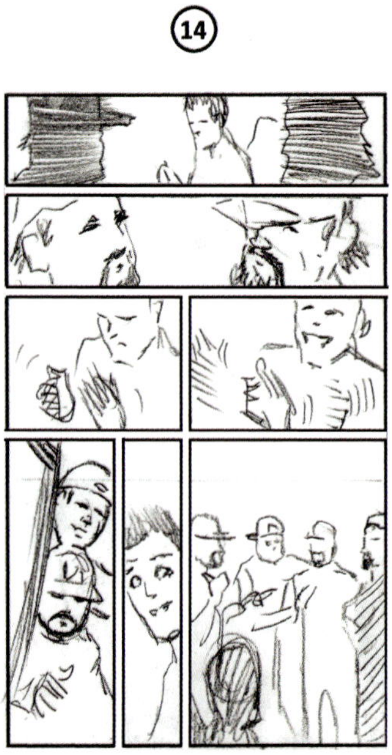
14

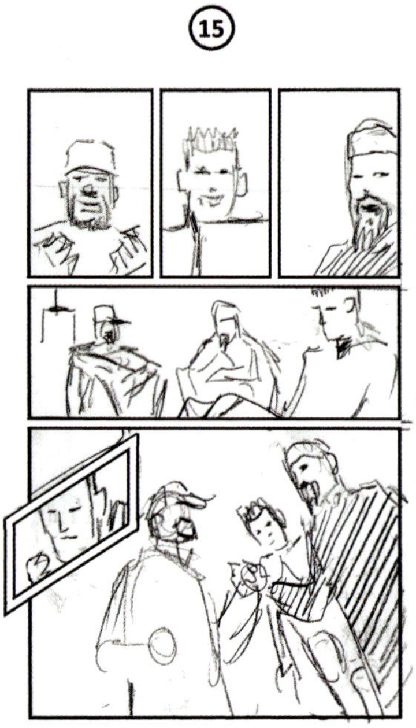
15

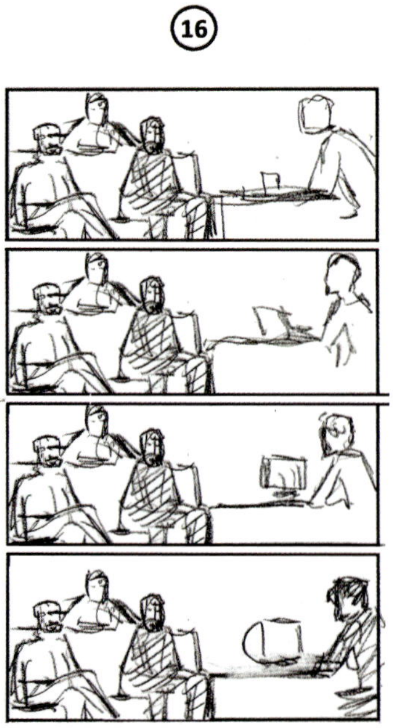
16

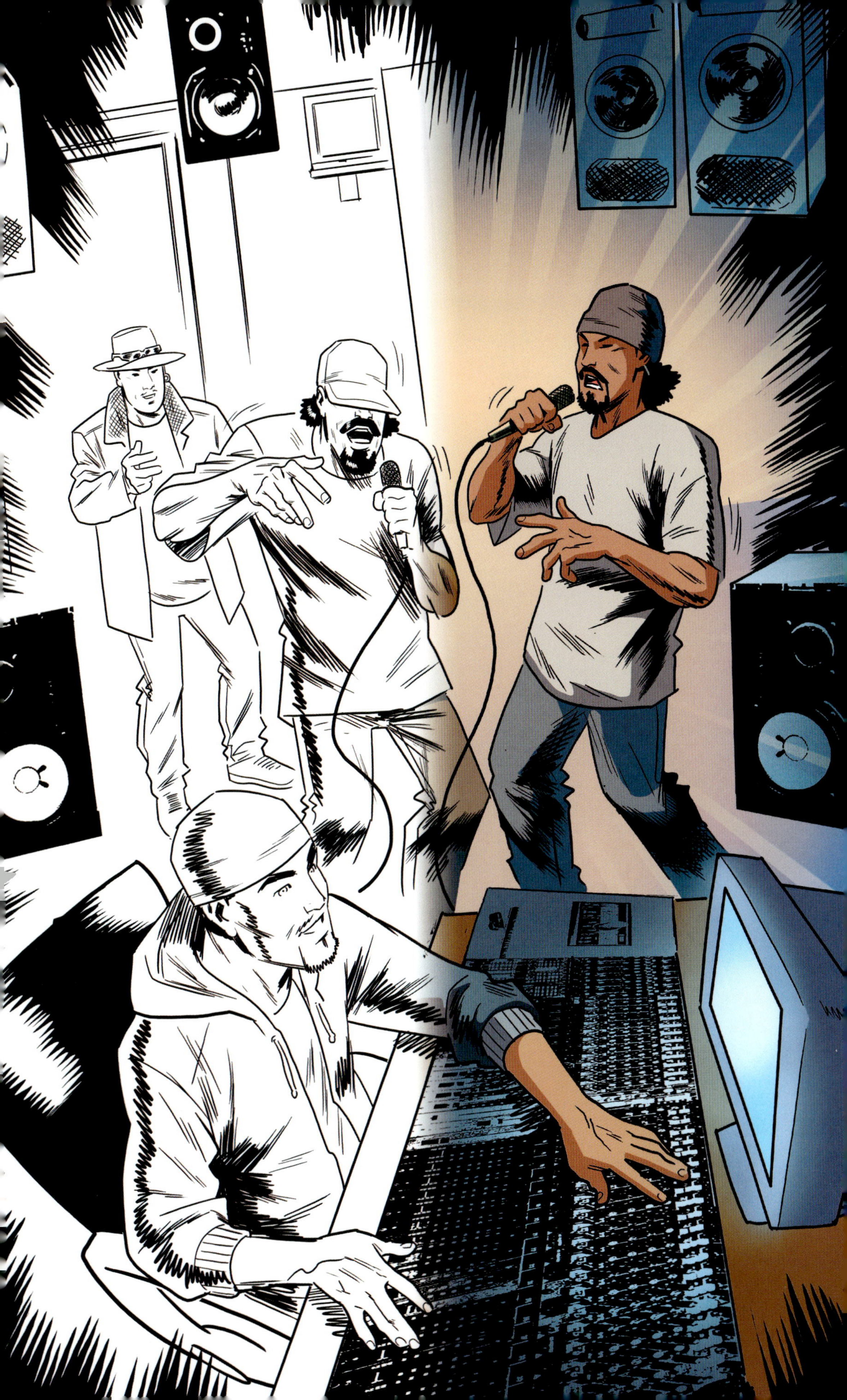

# PAGE 20

**PANEL 1 [1 of 3 on the top ⅓ ]:** The guys are in a circle talking and we're looking up at them. Kinda like the N.W.A Straight Outta Compton album cover.

SEN: Yo, fuck it. You know what? We gotta be a group!

EVERYONE: WORD!

**PANEL 2:** Now we're looking over the guys shoulders at B-REAL who is excited, emphatic.

B-REAL: And I got the perfect name for us. We'll be called…

B-REAL 2: …Devastating Vocal Excellence!!! You know, DVX for short!

**PANEL 3:** SEN DOG, MELLOW, MUGGS and JULIO G all look back at him blankly. They're perplexed and totally silent.

**PANEL 4 [wide middle ⅓ ]:** We see the house from a similar framing as the beginning of the scene. The difference is that we're pulled back a liiiiittle further and we see a street sign in the foreground this time that says CYPRESS AVENUE. Everyone's laughing.

SEN: Bro, you might need to take that name back to the lab.

B-REAL: It's a work in progress!

**PANEL 5 [1 of 2 on the bottom ⅓ ]:** We see SEN DOG looking down at his pager. B-REAL is also in the frame.

SEN: Ay, B, we gotta roll out…

B-REAL: Now what?

SFX: BZZT

**PANEL 6:** SEN DOG and B-REAL are walking off the porch towards the camera. They have grim looks on their faces.

SEN: We gotta go finish what we started.

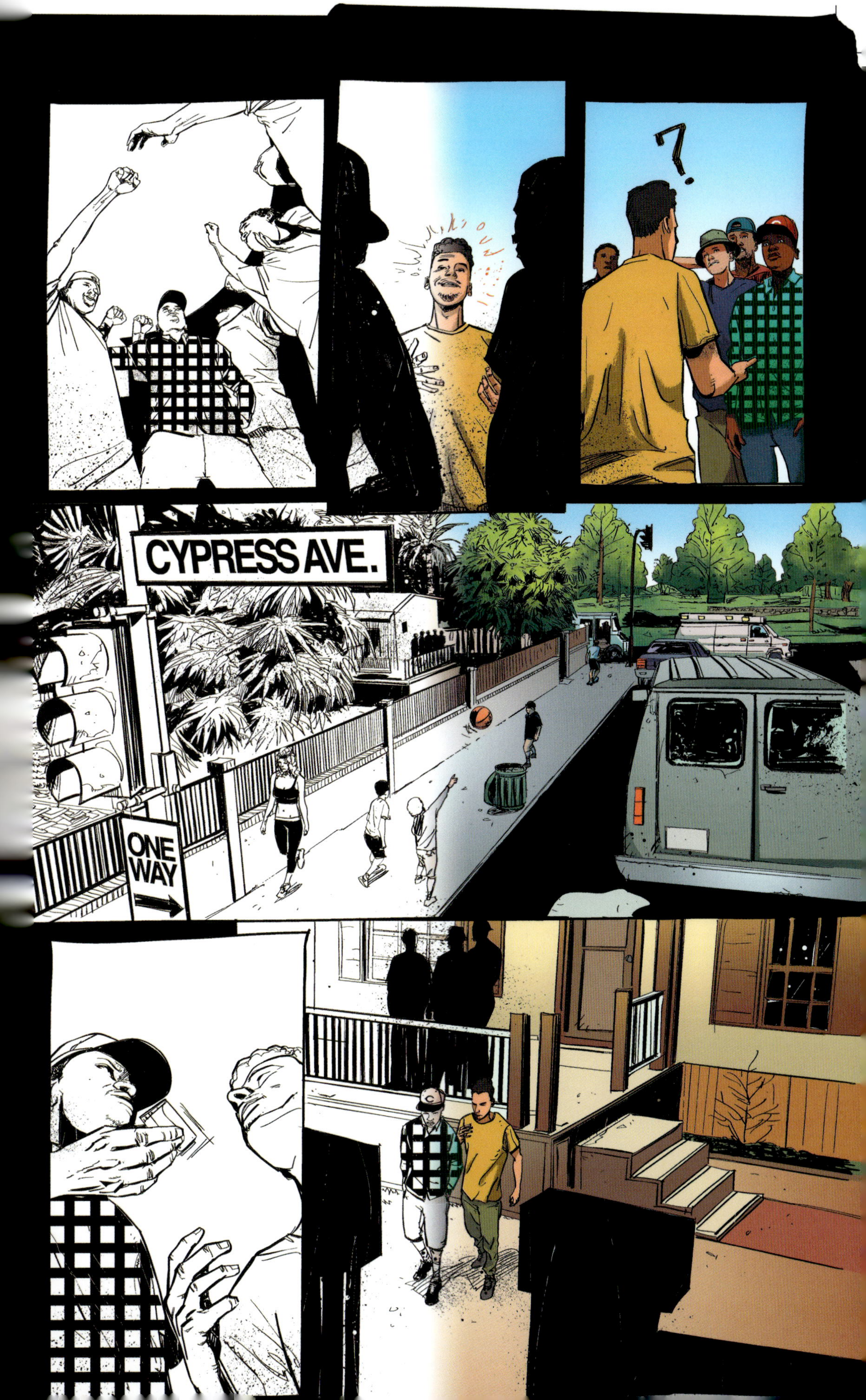
?
CYPRESS AVE.
ONE WAY

# PAGE 18

**PANEL 1 [1 of 3, top 1/2 ]:** We're close on SEN's face. It's tense and we see the light cast from the flashlights across his face and hat. The cops are close.

**PANEL 2:** We're close on MUGGS face. Same thing. The red and blue lights and flashlight are reflecting off of his sweaty skin.

**PANEL 3:** We're close on B-REAL. Same deal with the light, but he looks cool as a cucumber. We can see he's holding the shotgun.

**PANEL 4 [1 of 3, bottom 1/2 ]:** Repeat of PANEL 1, except the shadows and lights are moved (indicating the cops moving thru the space.

**PANEL 5:** Repeat of PANEL 2, except the shadows and lights are moved (indicating the cops moving thru the space.

**PANEL 6:** Repeat of PANEL 3, except the shadows and lights are moved (indicating the cops moving thru the space.

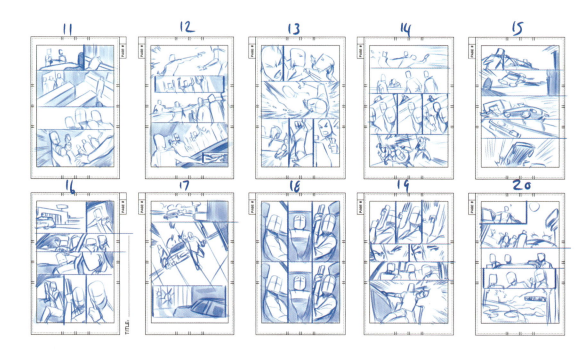

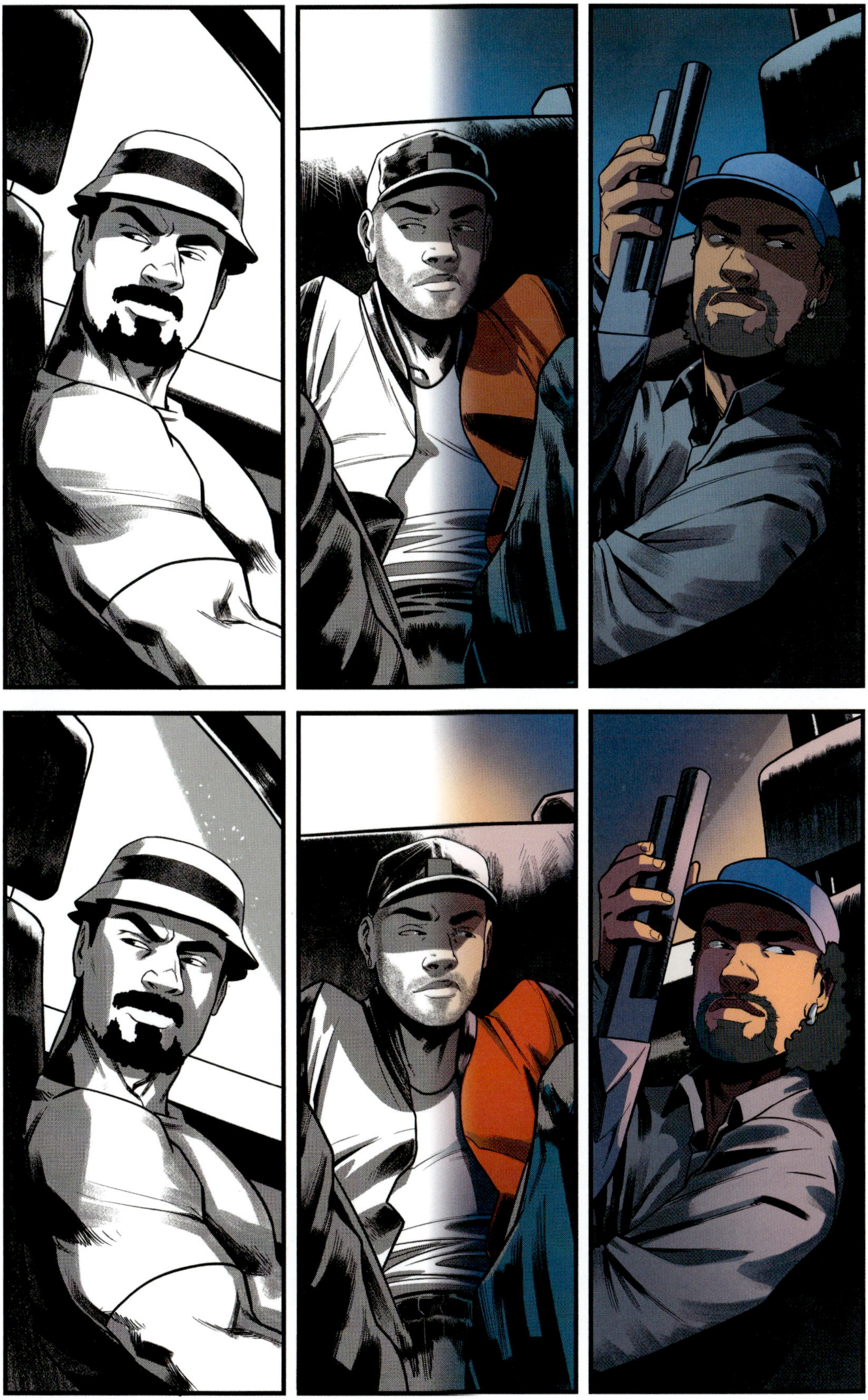

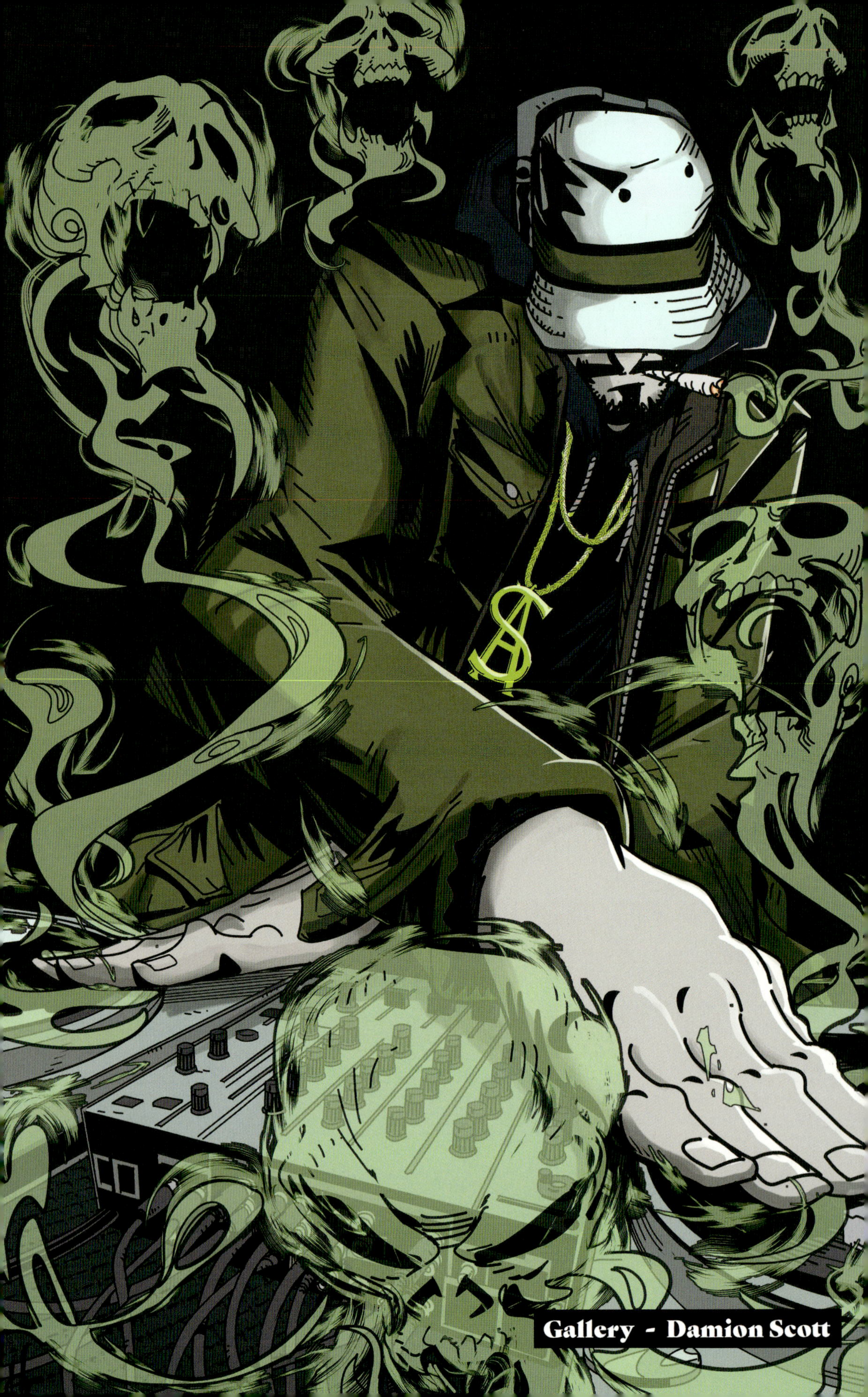

Gallery - Damion Scott

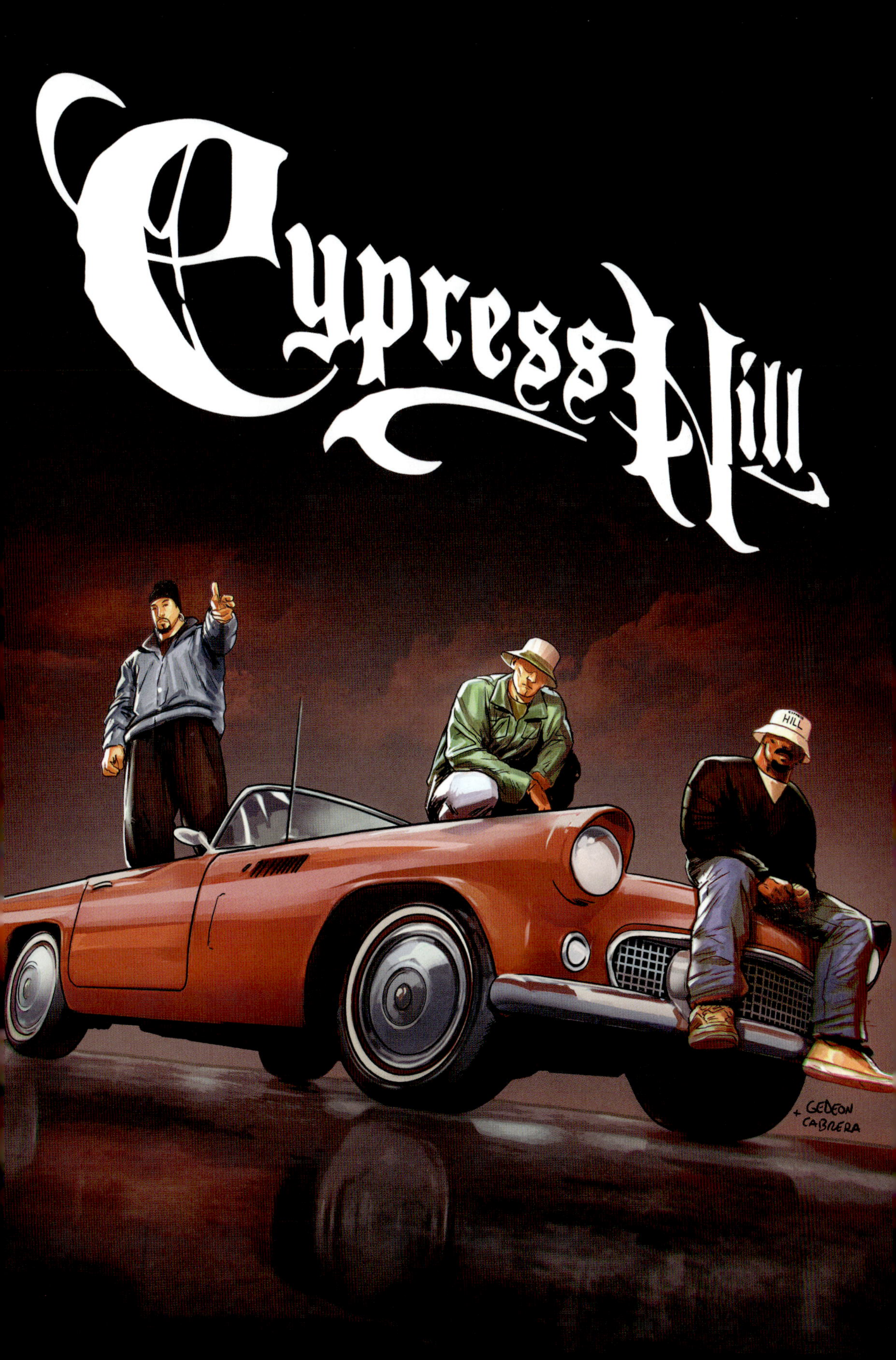
Cypress Hill
HILL
GEDEON
+ CABRERA

**Gallery - Juan Gedeon**

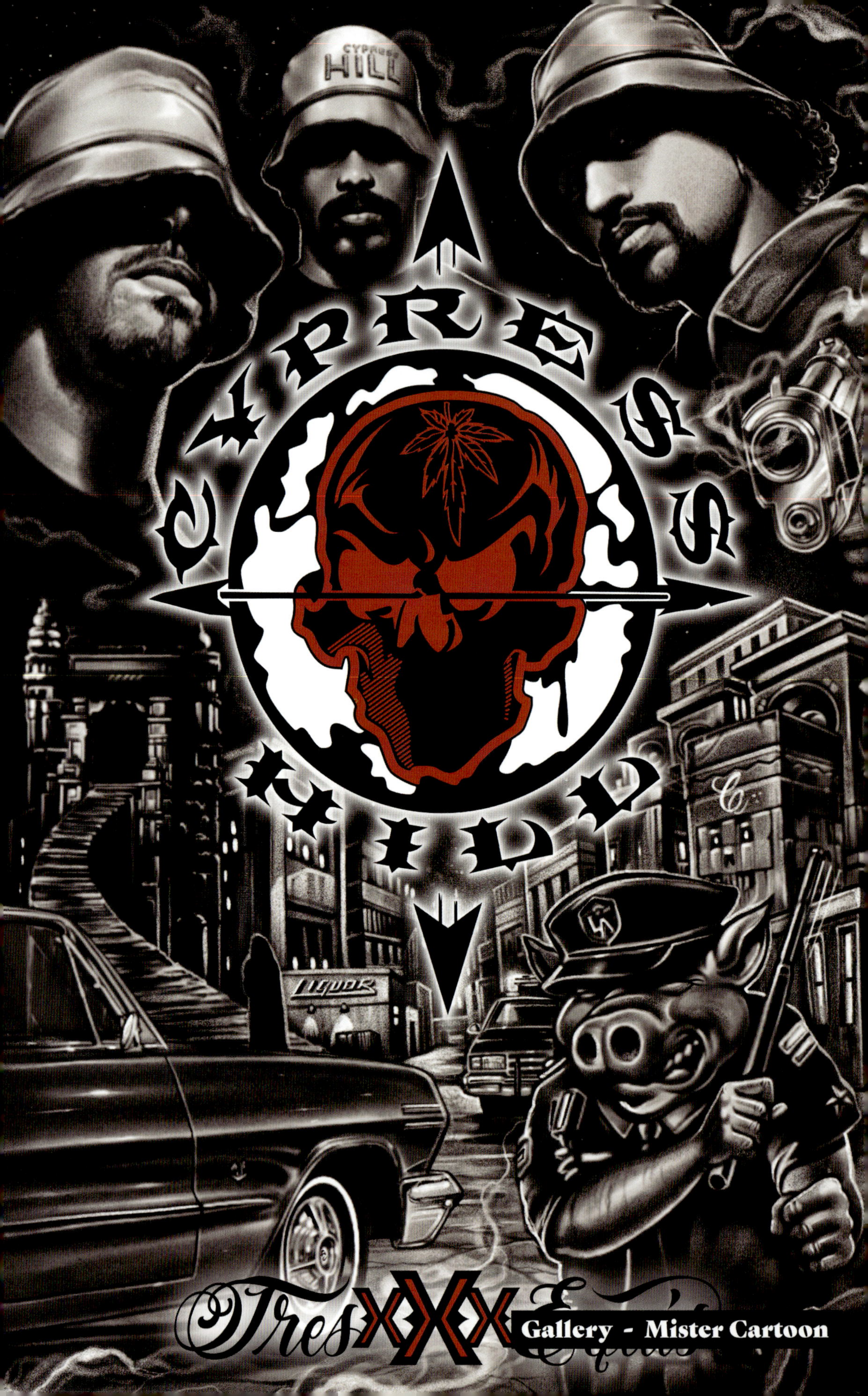
CYPRESS HILL
CYPRESS
HILL
LIQUOR
Tres XXX Equis
Gallery - Mister Cartoon

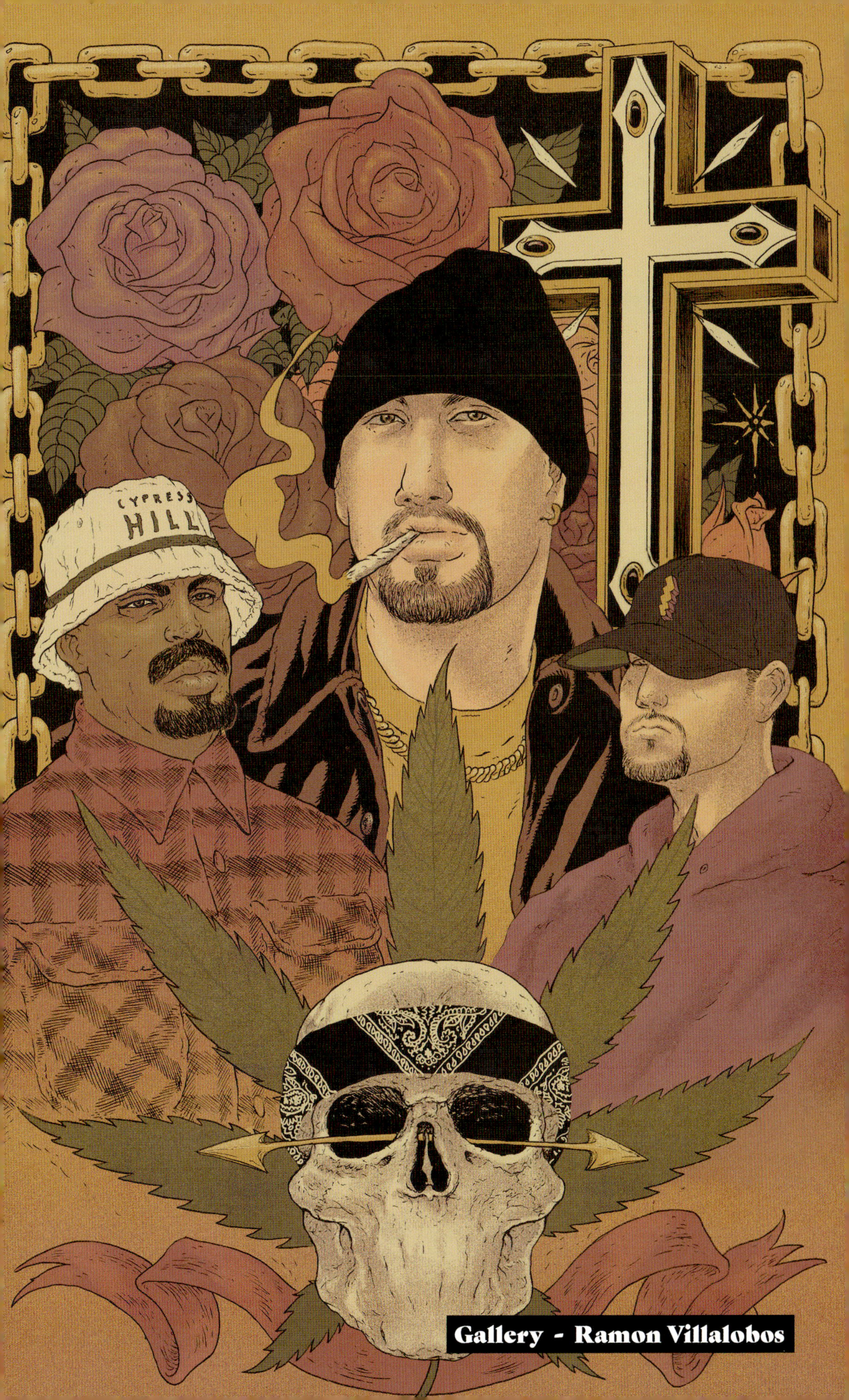
CYPRESS
HILL

**Gallery - Ramon Villalobos**

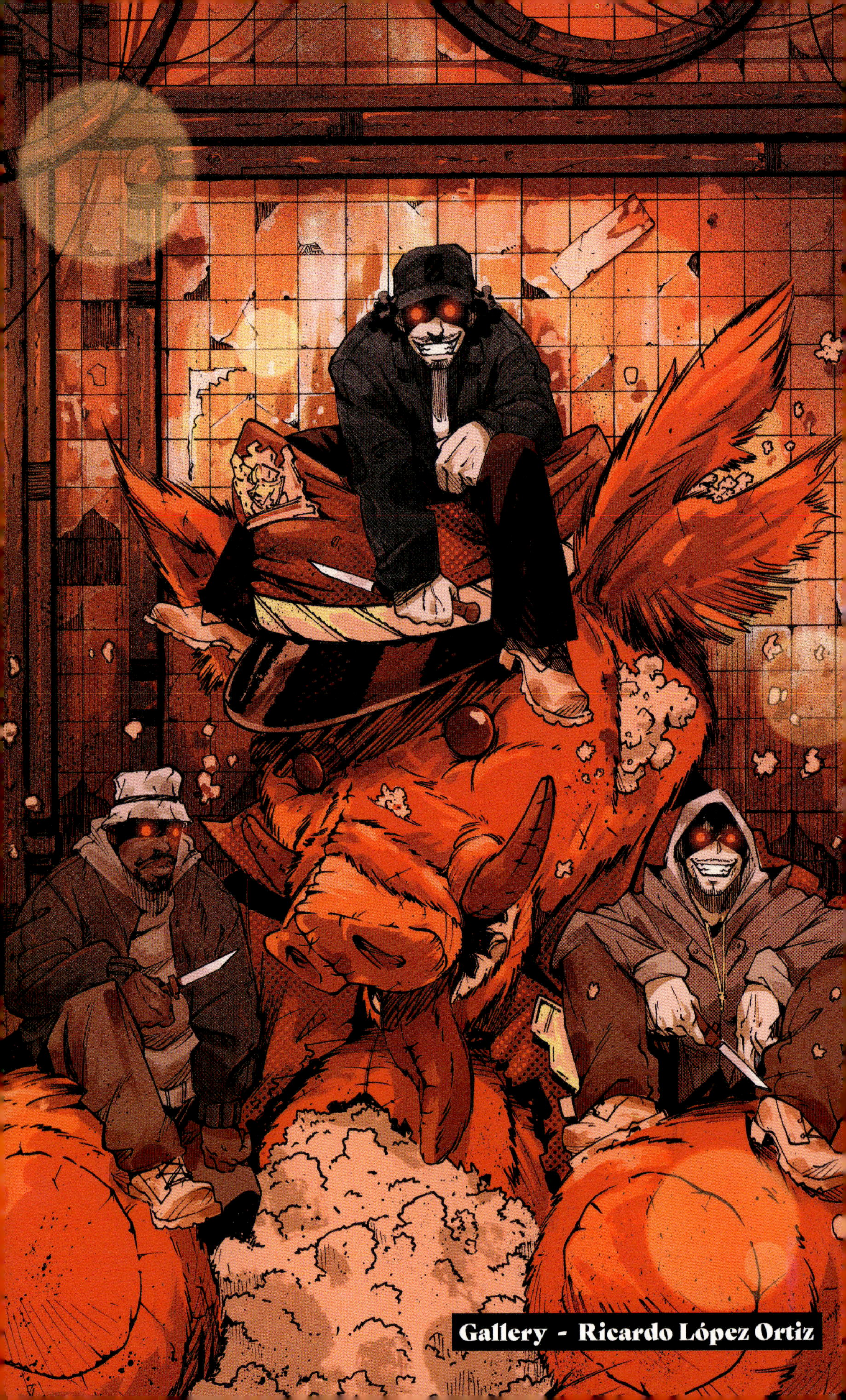

Gallery - Ricardo López Ortiz

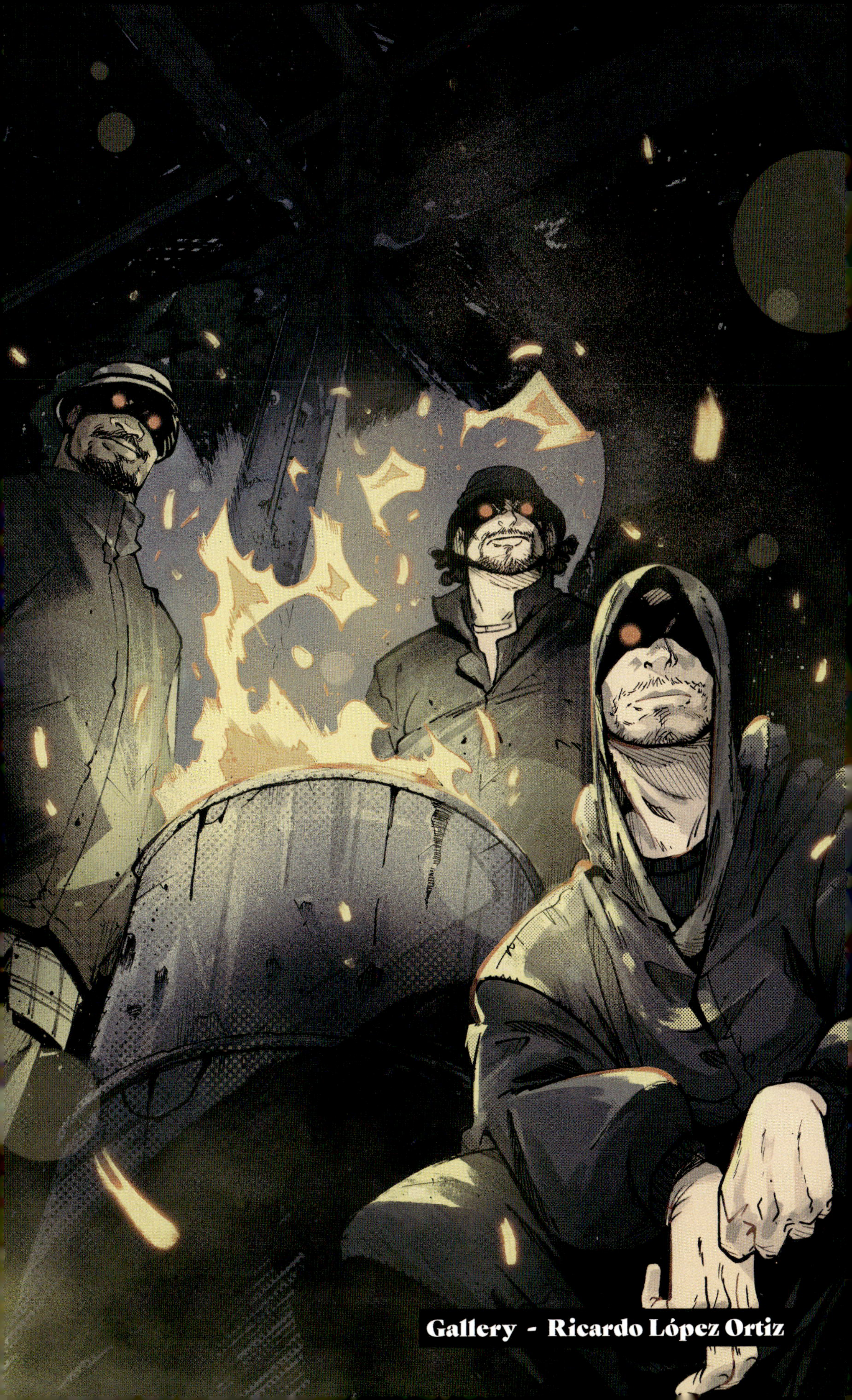

Gallery - Ricardo López Ortiz